Territory and Ideology in Latin America

Transformations in Governance

Transformations in Governance is a major new academic book series from Oxford University Press. It is designed to accommodate the impressive growth of research in comparative politics, international relations, public policy, federalism, and environmental and urban studies concerned with the dispersion of authority from central states up to supranational institutions, down to subnational governments, and sideways to public–private networks. It brings together work that significantly advances our understanding of the organization, causes, and consequences of multilevel and complex governance. The series is selective, containing annually a small number of books of exceptionally high quality by leading and emerging scholars.

The series targets mainly single-authored or co-authored work, but it is pluralistic in terms of disciplinary specialization, research design, method, and geographical scope. Case studies as well as comparative studies, historical as well as contemporary studies, and studies with a national, regional, or international focus are all central to its aims. Authors use qualitative, quantitative, formal modeling, or mixed methods. A trade mark of the books is that they combine scholarly rigor with readable prose and an attractive production style.

The series is edited by Liesbet Hooghe and Gary Marks of the University of North Carolina, Chapel Hill, and Walter Mattli of the University of Oxford.

Organizational Progeny: Why Governments are Losing Control over the Proliferating Structures of Global Governance
Tana Johnson

Democrats and Autocrats: Pathways of Subnational Undemocratic Regime Continuity within Democratic Countries
Agustina Giraudy

A Postfunctionalist Theory of Governance (5 Volumes)
Liesbet Hooghe and Gary Marks et al.

Constitutional Policy in Multilevel Government: The Art of Keeping the Balance
Arthur Benz

With, Without, or Against the State? How European Regions Play the Brussels Game
Michaël Tatham

Territory and Ideology in Latin America

Policy Conflicts between National and Subnational Governments

Kent Eaton

OXFORD
UNIVERSITY PRESS

OXFORD
UNIVERSITY PRESS

Great Clarendon Street, Oxford, OX2 6DP,
United Kingdom

Oxford University Press is a department of the University of Oxford.
It furthers the University's objective of excellence in research, scholarship,
and education by publishing worldwide. Oxford is a registered trade mark of
Oxford University Press in the UK and in certain other countries

First Edition published in 2017

Published in the United States of America by Oxford University Press
198 Madison Avenue, New York, NY 10016, United States of America

British Library Cataloguing in Publication Data
Data available

Library of Congress Control Number: 2016958027

ISBN 978–0–19–880057–6

For Karl

Acknowledgments

Over the decade I worked on this project, including years when I did not yet realize that it would take the form of a book, I benefited from all kinds of support, feedback, and assistance—both in the Andes and in the USA. I am grateful to all those who contributed to my research and for the variety of the contributions they made, which ranged from financial support to analytical insights, and from interview contacts to critical feedback. Sometimes this feedback took the form of detailed comments on chapter drafts, but it also came as one-off conversations or question-and-answer sessions that fundamentally changed the way I thought about my material.

For helping to support and guide my research in Bolivia, I would like to thank Helena Argirakis, Mauricio Bacardit, Eliane Capobianco, Norma Yalila Casanova, Alejandro Colanzi, Gabriel Dabdoub, Marcelo Dabdoub, Pablo Deheza, Gisela López, Gilber Mamani, Juan Pablo Marca, José Abel Martínez, Hugo Carlos Molina, Oscar Ortíz, Gustavo Pedraza, Claudia Peña, Paula Peña, Carlos Rocabado, Dunia Sandoval, Vania Sandoval, Carlos Schlink, Hugo Siles, Leonardo Tamburini, Juan Carlos Urenda, Carlos Valverde, and Moira Zuazo. Like so many US-based academics conducting field research in Bolivia, I am especially thankful for the generosity of Diego Ayo, both for his help in navigating La Paz, where he is based, and for helping me understand the complexities of Santa Cruz.

In Ecuador, I am grateful to Maribel Almeida, Pablo Andrade, Xavier Andrade, Guillermo Arosemena, Orazio Belletini, Joffre Campana, Hector Chiriboga, Russell Crawford, Lois Crawford de Roberts, Jaime Damerval, Francisco Franco, Jonas Frank, Simon Jaramillo, Henry Kronfle, Victor Maridueña, Billy Navarrete, Andrea Ordoñez, Emilio Palacio, Willington Paredes, Benjamin Rosales, Carlo Ruiz Giraldo, Walter Spurrier, Roberto Vernimmen, and Tina Zerega. Most of all, I want to thank Felipe Burbano de Lara, whose fascination with the Guayaquil-Santa Cruz comparison rivals my own, whose work has long served as an inspiration, and whose invitations enabled me to present my work on several occasions in Quito.

In Peru, I sincerely appreciate the help I received from César Acurio, Carlos Anderson, Javier Azpur, Carmen Bedoya, Violeta Bermúdez, Analía Calmell, Luís Chirinos, Jorge Chumpitaz, Elena Conterno, Mercedes Cruz, Vladimir

Gil, Efraín González, Rolando Luque, Raúl Molina, Carlos Monge, Mirian Morales, Paula Muñoz, Humberto Olaechea, Giannina Pastor, Patricia Pinto, Cynthia Sanborn, Javier Torres, Dante Vera, Alberto Vergara, Luís Alberto Villafranca, and Johnny Zas Friz. I particularly want to thank Eduardo Dargent and Martiza Paredes for inviting me to spend time as a visiting scholar at the Catholic University in Lima in 2014, which gave me the opportunity to engage with their very talented colleagues, including José Carlos Orijuela, Aldo Panfichi, Stephanie Rousseau, and Martín Tanaka.

Back in the USA, I credit David Collier for pushing me to think about how I might combine the research I was doing on Bolivia and Ecuador with what I had, until then, thought of as an entirely separate project on Peru. I am glad I took his advice. Tyler Dickovick, my former student, co-author, and cherished friend, is the person who has most influenced my thinking about this topic, including during the long months we spent drafting together a handbook on democratic decentralization for USAID. I also benefited from several hard-working research assistants at UC Santa Cruz, including Matthew Boitano, Leonardo de Haro, Alicia Dolan, Shawn Nichols, Fernando Nuñez, and Sarah Romano. Also at UC Santa Cruz, I want to thank the participants in my department's comparative politics workshop, especially my colleagues Lamis Abdelaaty, Mark Massoud, Eleonora Pasotti, Ben Read, and Roger Schoenman. Likewise, I am grateful to the members of the interdisciplinary research cluster that I organized at UC Santa Cruz for several years on Transnational and Local Dynamics in the Andes (TILDA), including Jeff Bury, Adam French, Flora Lu, Tim Norris, and Aviva Sinervo. I also want to thank our terrific departmental staff, including Marianna Santana, Glenda Dixon, Jerry Díaz, Cindy Bale, Maya Woolfe, Tammy Tooley-Chelossi, and especially Dana Rohlf, who made it possible for me to continue to make progress on this book even in the years when I served as chair of the department.

For comments, questions, suggestions, and advice on the book project at various stages along the way, I would like to thank Carla Alberti, Naazneen Barma, Will Barndt, Mattias Bianchi, Aimee Bourassa, Pasha Bueno-Hansen, Christopher Chambers-Ju, Sarah Chartock, Ruth Collier, Catherine Conaghan, Jennifer Cyr, Carlos de la Torre, Diego Díaz, Rodolfo Disi Pavlic, Jorge Domínguez, Thad Dunning, Tasha Fairfield, Tulia Falleti, Tracy Beck Fenwick, Franz Flores, Jonathan Fox, Candelaria Garay, Edward Gibson, Agustina Giraudy, Maria-Therese Gustafsson, Patrick Heller, Maiah Jaskoski, Margaret Keck, Atul Kohli, Pablo Lapegna, Adrienne Lebas, Steve Levitsky, James Loxton, Juan Pablo Luna, Sebastián Mazzuca, Stephanie McNulty, Gabe Paquette, Tianna Paschel, Deborah Poole, Grigo Pop-Eleches, Mathias Poertner, Alison Post, Juan Diego Prieto, Andrew Schrank, Adam Sheingate, Jazmin Sierra, Erica Simmons, Alberto Simpser, Dan Slater, Paul Smoke, Rich Snyder, Mariela

Szwarcberg, Brandon Van Dyck, Matthias vom Hau, Steven Wuhs, Deborah Yashar, Yue Zhang, and Nick Ziegler.

I am very grateful for invitations from colleagues to present my research on the book, as it unfolded and evolved over multiple phases, at Brown University, the Catholic Universities of Lima and Santiago, FLACSO/Ecuador, Harvard University, Johns Hopkins University, Princeton University, Reed College, University of Arizona, University of Chicago, University of Delaware, University of California Berkeley, University of California Riverside, University of Redlands, and University of Toronto. I would also like to thank Ed Connerley at the US Agency for International Development and Kai Kaiser, Ghazala Mansuri, and Vijayendra Rao at the World Bank for consulting and research opportunities within their organizations over the years that have significantly enriched my thinking about the territorial dimensions of economic development.

For defraying the financial costs of the many research trips to Bolivia, Ecuador, and Peru upon which this book is based, I am deeply indebted to my home institution, both for annual grants from the Committee on Research at the University of California Santa Cruz, and for the grant I received from the UC-wide Pacific Rim research program. I am especially grateful to the Woodrow Wilson International Center for Scholars for the 2015–16 residential fellowship in Washington, DC, which enabled me to complete a full draft of the book. At the Center I would like to thank Kim Conner, Lindsay Collins, Verónica Colón-Rosario, Karla Peña, and Janet Spikes, along with my very helpful research assistant Victor Cruz, and the indefatigable Cynthia Arnson, whose leadership makes the Center such a vibrant place for the study and analysis of Latin America.

Finally, I am grateful to Dominic Byatt, my editor at Oxford University Press, to the two anonymous reviewers who took the time to prepare constructive and detailed comments on the book, and to the editors of the series on *Transformations in Governance*, Gary Marks and Liesbet Hooghe—from whose pioneering work on multilevel governance I have learned so much. I also wish to acknowledge that Chapter 3 of this book is derived, in part, from an article entitled "Disciplining Regions: Subnational Contention in Neoliberal Peru" published in *Territory, Politics, Governance* on February 17, 2015, available online: <http://www.tandfonline.com/10.1080/21622671.2105.1005126>.

Contents

List of Maps

List of Tables

List of Abbreviations

ACORVOL	*Asociación Coordinadora del Voluntariado del Guayas* (Association of Voluntary Organizations of Guayas)
ADN	*Acción Democrática Nacionalista* (Nationalist Democratic Action)
AHG	*Archivo Histórico de Guayaquil* (History Archive of Guayaquil)
AMPE	*Asociación de Municipalidades del Perú* (Association of Peruvian Municipalities)
ANGR	*Asociación Nacional de Gobiernos Regionales* (National Association of Regional Governments)
AP	*Alianza Patria Altiva y Soberana* (Proud and Sovereign Fatherland Alliance)
APRA	*Alianza Popular Revolucionaria Americana* (American Popular Revolutionary Alliance)
CADEX	*Cámara de Exportadores de Santa Cruz* (Santa Cruz Chamber of Exporters)
CAO	*Cámara Agropecuaria del Oriente* (Eastern Agricultural Chamber)
CAINCO	*Cámara de Industria y Comercio* (Chamber of Industry and Commerce)
CCI	*Consejo de Coordinación Inter-Gubernamental* (Inter-Governmental Coordination Council)
CCR	*Consejo de Coordinación Regional* (Regional Coordination Council)
CEDISA	*Centro de Desarrollo e Investigación de la Selva Alta* (Center for Development and Research on the Highland Jungle)
CEJIS	*Centro de Estudios Jurídicos e Investigación Social* (Center for Juridical Study and Social Investigation)
CEPB	*Confederación de Empresarios Privados de Bolivia* (Confederation of Private Entrepreneurs of Bolivia)
CEPLAN	*Centro Nacional de Planeamiento Estratégico* (National Center for Strategic Planning)
CFP	*Concentración de Fuerzas Populares* (Concentration of Popular Forces)
CGTP	*Confederación General de Trabajdores del Perú* (General Confederation of Workers of Peru)

CIDOB	*Confederación de Pueblos Indígenas de Bolivia* (Confederation of Indigenous Peoples of Bolivia)
CIPCA	*Centro de Investigación y Promoción del Campesinado* (Center for Research and Promotion of the Peasantry)
CND	*Consejo Nacional de Descentralización* (National Council of Decentralization)
COB	*Central Obrera Boliviana* (Bolivian Labor Confederation)
COD	*Central Obrera Departamental* (Departmental Labor Federation)
COMEXI	*Consejo de Comercio Exterior e Inversiones* (Council of Foreign Trade and Investment)
COMF	*Código Orgánico Monetario y Financiero* (Organic Monetary and Financial Code)
CONAIE	*Confederación de Nacionalidades Indígenas del Ecuador* (Confederation of Indigenous Nationalities of Ecuador)
CONALDE	*Consejo Nacional Democrático* (National Council for Democracy)
CONAM	*Consejo Nacional de Modernización* (National Council on Modernization)
CONFIEP	*Confederación Nacional de Instituciones Empresariales Privadas* (National Confederation of Private Business Institutions)
COP	*Comité de Obras Públicas* (Public Works Committee)
CORDECRUZ	*Corporación Regional de Desarrollo de Santa Cruz* (Regional Development Corporation of Santa Cruz)
COTAS	*Cooperativa de Telecomunicaciones Santa Cruz* (Telecommunications Cooperative of Santa Cruz)
CPESC	*Coordinadora de Pueblos Étnicos de Santa Cruz* (Coordination of Ethnic Peoples of Santa Cruz)
CPSC	*Comité Pro-Santa Cruz* (Pro-Santa Cruz Committee)
CRE	*Cooperativa Rural de Electrificación* (Rural Electrification Cooperative)
CSC	*Corporación de Seguridad Ciudadana* (Citizen Security Corporation)
CSR	corporate social responsibility
CSUTCB	*Confederación Sindical Única de Trabajdores del Campesinado de Bolivia* (Unified Syndical Confederation of Rural Workers of Bolivia)
CTG	*Comité de Transito de Guayas* (Transit Committee of Guayas)
DASE	*Dirección de Acción Social y Educación* (Department of Social Action and Education)
EIA	Environmental Impact Assessment
EMAPA	*Empresa de Apoyo a la Producción de Alimentos* (Company to Support the Production of Foodstuffs)

FEPB-SC	*Federación de Empresarios Privados de Bolivia–Santa Cruz* (Federation of Private Entrepreneurs of Bolivia–Santa Cruz)
FES	*función económico y social* (economic and social function)
FEXPOCRUZ	*Feria Exposición de Santa Cruz* (Exhibition Fair of Santa Cruz)
FINDESA	*Financiera de Desarrollo de Santa Cruz* (Development Finance Company of Santa Cruz)
GRUFIDES	*Grupo de Formación e Intervención para el Desarrollo* (Group for Interventions in Development)
IESS	*Instituto Ecuatoriano de Seguridad Social* (Ecuadorian Social Security Institute)
IU	*Izquierda Unida* (United Left)
JBG	*Junta de Beneficiencia de Guayaquil* (Guayaquil Charity Board)
JCG	*Junta Cívica de Guayaquil* (Civic Board of Guayaquil)
JCP	*Junta Cívica Popular* (Popular Civic Board)
JNE	*Jurado Nacional de Elecciones* (National Board of Elections)
MAS	*Movimiento al Socialismo* (Movement for Socialism)
MEF	*Ministerio de Economía y Finanzas* (Ministry of Economy and Finances)
MG	*Madera de Guerrero* (Wood of the Warrior)
MIES	*Ministerio de Inclusión Económica y Social* (Ministry of Economic and Social Inclusion)
MINAM	*Ministerio del Ambiente* (Ministry of the Environment)
MINEM	*Ministerio de Energía y Minas* (Ministry of Energy and Mines)
MIR	*Movimiento de Izquierda Revolucionaria* (Revolutionary Left Movement)
MNR	*Movimiento Nacionalista Revolucionario* (Nationalist Revolutionary Movement)
NAFTA	North American Free Trade Agreement
ONDS	*Oficina Nacional de Diálogo y Sostenibilidad* (National Office for Dialogue and Sustainability)
ONPE	*Oficina Nacional de Procesos Electorales* (National Office of Electoral Processes)
OT	*ordenamiento territorial* (territorial regulation)
PASOC	*Pastoral Social Cáritas* (Cáritas Social Pastorate)
PRE	*Partido Roldosista Ecuatoriano* (Ecuadorian Roldosist Party)
PSC	*Partido Social Cristiano* (Social Christian Party)
REMURPE	*Red de Municipalidades Urbanas y Rurales del Perú* (Network of Urban and Rural Peruvian Municipalities)
SAGUAPAC	*Servicio de Agua Potable* (Potable Water Service)

SENPLADES	*Secretaría Nacional de Planificación y Desarrollo* (National Secretariat for Planning and Development)
SNIP	*Sistema Nacional de Inversión Pública* (National System of Public Investment)
SNMPE	*Sociedad Nacional de Minería, Petróleo y Energía* (National Society for Mining, Petroleum, and Energy)
SOLCA	*Sociedad de Lucha Contra el Cáncer del Ecuador* (Ecuadorian Society to Fight Cancer)
SUNAT	*Superintendencia Nacional de Administración Tributaria* (National Superintendency of Tax Administration)
SUTEP	*Sindicato Único de Trabajadores de la Educación del Perú* (Unified Union of Education Workers of Peru)
TIPNIS	*Territorio Indígena y Parque Nacional Isiboro Sécure* (Isiboro Sécure National Park and Indigenous Territory)
UCS	*Unidad de Conflicto Social* (Social Conflict Unit)
UJC	*Unión Juvenil Crucenista* (Crucenista Youth Union)
UNASUR	*Unión de Naciones Suramericanas* (Union of South American Nations)
UNSA	*Universidad Nacional de San Agustín* (National University of San Agustín)
USAID	United States Agency for International Development
ZEE	*Zonificación Ecológica Económica* (Ecological and Economic Zoning)

1

Introduction

One of the most consequential recent developments in global politics is the shift toward multilevel governance that has taken place in countries around the world. Thanks to the twin processes of decentralization and integration, national governments have lost authority both downward to subnational governments and upward to supranational bodies (Hooghe and Marks 2001; Bache and Flinders 2004). Although this ongoing phenomenon has been extensively studied, questioned, and debated, one of its most important consequences remains unexamined and poorly understood. The shift toward multilevel governance means that ideological conflicts over the market, which have long dominated the political life of so many countries, are being shaped in newly important ways by territorial conflicts between levels of government—especially national and subnational governments. Empowered by various types of decentralization, subnational governments now have the power not only to make use of significant new forms of authority, but to do so in ways that contest the economic development model in place at the national level. More and more, subnational governments are challenging national governments in the field of policy.

We are at the dawn of a period of far greater complexity in the relationship between territory and ideology. This new era is marked by subnational policy challenges of growing strength, and policy conflicts between national and subnational governments of increasing relevance. Even if "reports of the death of the national economy are greatly exaggerated" (Wade 1996), the supremacy of the national government as the sole arena for conflict over economic development strategies has been seriously called into question. In numerous countries, gone are the days when the center could safely ignore the economic policy preferences of officials who operate at lower levels of government. Making sense of this phenomenon requires that we more fully integrate the literature on multilevel governance, which has focused on why politicians decide to reallocate policymaking authority between different levels of government, with the literature on the politics of economic development, which has focused on why politicians use this authority to adopt or discard rival development models.

In most countries, the contemporary debate between advocates of market-centered and state-centered models is anything but new, and has produced instead a strong sense of déjà vu as national governments over time tend to tack back and forth between more liberal and more statist conceptions. In the current period, however, this by now familiar ideological conflict is generating qualitatively new and significant forms of territorial friction, dissonance, and heterogeneity. As the political science literature on economic development has demonstrated, the replacement of one policy regime with another has always produced political resistance, opposition, and struggle—as one would expect given the high stakes associated with the reorientation of a country's overarching economic development model (Haggard 1990; Murillo 2003; Kohli 2004; Roberts 2015). But more than at any time in the past, political conflict over the content of these models now involves much more prominent and dynamic roles for subnational governments, whose elected authorities are increasingly using their independent control over subnational territories to contest national development models and/or to pursue their own preferred approaches at the subnational level.

It is not that ideological struggles over the appropriate role of the state in the economy did not have consequential, often heavily redistributive, impacts on subnational territories in the past. Quite the contrary. Liberalism has typically benefited those subnational regions that produce commodities in high demand globally (Cardoso and Faletto 1979; Saylor 2014). Statism, meanwhile, has often led to the concentration of new industrial opportunities in and around national capital regions, leading to territorially lopsided patterns of industrialization and contributing in no small measure to the emergence of megacities across the global South (Evans 2002; Portes and Roberts 2005). Economic development models have always had profound territorial consequences, but in the opening years of the twenty-first century governing officials in subnational territories have much greater scope to challenge national policy directions, and to express and act on their own policy preferences in their own subnational jurisdictions. In the past, subnational officials who dared to criticize, resist, or subvert national policy approaches often did so at their own peril since they served at the pleasure of national patrons who appointed them to their posts, whether these patrons were democratically elected presidents or de facto military leaders. By the end of the twentieth century, however, a global wave of political decentralization to both local- and intermediate-level governments had replaced appointments with elections as the main mechanism through which most subnational executives hold their offices, a shift that has widened the scope for and significance of territorial conflicts over the market.[1] As a result, while the search for appropriate economic development strategies remains a highly salient one in the world today, no longer is it affected only by political actors who operate chiefly at the national level, such as presidents and legislators, party and interest group leaders, or business chamber executives and labor bosses. Instead, subnational actors such as mayors and governors are shaping the contours and outcomes of these ideological conflicts to a far greater degree than was typically the case in the twentieth century.

Examples abound of the growing incidence of territorial actors and issues in the ideological debates that continue to rage over the market, starting with Europe. A "Europe of the regions" may have been slower to emerge than many anticipated, but subnational regional governments now commonly form coalitions with the European Commission in ways that challenge national governments, and the Europeanization of particular policy sectors has increased the autonomy of subnational actors (Hooghe 1996; George 2004; Piattoni and Schönlau 2015).[2] Although the literature on regionalism in Europe has tended to focus on linguistic, ethnic, and cultural demands, European regions have also articulated distinctive ideological demands vis-à-vis the market—on both the left and the right. On the left, French-speaking Socialists in Belgium's lesser-developed southern region of Wallonia worry that Flemish liberals in the north will use their influence in national institutions to undo the welfare state (Coffe 2008). In the UK, it is not just national identity that has animated the push for Scottish independence, but widespread ideological preferences for forms of social solidarity that seem incompatible with Conservative rule from London (Salmond 2014). On the right, the hegemony in Bavaria of the conservative Christian Social Union, which has governed the state without interruption since the Second World War, reflects both the lowest levels of unionization in Germany as well as strong local preferences for free market economics

[1] According to Rodden (2004), over the three decades that began in 1970, the percentage of local governments that were directly elected increased from 30% to 86%, whereas the percentage of elected regional governments increased from 25% to 55%. According to Hooghe and Marks, 79% of central governments could override the decisions of subnational governments in 1975, but only 40% could by 1995 (Hooghe and Marks 2010: 22).

[2] In the debate over the evolution of the EU that has taken place between "inter-governmentalists" and "supranationalists," the former have questioned the possibility of robust regions that might escape the control of national governments (Moravcsik 1998), whereas the latter have emphasized the important role of regions in the EU's new three-tiered system of multilevel governance (Hooghe and Marks 2001). While some dismiss the Committee of Regions owing to its merely advisory status and view the regions as "hype" (Greenwood 2011: 176–7; Luedtke 2005), others argue that subnational governments are actively claiming a role in EU policy, and not merely as passive beneficiaries of a struggle over competencies between national governments and European institutions (Jeffery 2000; Piattoni and Schönlau 2015).

(Gunlicks 2003: 292).[3] In Italy, the Northern League has sought to use its control over regional governments such as Lombardy and Veneto to articulate an anti-statist ideology that seeks to reduce redistribution to lesser-developed regions (Spektorowski 2003).

The territorial dimension within the larger ideological debate over development models has also become more salient in Asia. One of the key questions that dominated the transfer of Hong Kong back to Chinese rule in 1997 was whether the city's distinctly liberal economic model could survive reincorporation into China, as reflected in the aspirational phrase "one country, two systems" (Davis 2015). Elsewhere in China, policy decentralization led to the development of territorially distinct local models of development. For example, according to Thun's study of the auto sector (2004: 1291), while "Shanghai became the local version of a developmental state... Guangzhou took a more laissez faire approach [by forcing] firms owned by different ministries to compete with each other for business and investment capital."[4] In India, scholars have documented the performance of the economic development model designed and implemented by the Communist Party of India (Marxist) over the course of many decades in the states of Kerala and West Bengal—in both cases on the basis of strong mass support among peasant and working-class populations (Isaac 2000; Parayil 2000). The distinctive features of the Kerala model, according to Heller (1999, 2001), include extensive investments in public infrastructure, increases in planning capacity centered in the state-level Planning Board, and working-class empowerment in the form of new participatory mechanisms. On the opposite side of the ideological spectrum, the Gujarat model that crystallized under the auspices of the right-of-center Bharatiya Janata Party looks quite different. Administered by Narendra Modi, who leveraged his territorial experience as the Chief Minister of Gujarat between 2001 and 2014 to launch a successful bid for Prime Minister in 2014, the Gujarat model is characterized by business-friendly policies, cuts in state subsidies, hikes in electricity rates, and declining state budget deficits (Sharma 2013).[5]

[3] See Jeffery et al. (2014) for the argument that partisan and structural differences among the *länder* have led to significant policy variation at the subnational level in Germany—against the dominant view of high levels of policy coordination between federal and state governments.

[4] Whereas Thun sees local divergence as the response to policy decentralization, Montinola, Qian, and Weingast (1995) predict convergence on the part of subnational governments in China in response to the incentives generated by "market preserving federalism." For more on regional variation within China, see Blecher (1991), Qian and Stiglitz (1996), Yang (1997), and Oi (1999).

[5] For the argument that "some regional states have managed to escape the adverse effects of the *dirigiste* regime" at the national level in India, see Sinha (2003: 460). According to Sinha, while "some regional states emphasized the role of the public sector, others encouraged synergistic public–private coordination" (p. 460). Still, because subnational states "cannot be treated like nation-states" (p. 461), Sinha insists on the existence in India of a "single policy framework"

While a noticeable tightening in the connection between territorial politics and ideological conflict can be seen around the world, this phenomenon is particularly striking in Latin America, in part because of the region-wide oscillation in economic policy that took place across the twentieth century. Virtually all Latin American countries began that century governed by fundamentally liberal development models, followed by widespread experimentation with statism in the middle fifty years of the century, and ending with the subsequent return to market-centered approaches in the century's closing decades. Individual countries differed in the exact timing, scope, and depth of the policy reforms they adopted as part of each successive shift, but to a striking degree Latin America as a region moved in concert as national governments adopted and then shed common approaches (Sheahan 2002; Corrales 2003). Indeed, these region-wide shifts help account for much of the coherence that characterizes Latin American political economy as a field of study.[6] One important pattern of continuity as the policy pendulum swung back and forth between liberalism and statism in the twentieth century was the unimportance of subnational actors such as mayors and governors, who did not meaningfully influence the ideological debate over the market, even as this debate triggered frequent regime changes, extensive social mobilization, and in some cases high levels of political violence (Smith, Acuña, and Gamarra 1994; Oxhorn and Ducatenzeiler 1998; Kurtz 2004). This twentieth-century backdrop sets into sharp relief the protagonism that subnational elected officials are now exerting in the twenty-first century, which as a result is starting to look much more like the nineteenth century—a period in which subnational *caudillos* routinely took up arms against the center over a range of matters, including economic policy (Bethell 1985).[7]

Particularly with respect to the European cases that have figured so prominently in the literature on multilevel governance, Latin America is an important region for theory-building because of two further reasons. First is the relative absence of successful EU-like integration efforts in Latin America (outside of NAFTA). If the development of supranational institutions had the effect of strengthening subnational regions in Europe (Hooghe 1996; George 2004), subnational governments in Latin America have largely been

that is the "product of central rules, provincial strategic choices and subnational institutional variation" (pp. 460–1).

[6] Further, as scores of political scientists have argued, this oscillation in economic policy interacted in significant ways with some of the region's most important political developments, including the emergence, collapse, and reshaping of democratic rule (O'Donnell 1973; Collier and Collier 1991; Haggard and Kaufman 1995; Roberts 2015).

[7] While the territorial dimensions of ideological conflict were salient in nineteenth-century Latin America as well, especially in the post-independence period, this was often the result of attempts by national governments to challenge the authority of local governments, as opposed to the opposite configuration now dominant. I thank Gabriel Paquette for this point.

denied this possible source of support in their struggles with national governments. Also, not having lost much authority upwards to supranational regional bodies means that national governments in Latin America have been freer to concentrate their efforts on how they want to respond to policy threats from below.

The second factor runs in the opposite direction by encouraging rather than discouraging subnational policy challenges. Lower levels of state capacity in Latin America relative to Europe should be understood as a permissive factor for the development of these challenges. Limited state capacity and highly incomplete processes of state formation have created a fertile landscape for the emergence of much more significant and destabilizing forms of territorial heterogeneity in Latin America. It is no coincidence that the most powerful subnational policy challenges in Latin America have emerged in countries with especially low levels of state capacity, including the three countries that I focus on in this book: Bolivia, Ecuador, and Peru. Interestingly, all three of these countries are unitary and not federal systems, which suggests that the design of state institutions may actually be less important than their underlying strength. By focusing on policy conflicts and multilevel governance in unitary countries, my research complements and extends a vibrant body of scholarship on federal countries in Latin America (Argentina, Brazil, and Mexico) that has demonstrated how subnational officials shape industrial policy (Montero 2002), macroeconomic stability (Wibbels 2005), regulation (Snyder 2006), democracy (Gibson 2012; Giraudy 2015), privatization (Post 2014), poverty alleviation (Fenwick 2016), and social policy implementation (Niedzwiecki, forthcoming).

Based on in-depth field research between 2005 and 2015 in three Andean countries, this book seeks to understand the nature of the new policy challenges that subnational governments are now posing, and to explain the relative success or failure of these challenges. To set up the book, this introductory chapter is organized into four main sections. The first section conceptualizes the two main types of subnational policy challenges I seek to explain, along with the two most common territorial and ideological configurations that have resulted from these challenges. What are the distinctive possibilities and limitations of "subnational neoliberalism" and "subnational statism" as two prominent types of subnational policy regimes? The second section examines the general causes that have made subnational policy challenges more common in the world today. Why are we seeing more territorial heterogeneity within countries in terms of the pursuit of ideologically disparate economic development models? This discussion of the main causes of subnational policy challenges serves as the background for my core research question, which is not the easier question of why these challenges have emerged but the harder question of why they succeed or fail. The third section assesses the importance of this trend by analyzing the chief advantages and disadvantages of the shift toward greater territorial heterogeneity. Regardless of why it has become more common, is this kind of heterogeneity positive or negative? The fourth section describes the plan of the book, including a brief overview of the theoretical framework, which stresses the importance of structural, institutional, and coalitional factors to explain variation in the success of subnational policy challenges.

Subnational Policy Challenges

The claim that ideological conflict over the market has become progressively more territorialized leads me to focus in this book on the policy challenges that are being articulated by *subnational governments*. I conceptualize these challenges as coming in two related but distinct forms. The first stems from elected subnational officials who use their authority, resources, and legitimacy to design, implement, and defend subnational policy regimes that deviate ideologically from national policy regimes.[8] The second occurs when these same officials use their authority, resources, and legitimacy to question, oppose, and alter the ideological content of national policy regimes. "Policy regime" here refers to a package of public policies and institutional practices that together reflect a common set of ideas and beliefs about the appropriate role for market forces and the appropriate levels and types of state intervention in economic life (May and Jochim 2013).[9] While the focus in this book is on economic policy regimes rather than other types of policy regimes, ideological struggles between national and subnational politicians are also playing out in other policy fields, including vis-à-vis controversial social policies in issues such as reproductive rights and same-sex marriage. Subnational governments can and do articulate challenges in a whole range of policy fields, and intergovernmental relations should not be reduced to economic issues alone, but here I focus solely on economic policy disputes between territorial actors with rival views of the market.

[8] Throughout the book, I use "policy regime" and "development model" as interchangeable terms.

[9] According to May and Jochim (2013), policy regimes are "governing arrangements for addressing policy problems" (p. 428), and "the breadth of a policy regime is largely determined by the boundaries that one establishes in conceptualizing the problem or set of problems" (p. 437). Whereas the American politics and international relations literatures often conceptualize policy regimes as being organized around specific issue areas such as the environment, civil rights, or education (Wilson 2000: 257), I use the term to refer not to any one policy area but rather to a broader set of economic policies (taxation, regulation, privatization, and trade and financial policies) that together reflect either a state-centered or market-centered approach to the "problem" of economic development.

My conceptualization of the two distinct types of policy challenges posed by subnational officials reflects the reality that these officials can develop and act on preferences vis-à-vis both subnational and national policies; their subnational identities do not prevent them from espousing views about national policy regimes, and their constituents (now that these officials are elected) may indeed push them to do so. Each type of challenge can trigger ideological conflict with national authorities, who are now much more frequently in the position of having to spend significant amounts of time, energy, and resources either suppressing or accommodating these challenges. Analytically distinguishing between these two main types of subnational policy challenges is important because each must overcome different sorts of obstacles in order to succeed vis-à-vis the national government. Which of the two main types of challenges emerge in particular points in time and how exactly they threaten the national government will vary from country to country, but what is clear is that new theories are needed to understand these newly salient challenges.[10]

The chief significance of the first type of challenge is that it potentially represents a threat to one of the central state's defining attributes—namely, the prerogative of imposing its preferred policies uniformly throughout the national territory (Mann 1986; Soifer and vom Hau 2008). Subnational governments that are able to develop discordant policy regimes in effect introduce territorial limits on the scope of the national government's policy authority. Subnational governments are by no means independent states; what they are challenging is not the sovereignty claims of the national government but rather its ability to enforce a single development model across the national territory. When these subnational policy regimes manage to persist, the result is policy regime juxtaposition, a term I use to refer to the simultaneous pursuit of ideologically divergent policy regimes at different levels of government within the same country. It is important to clarify here that the emergence of this phenomenon by no means requires federalism, even if the kinds of powers assigned to intermediate-level governments under federalism theoretically augment their ability to build subnational policy regimes. Whenever two separately elected governments—one national and one subnational—can jointly claim governing authority over the same territory, this arrangement opens up the possibility of policy regime juxtaposition. It is also important to note that this first type of subnational policy challenge is likely to be especially threatening in developing countries, where national leaders are typically under intense pressure to select and execute strategies that

[10] One important new argument is that of Sara Niedzwiecki (2016 and forthcoming), who focuses on a related but distinct type of subnational challenge that occurs when subnational governments obstruct the *implementation* of national policies. According to Niedzwiecki, opposition-controlled subnational governments will oppose national policies like conditional cash transfers when voters can clearly attribute responsibility to the national government.

will generate economic development, and thereby lessen the widening gap with the developed world.

The second type of subnational policy challenge, however, can be just as significant. In fact, in some situations the center may more easily tolerate deviant subnational policy regimes, and perceive instead as the greater threat those subnational officials who are trying to use their powers to influence the content of the national policy regime. Ideologically divergent models in marginalized local districts that are deemed politically or economically irrelevant by the national government may well be dismissed as a mere nuisance to the center. In contrast, when mayors and governors in politically and economically significant subnational districts try to take on the center by contesting its policy direction, such a challenge will probably be taken very seriously. From the perspective of presidents who can count on congressional majorities and compliant judiciaries—not uncommon realities in Latin America owing to the region's long experience with hyper-presidentialism—the most significant obstacle to the pursuit of their preferred policy preferences may well come from subnational challengers. Subnational officials now have their own electoral mandates to point to in articulating and justifying ideological opposition to the president's policy orientation, especially (but not only) when they belong to parties other than the president's. While I focus on efforts by subnational challengers to alter the orientation of national policies by forcing changes in the content of policy, others have focused on how subnational opponents can sabotage the *implementation* of national policies (Fenwick 2016; Niedzwiecki, forthcoming).

Just as the nature of the significance of these two types of challenges differs, so too do the obstacles they tend to face. For instance, developing and implementing a coherent and deviant subnational policy regime (subnational policy challenge no. 1) probably requires more in the way of institutional capacity than challenging that of the national government (subnational policy challenge no. 2). It also usually depends on longer time horizons, which are not necessary in order for subnational officials to be able to lead effective protests against the policies of the national government, but are essential in order for them to build distinctive local models. On the other hand, successfully challenging the national policy regime usually requires coalitions with other subnational units, which might not be necessary when a subnational government "merely" seeks to develop its own distinctive model. Alliances among the governors or mayors who preside over separate subnational jurisdictions have to surmount all of the differences that otherwise divide these jurisdictions, including partisan orientation, level of economic development, and size—to name just a few. What explains the success or failure of these two types of subnational policy challenges is the central theoretical challenge that I tackle in the next chapter.

Although it is important to refrain from assigning greater significance, a priori, to either type of challenge, it is also critical to note that neither type of challenge is a necessary condition for the other. In other words, for subnational officials to seek to change the national policy regime does not require that they have already built and are simultaneously defending a deviant local model. Likewise, subnational officials who are engaged in the design, implementation, and/or defense of an ideologically discordant subnational policy regime may or may not be actively engaged in efforts to alter the ideological content of the national policy regime. According to my conceptualization, any given elected subnational official can articulate either type of challenge, both types of challenges, or neither type of challenge. While it is thus important to appreciate the conceptual separateness of these two types of challenges, in the real world they can generate complicated interactions. For example, subnational officials who can successfully defend their preferred policies locally may be less preoccupied with altering the national policy regime, and national officials may well accept local deviations if they conclude it might help them head off challenges to the content of the national development model.

In the conceptual framework on which this book rests, I take ideology seriously by emphasizing the deeply held ideological commitments that motivate politicians at both the national and subnational level, and that lead them to clash over policy with politicians who are motivated by rival ideologies. Rather than see politicians as exclusively strategic actors who instrumentally adopt the ideological positions that best serve the interests of the jurisdictions they govern at any given moment, I argue that ideological differences structure political conflict, and show how genuine and protracted ideological disagreements are now playing out across territory. The reality is that mayors, governors, and presidents are all pursuing both ideological and territorial interests, which sometimes align and sometimes diverge. But, by highlighting the substance and seriousness of their ideological disagreements, I underscore how politicians who lose ideological battles at the national level are increasingly able to shelter in subnational spaces—from which they can keep up the fight. Finally, although I see ideologically motivated policy challenges by subnational officials as real threats that inflict real damage upon national officials when they succeed, a less zero-sum dynamic may also obtain, especially in ideologically charged settings. For example, subnational policy challengers may function as useful domestic enemies for national incumbents to rail against and thereby better connect with their own ideologically motivated voters.[11] More generally, whipping

[11] In a similar vein, the literature on the juxtaposition of political regimes (as opposed to policy regimes) has demonstrated that the persistence of subnational authoritarianism may be functional

the flames of ideological conflict may redound to the electoral benefit of both national and subnational politicians, which can be true without calling into question the genuineness of their core ideological disagreements.

Moving from the conceptual level to the empirical, consider the cases of Bolivia and Ecuador as countries that have witnessed powerful examples of the first type of subnational policy challenge. In both countries, the adoption of state-centered development models by Presidents Evo Morales and Rafael Correa in the first decade of the twenty-first century triggered attempts by local authorities to defend market-oriented strategies in each country's most economically vibrant subnational jurisdiction: Santa Cruz in Bolivia and Guayaquil in Ecuador. In these countries, separately elected subnational authorities in alliance with local business elites have sought to preserve within their jurisdictions the neoliberal policy regimes that have been developed and implemented over the course of many decades, and that arguably have helped each region achieve its predominant economic status within the country. Market-oriented approaches in Santa Cruz and Guayaquil, however, have clashed with the more statist course set by left-leaning presidents, both of whom have responded aggressively to the subnational policy challenges that they have faced from below, though with differing degrees of success.

For an example of the second type of subnational policy challenge, consider the case of Peru, where a succession of national governments has consistently implemented and defended a neoliberal policy framework since its adoption by President Alberto Fujimori in the early 1990s. After the end of the Fujimori regime and the return to democracy in 2000, Presidents Alejandro Toledo (2001–6), Alán García (2006–11), and Ollanta Humala (2011–16) all maintained the core elements of Peru's neoliberal model—even as this model has been called into question and significantly altered in most neighboring countries. Against this backdrop, it is subnational governments in Peru that have emerged as important spaces for the expression of opposition to and frustration with neoliberalism, as well as experimentation with more vigorous forms of state action in the economy. The remarkable stability of the neoliberal policy regime at the national level in Peru thus belies a great deal of subnational resistance and contention. Distinct and fully-formed subnational policy regimes have yet to emerge in Peru—at either the regional or the municipal level—but the critics of neoliberalism who are embedded in Peruvian subnational governments have tried to use those offices to push back against neoliberalism as a national policy regime. In this way, Peru shows that territorial friction over economic

to the national democratic regime, as when subnational autocrats deliver vote blocs to national politicians (Gibson 2013; Giraudy 2015).

development models can result in the opposite ideological configuration from Bolivia and Ecuador; in Peru advocates of neoliberalism in control of the national government seek to defeat its subnational critics, while in Bolivia and Ecuador subnational exponents of neoliberalism seek to preserve it vis-à-vis the critics of neoliberalism who govern nationally.

These three neighboring Andean countries illustrate a broader and striking phenomenon, which is the reality that subnational officials in the contemporary period are using their newfound powers to pursue very different policy approaches, ranging all the way from neoliberalism to statism. To date, we know very little about what these heavily studied models look like, much less how they perform, when they are being crafted, adopted, and defended by subnational rather than national politicians. Political scientists who study the design, adoption, and implementation of economic development models have tended to assume a national stage, and often to question the very possibility of subnational models.[12] If, as Evelyn Huber (2002: 468) argues in her influential work on models of capitalism in Latin America, coherent development models require "a considerable degree of centralization of political institutions," then it might be well-nigh impossible for subnational politicians to articulate and pursue coherent subnational models. At the same time, such a view would render invisible the increasingly serious and systematic attempts by subnational officials not just to influence the national policy regime, but to design their own coherent policy regimes.

According to a vibrant literature based largely in geography and urban studies, subnational governments have indeed become important spaces for neoliberalism around the world (Brenner and Theodore 2002; Harvey 2009; Brenner, Peck, and Theodore 2010).[13] According to Paul (2002), the subnational state is playing an increasingly important role in the promotion of transnational liberal production and circulation. Borrowing from Gramsci, Jessop (1997) examines the "local hegemonic projects" that are created when transnational capital and its local allies link up with subnational states. Sassen's work on global cities operates in a similar mode by describing the partnerships that have developed between transnational capital and decision-makers in cities that host the world's leading financial firms (Sassen 1998). Geddes and Sullivan (2012) identify a range of behaviors that local leaders around the world have adopted to further "neoliberalization," prioritizing goals such as efficiency and competitiveness over social cohesion and distributive justice. In

[12] Meanwhile, political scientists who study the administrative performance of subnational governments tend to overlook the significance of their ideological orientations. See, e.g., Sabel and Zeitlin (2012).

[13] See also Logan and Molotch (1987) for a classic critique of how "conventional market reasoning" in cities has produced "growth machines" marked by high levels of stratification and inequality.

Latin America, Goldfrank and Schrank (2009) show how the turn toward neoliberalism that took place at the national level in the 1990s was actually foreshadowed in many cases by the earlier introduction of free enterprise zones by local authorities.[14]

Not controlling the national government is a serious drawback for neoliberals—among other things, it means that they cannot reduce tariffs, quotas, or capital controls, and that they cannot devalue the currency to promote export-driven growth. Reducing state intervention in the economy, a hallmark of neoliberalism, is difficult to achieve if the national government is actively expropriating private firms and pursuing vigorous industrial policies. Nevertheless, it is important to recognize the wide scope for neoliberal action that exists at the subnational level across three main fields of public policy, including economic, social, and security policies. With respect to economic policy, neoliberal precepts encourage subnational officials to endorse private-sector entrepreneurship vis-à-vis those infrastructural needs (roads, highways, ports, and irrigation systems) that are paramount for the success of export-oriented economic activities. Precisely because of the decentralization of many of these responsibilities during the neoliberal era, Latin America's subnational governments often retain important control vis-à-vis the infrastructure that is critical for these activities (Oxhorn, Tulchin, and Selee 2004; Smoke, Gomez, and Peterson 2007). To turn to social policy, subnational neoliberals favor a more targeted and less fiscally generous approach to social investments—as opposed to the holistic and universalistic policies that characterize more state-centered approaches (Pribble and Huber 2011; Garay 2016). They also depend heavily on partnerships with the private sector in the provision of social services and/or the outright privatization or concession of utilities, including electricity, water, and sewerage. The same emphasis on cost recovery and the preference for private as opposed to public action also characterize the security field, where neoliberal tenets favor the privatization of security and the expansion of roles for private security guards relative to publicly financed police officers (Spitzer and Scull 2001; Ungar 2007–8). Across all policy domains and service fields, subnational neoliberals try to pare down public-sector payrolls as they aspire for higher levels of efficiency and productivity.

Committed liberals thus have good reason to set their sights on subnational governments, but these governments can also lend themselves to the pursuit of approaches that are decidedly illiberal.[15] Based on research in a number of

[14] See also Herrera (forthcoming) for a comparative study of how nine different Mexican municipalities responded to pressures to adopt neoliberal cost-recovery reforms in the water sector.

[15] See Parnell and Robinson (2012) for the argument that Northern scholars in urban studies have been too quick to use neoliberalism as the dominant lens through which to study urban environments in the Global South, ignoring other perspectives, including developmentalism and

Latin American countries, scholars in recent years have identified a range of policy behaviors by subnational governments that confound rather than promote neoliberal outcomes.[16] In Brazil, Montero (2002) documents the conditions that enable state-level governments to succeed in their efforts to promote economic transformation via subnational industrial policy. Snyder (2006) analyzes the new forms of subnational corporatism that emerged in a variety of Mexican states in the aftermath of national-level economic liberalization.[17] In Argentina, Wibbels (2005) shows how profligate provincial behavior challenged attempts by neoliberal national governments to defend fiscal balance, and Post (2014: 33) demonstrates how governors with statist orientations and fiscal resources were "less likely to negotiate constructively with private providers" of water and sanitation infrastructure. In Peru, Eaton (2010) argues that societal opposition to the sale of state-owned enterprises to foreign firms has encouraged, ironically, postures of economic nationalism on the part of *subnational* elected officials. Across the region, according to Goldfrank and Schrank (2009), national-level free-market reform has triggered the spread of new forms of municipal socialism that focus on long-neglected urban peripheries, at-risk schoolchildren, and social programs from which neoliberal national governments have retreated.[18] While some illiberal behaviors by subnational government may thus be considered forms of socialism (Quilley 2000; Goldfrank and Schrank 2009) or nationalism (Eaton 2010), I use subnational statism in this book as a broader term meant to capture a range of anti-neoliberal positions adopted by subnational elected officials.

As an economic development model, statism typically requires higher levels of state capacity than does neoliberalism, and as a result subnational officials will probably have a more difficult time acting on statist as opposed to neoliberal preferences. According to Evelyne Huber's exploration (2002: 473) of the possibility of more interventionist social policies in Latin America, "local governments typically do not have sufficient resources to experiment successfully with comprehensive social policies." Building statist policy regimes at the subnational level is likely to be harder than building neoliberal policy regimes for this reason, but there is much that can be done subnationally

the legacies of the "local state." On the zeal of subnational states for "re-regulation" in the aftermath of national-level liberalization in India, see Sinha (2004) and Snyder (2006).

[16] According to Fitzgerald (2005: 102), local and regional governments across Latin America continued to engage in planning activities even as neoliberal doctrines came to dominate at the national level in the 1980s and 1990s.

[17] At the municipal level in Mexico, Mahon and Macdonald (2010) examine attempts by city governments in Mexico City to implement anti-poverty policies that are embedded in norms of social citizenship, and that therefore directly challenge the neoliberal anti-poverty approach favored by national governments. For other left experiences at the municipal level, see Carrión and Ponce (2015).

[18] On the perils of "socialism in one borough," see Davies (1988) and Leopold and McDonald (2012).

to contest or derail national-level neoliberal frameworks, notwithstanding Vladimir Lenin's views of municipal socialism as "incapable of bringing about larger socialist transformation" (Leopold and McDonald 2012: 1838).[19] Subnational governments, for example, often enjoy the power to set property taxes, maintain local cadastres, grant (or deny) land-use permits, and allow (or prohibit) the (re)zoning of land for various purposes (Campbell 2009; Faguet 2013). These powers still pale in comparison to national-level prerogatives over tariffs, currencies, and capital controls, but, if subnational officials choose, they can be used to target and complicate the investment projects by private-sector actors (foreign or domestic) that neoliberal policies are seeking to promote at the national level. Particularly in extractive sectors, private investment often depends on securing a "social license" in the form of sufficient levels of societal support locally for projects to go forward (Bebbington and Bury 2013). Elected subnational officials can ally with local groups seeking to deny this informal but important license, and they can endorse, support, and even lead local protests against private companies. In addition to using their offices to throw up obstacles to the private-sector investments that are favored by national neoliberals, subnational officials can also sometimes act on statist preferences by establishing banks and enterprises that are owned and operated by subnational states (Tendler 1968; Trebat 1983; Eaton 2006). More generally, if Leopold and McDonald (2012: 1848) are correct and it was "the emergence of *national* welfare states [that] took the wind out of the municipalist socialist sails" in the early twentieth century, then one can argue that the subsequent decline of the national welfare state model has created space once again for the pursuit of more statist approaches at the local level.

At the subnational level no less than at the national level, "neoliberalism" and "statism" are ideal types that are useful as guides to empirical analysis. No policy regime in the real world is either purely neoliberal or purely statist, and many blend features of both. Furthermore, each analytical category includes a gamut of approaches that range from more moderate to more extreme. For example, neoliberals who advocate aggressive export promotion policies can be differentiated from those who strictly prefer to be price-takers from international markets, and likewise statists who support horizontal policies to foment innovation can be distinguished from those who advocate heavy subsidization and import substitution.[20] These gradations matter for the likelihood of serious and sustained ideological struggle in specific countries; we

[19] According to Lenin, "the bourgeois intelligentsia elevates municipal socialism to a special 'trend' precisely because it dreams of social peace, of class conciliation, and seeks to divert public attention away from the fundamental questions of the economic system as a whole, and of the state *structure* as a whole, to minor questions of *local government*" (Leopold and McDonald 2012: 1845).

[20] I am grateful to an anonymous reviewer for this point.

should not expect to see sharp conflict where neoliberals want to use the state to promote exports and where their statist counterparts only push innovation policies. But in other cases it is possible to identify well-defined and irreconcilable differences between neoliberals and statists, and my core contention is that this kind of conflict increasingly unfolds along territorial lines.

The Emergence of Subnational Policy Challenges

According to the previous section, although they have appeared in the development literature only recently, subnational governments do indeed operate as meaningful and attractive spaces for advocates of liberalism and statism alike, who can use their control over these governments to articulate subnational policy challenges. But why have these challenges become so much more common, in Latin America and elsewhere? A number of factors, some global in their reach and some more specific to the region, help account for the growing importance of territorial heterogeneity in the search for effective economic development strategies.

One key driver is globalization, which has increased opportunities for some subnational regions to insert themselves into the world economy as exporters of the goods that they have comparative advantages in producing, more or less independently from their respective national governments (Piore and Sabel 1986; Scott 1998). Less fortunate subnational regions, in contrast, have been left further behind by globalization in ways that have triggered the defensive creation of distinct subnational policy regimes (Brenner 2004; Geddes 2014). In other words, globalization is especially potent because it can trigger subnational challenges on the part of regional winners *and* losers (Castells and Borja 2004). The globalization of capital markets has also tended to enhance the financial independence of subnational officials, who increasingly can circumvent national governments in their attempts to raise money abroad to fund distinct subnational projects and approaches (Savitch and Kantor 2004; Rodrik 2010). The transition to post-Fordist production with the attendant need to target niche markets has heightened the importance of agile local governments and lessened the importance of the services provided by less flexible national governments (Doner and Hershberg 1999). According to Keating (1999: 4), "free trade, sectoral restructuring, and changes in production technology have in some ways reduced the importance of territory, notably by reducing transportation costs, but in other respects they have enhanced it by increasing the importance of non-traded interdependencies, and reshaped it by fostering new systems of production and innovation." In addition to unleashing these economic changes, globalization has also triggered sustained political efforts at regional integration through the construction of supranational institutions. In Europe, supranational regionalism has strengthened subnational regionalism (Hooghe 1996; Jeffery 2000), thereby potentially enhancing the power and reach of subnational policy challenges.

Democratization has also increased the scope for serious subnational policy challenges and for the possibility of policy regime juxtaposition. Democratically elected national officials may not like the emergence of distinct subnational policy regimes and, as documented in the following chapters, they can use the full range of their powers in the attempt to attenuate policy challenges from below. Authoritarian national governments, however, are even less likely to tolerate subnational deviations, particularly in cases where authoritarian actors like the armed forces have taken power to fix the national economy or to pursue a particular vision of economic development (O'Donnell 1973; Hirschman 1979).[21] Even if the third wave of democratization has tended to produce thin and feeble democratic regimes more often than robust consolidated democracies (Hagopian and Mainwaring 2005), transitions to democracy in the 1980s and 1990s created permissive conditions for the generation of subnational policy challenges.

Particularly where voters can cast separate ballots in national and subnational races, and where these races are held at different times in the electoral calendar (Carey and Shugart 1992), democracy may well encourage policy regime juxtaposition. After all, voters may look to different levels of government for different policy solutions and for different levels of engagement in the economy. For instance, voters might prefer more interventionism from local governments and less interventionism on the part of the more distant national government, whose actions may be deemed disproportionately to benefit residents in other parts of the country. Or, conversely, doubting the competence of local authorities whom they can observe up close, voters may prefer greater intervention by the national government officials whom they consider to be better trained or more competent. In fact, we should expect that this type of split-ticket voting will more frequently produce "divided government" between national and subnational levels than "divided government" between executive and legislative branches at the national level. Whereas the latter is possible only under presidentialism (Haggard and McCubbins 2001), the former is theoretically possible in both presidential and parliamentary systems alike. The tendency of democracy to generate vertically divided government between national and subnational levels is important in all three of my country

[21] At the same time, while authoritarianism probably limits the space within which subnational policy challenges can emerge, under certain conditions the pursuit of subnational policy regimes that deviate from the national policy regime may actually serve the interests of authoritarian national governments. I am grateful to Yue Zhang for this point. See also Snyder (2006) on Mexico, where subnational corporatism was functional to the interests of the (authoritarian) governing party at the national level.

cases, but especially in Ecuador and Bolivia, where many voters in Guayaquil and Santa Cruz have supported the right locally but the left nationally.

By definition, the ability to mount subnational policy challenges depends on some degree of decentralization, which I consider to be the main driver of the tighter connection that has emerged between ideological and territorial conflicts. The late twentieth-century trend toward political, fiscal, and administrative decentralization has almost certainly increased the significance of the two types of subnational policy challenges that are examined in this book (Eaton 2004; Falleti 2010; Goldfrank 2011). Typically taking the form of separate elections for subnational officials, political decentralization has introduced an entirely new arena for ideological contestation over the market, creating the possibility that subnational officials will win electoral mandates to pursue very different economic models relative to the national level. Fiscal decentralization, meanwhile, provides a double impetus in that it both enhances the resources that elected subnational officials can devote toward the pursuit of their preferred approaches, while also endowing them with fiscal policy tools they can use to behave in either a liberal or a statist fashion (that is, either lowering taxes to promote investment or raising taxes to finance expenditure).[22] Administrative decentralization has also contributed to this phenomenon since it gives subnational officials real choices in terms of how much of a role they want the private sector to play in the provision of critical public services such as health, education, and infrastructure. While decentralization typically refers to the transfer of political, fiscal, and administrative authority to existing subnational governments, it can also take the form of creating these governments wholesale and/or transforming subnational administrative units into governmental entities. In their comprehensive study of eighty countries between 1950 and 2010, Hooghe and Marks document a clear trend toward the creation of regional authority; while thirty-four new tiers of government were created in this period, only seven were eliminated (Hooghe and Marks 2016: 48).[23]

Decentralization has undeniably set the stage for more meaningful subnational policy challenges around the world, and yet it does not necessarily imply that distinct subnational policy regimes will automatically take shape. Subnational officials can make extensive use of newly decentralized authorities without their policy choices congealing into an identifiable and coherent policy regime or challenge. The key question explored in this book is whether

[22] For a contrary view see Harbers (2015: 379), who argues that ideology influences tax policy choices at the national level far more than at the local level, where she assumes that the authority "to set tax policy is limited . . . because municipal governments are subject to the same tax regime."

[23] In addition to the creation of new tiers of subnational government, new governance structures have emerged that bring together multiple tiers of government along with non-governmental actors. See Abers and Keck (2013).

subnational officials who are committed to either liberalism or statism can use the powers of their offices to act on those ideological commitments. In and of itself, decentralization does not tell us enough about the outcome of attempts by subnational officials to use their powers in this fashion. Furthermore, it is important not to overstate the significance of formal decentralization because the reality is that subnational elected officials, particularly in the context of weak central states, often enjoy significant *de facto* autonomy to act on their ideological preferences, even in the absence of high levels of *de jure* policy decentralization. As developed in greater detail in the following chapter, I find that subnational capacity is a more critical factor than subnational authority in explaining when elected officials can act on their discordant preferences.

In addition to worldwide trends such as globalization, democratization, and decentralization, several other developments that are especially salient in Latin America have increased the likelihood of subnational policy challenges and distinct subnational policy regimes.[24] Across the region, countries have experienced high levels of party system instability, characterized by the collapse of traditional political parties in some cases (Tanaka 2006; Seawright 2012). Party system turmoil has threatened the ability of powerful economic interests to achieve representation in the national government through the same political parties they previously relied on for this purpose. In some countries, the traditional parties that contested national elections have not disappeared altogether but rather survive at the subnational level (Freidenberg and Suárez-Cao 2014; Cyr 2017). Where parties that formerly represented elite interests can no longer hope to win national elections or can no longer be expected to exert great influence in national level policymaking processes, one response might be to pay greater attention to the types of policy solutions that subnational governments can provide. Economic elites in this situation certainly have other options, including the pursuit of non-partisan mechanisms of representation at the national level (Levitsky, Loxton, and Van Dyck 2016), but the greater difficulty of accessing national power via parties should throw into greater relief the potential importance of subnational policy regimes. Party system turbulence has taken different forms in Bolivia, Ecuador, and Peru, but in all three cases the collapse of the national party system has increased the importance of being able to shape and defend distinct policy approaches at the subnational level. Control over subnational governments may be one means of partially restoring the influence in national policy debates that at least some leading economic actors lost in the wake of

[24] In other world regions, the relative weakness of the global trends emphasized here may account for the relative absence of subnational policy challenges. The limited nature of democratization and decentralization in the Middle East, for example, may help explain why these challenges have yet to appear in a significant way.

party system collapse; for others, investing in subnational policy regimes can represent a form of "exit" from a national political system they can no longer dominate and instead find threatening (Hirschman 1970).

Looking across the region brings into focus another common cause of the greater frequency of subnational policy challenges in Latin America today: ethnic mobilization. Against a backdrop of centuries of political subordination, new indigenous social movements in recent decades have dramatically expanded their capacity to influence national level policy debates, not just by placing indigenous leaders in key bureaucratic positions but by winning presidential and legislative elections as well (Yashar 2005; Van Cott 2008; Madrid 2012; Chartock 2013). While the perhaps more dramatic story here is that indigenous mobilization has led to the transformation of *national* policy regimes, it has also triggered the articulation of demands for alternative *subnational* policy regimes. This can even happen simultaneously in the same country, as in Bolivia, where eastern indigenous communities have sought to enhance the policy authority of subnational units even as western indigenous groups enjoy unprecedented control over national policy levers through the dominance of the governing Movement for Socialism (*Movimiento al Socialismo* or *MAS*) party (Postero 2006, 2010). More generally, where ethnic claims overlap with territorial demands for autonomy, as in the lowland areas of the Amazonian basis, the political mobilization of ethnic identities has prioritized not so much the transformation of national policy regimes as the right to pursue territorially distinct local models (Tockman and Cameron 2014). Specific policy outputs are not the only (nor perhaps even the most important) demands made by indigenous actors, who instead are articulating a number of proposals that range from legal system reform to far-reaching cultural changes (Yashar 2005; Lucero 2008). Nevertheless, ethnic mobilization is appropriately understood as an important new source of the subnational policy challenges that Latin America is witnessing. Indeed, when articulated by indigenous communities, these challenges in many respects represent a more radical critique of economic development, along with its associated negative impacts on cultural survival and environmental sustainability, than the more familiar (but no less significant) struggles between liberal and statist approaches highlighted in this book.

Advantages and Disadvantages of Policy Regime Juxtaposition

If, for whatever combination of reasons, the articulation of subnational policy challenges has become more common around the world, is this a desirable trend? From a normative perspective, what are the various advantages and disadvantages of the first type of challenge that is examined in this book, that of territorially juxtaposed policy regimes? A more thorough, but necessarily speculative, exploration of the costs and benefits that might be generated by policy regime juxtaposition underscores the importance of better understanding this growing phenomenon. In contrast to the literature on the juxtaposition of *political* regimes (Gervasoni 2010; Gibson 2013; Giraudy 2015; McMann 2006), which is animated by a widely shared normative desire to promote the democratization of subnational authoritarian enclaves, the relative merit of market-oriented versus state-centered approaches has remained an open debate among scholars. As a result, greater normative discord may characterize the study of the phenomenon of policy regime juxtaposition relative to political regime juxtaposition.

There are a number of reasons to emphasize the positive effects generated by territorially juxtaposed policy regimes. First, the phenomenon reflects movement away from a one-size-fits-all dynamic in which subnational governments are not allowed to pursue development models that may elicit majority support subnationally but not nationally. In some respects, policy regime juxtaposition is simply an outcome that follows logically from one of the primary motives behind decentralization, which is that it enables policy innovation and experimentation (Cheema and Rondinelli 2007; Sabel and Zeitlin 2012). If there are strong normative reasons to support decentralization, including meaningful variation in citizen preferences across subnational units and the likelihood that local politicians have better local knowledge than do national politicians (Oates 1972; Weingast 2014), then there are likewise strong reasons to conclude that it is positive when subnational officials can craft coherent models with their policy authority.

A second possible benefit of policy regime juxtaposition is that it may enable voters at a given point in time to make comparative assessments of the two regimes in contention. When only a single, national policy regime is in place, voters can engage only in retrospective comparisons, comparing their information about the current national model with their memories of the relative merits of the previous national model. Cross-temporal comparisons are complicated, however, not just by the quality of people's memories, but by the exogenous factors that impact the implementation of any model. How, for example, to compare the performance of statist models during the commodity boom of the 2000s in Latin America with the neoliberal model implemented during the 1980s and 1990s at a time of fiscal austerity and financial crisis? While the comparison of territorially juxtaposed policy regimes in real time suffers from other problems—namely, the difficulty of comparing models across scales of government—voters may be exposed to better and more useful information about the differences between statism and neoliberalism when they are repeatedly exposed to and reminded of these differences by the combative interactions of contemporary incumbents at different levels of government. This is especially likely if, as in my three cases, presidents, mayors, and governors regularly and sharply criticize one another's approaches in exchanges (covered extensively by the media) that can be personal and petty, but also more abstract and even illuminating and didactic.

Third, policy regime juxtaposition may reduce the size and/or the frequency of the often extreme policy swings that have been so destabilizing in Latin America. Writing on the instability of economic strategies in Latin America, John Sheahan (2002: 25) argues that "these countries change their versions of capitalism much more frequently, and more radically, than European countries do." With respect to the size of past swings, policy regime juxtaposition may moderate the tendency of national governments to experiment with extreme versions of either model, whether in the form of "Gerschenkron gone awry" in the mid-twentieth century (Corrales 2003) or the decision to privatize even profitable state-owned enterprises in some countries in the 1990s. Policy regime juxtaposition may have a dampening effect in either direction. With respect to the frequency of past swings, irrespective of one's ideological preferences and the value or lack thereof that one sees in the content of neoliberal or statist approaches, a case can be made that rapid and relatively short-lived changes are themselves negative. Furthermore, not unlike democracy, which lowers the stakes of electoral contests for losers by giving them an opportunity to win in the future (Przeworski 1991), the ability to construct subnational policy regimes can lower the stakes associated with losing the national-level battle over development models. This may be especially important for economic elites, whose past support for democracy in Latin America was often highly contingent (Gibson 1996), and whose ability to protect their economic interests through subnational policy regimes might increase their tolerance for the continuation of democracy at the national level. More generally, a country's political life may become more pluralistic when subnational officials are able to defend deviant local models from the national incumbents who would prefer to impose and enforce their own models; in other words, economic pluralism may beget political pluralism.

As a final possible advantage, the pursuit of ideologically distinct models at the national and subnational levels may enable and promote convergence between neoliberal and statist approaches in the medium to long term. Policy regime juxtaposition can bring into focus similarities rather than differences between market-oriented and state-centered approaches, particularly at a time when environmental and indigenous groups are articulating truly revolutionary critiques of both types of approaches. In this way, policy regime juxtaposition could appeal to pragmatists who would prefer a less ideologically charged and inflexible debate over economic development, and who wish to focus the conversation instead on the identification and emulation of practical solutions and effective partnerships between the state and the private sector. Ironically, more pragmatism and less ideology might be one of the side effects of policy regime juxtaposition.

On the other hand, there are significant potential disadvantages associated with successful subnational policy challenges and the territorial juxtaposition of distinct policy regimes. Furthermore, these disadvantages are likely to be especially acute in lesser developed countries, where the search for effective development strategies is of such paramount importance. In the context of policy regime juxtaposition, the territory circumscribed within a particular subnational unit (that is, municipality, department, region) is in effect being governed by two different regimes, which can generate substantial contradictions at both the policy and institutional level.[25] Especially where decentralization has taken the form of shared rather than exclusive competencies over public policy fields, which has been the dominant modality in many developing countries, juxtaposition may be a recipe for chronic uncertainty. But even where there is a clearer devolution of specific policy authorities to subnational levels, the national government still retains important oversight and monitoring roles in ways that can produce confusion for the local private sector. At a minimum, policy regime juxtaposition increases transaction costs by requiring economic actors to master and stay on top of the rules and incentives emanating from two rival models. These costs could be especially onerous for foreign investors, who have less access to high-quality information about domestic political realities and workarounds, along with fewer local relationships to help them navigate between disparate models.

A second disadvantage can be identified as the flip side of the presumed benefits of convergence and pragmatism already discussed. Firm believers in either neoliberalism or statism would argue that the strength of the incentives created by either model is undercut or diluted by the presence of a different set of incentives at another level of government within the same country. In this view, subnational governments should be prevented from being able to pursue deviant approaches that counter the logic of national models. In other words, that subnational policy regimes might have a moderating effect should be seen as a negative rather than a positive factor, and is precisely why they should be disabled. For example, defenders of neoliberal approaches at the national level might fear the market distortions created when important subnational governments establish their own state-owned enterprises or use

[25] While policy regime juxtaposition may lead to a chaotic institutional environment, it could also be an important source of the institutional layering dynamic described by Thelen (2003), to the extent that it encourages national and subnational governments to engage in the "partial renegotiation" of existing institutional arrangements.

state-owned banks to lend to preferred borrowers. In the opposite configuration, national advocates of statism might have a harder time encouraging private-sector actors to reorient their behavior toward industrialization, production for the domestic market, and/or the use of domestic (rather than imported) inputs if subnational governments are simultaneously providing vigorous support for exporting and importing activities.

Most importantly, policy regime juxtaposition in the Latin American context is likely to generate significant political conflict and consume scarce political resources that could be devoted to other pressing priorities. In the twentieth century, shifts between national models tended to produce acute political conflict in the period leading up to the shift, and then more low-grade conflict once the new model was in place (Fitzgerald 2005). In the contemporary period, marked by greater lag effects produced by territorial resistance and the greater persistence of distinct subnational models, political conflict may be intense and nearly constant. The politics of policy regime juxtaposition are often characterized by (1) aggressive national attempts to stamp out the subnational deviation, which understandably provokes stiff local resistance, and (2) equally aggressive subnational attempts to use subnational experiences as the basis for successful efforts to overthrow the national model. In more developed economies and in more institutionalized political settings, distinct subnational policy regimes may be less threatening to the center, and policy regime juxtaposition seems to have resulted in more stable equilibria and in less protracted forms of contention (Jones and Keating 1995). Cohabitation rather than contention may be the more accurate way to characterize the territorial heterogeneity that is being produced by ideological conflict over the market in Europe, for example. But in the less institutionalized contexts of the global south, where developmental challenges are often quite desperate and where the stakes are perhaps greater, territorially juxtaposed policy regimes are likely to be the source of deep, ongoing, and even violent political conflict, as in Bolivia and Peru and, to a lesser extent, Ecuador. When particularly acute, these quintessentially domestic conflicts between levels of government can even affect a country's external relations. In Bolivia, for example, the US Ambassador was expelled over charges he conspired with opposition governors against the national government in 2008, a conflict that then triggered the intervention of a new supranational body: the Union of South American Nations (UNASUR).

To summarize, a range of possible impacts—some positive, some negative—are likely to result from the global shift toward greater territorial heterogeneity in the search for economic development. More definitive judgments about the desirability (or otherwise) of this shift as it continues to unfold will depend in part on answers to the logically prior question that I ask in this book: under what conditions do subnational policy challenges actually succeed vis-à-vis the national government?

Plan of the Book

Now that I have defined in this chapter what I mean by subnational policy challenges, and explained why they have become more common and why that is important, the following chapter turns to my theoretical framework. Rather than aim for the parsimonious explanation of a multidimensional outcome that is probably the result of numerous causes, I set out instead to develop theoretical arguments inductively that can account for variation across my three cases, but that are also general enough to be applicable in contexts other than the central Andes. Given the paucity of research on the phenomenon I am studying, this book is an exercise in theory-building rather than theory-testing, and its overarching aim is to uncover the variables that appear most likely to shape the success or failure of subnational policy challenges. After a presentation of the theoretical framework, the second half of Chapter 2 then introduces my country cases: Bolivia, Ecuador, and Peru. I examine the core similarities that make these three countries a uniquely productive site for the small-N comparative study of how ideological conflict over the market has become increasingly territorialized. Drawing on a variety of sources of information gathered from a series of field research trips to Bolivia (2005, 2012, 2014), Ecuador (2008, 2010, 2014, 2015), and Peru (2007, 2014), the chapter closes with a section that scores each of these three cases on my two dependent variables (that is, the two types of subnational policy challenges conceptualized in this chapter).

To preview my theoretical argument, which taps into a wide variety of literatures in political science, I emphasize the importance of three sets of causal factors: structural, institutional, and coalitional. First is the structural significance of the region over which particular subnational elected officials govern. The greater the importance to the national economy of the jurisdictions that elected them, the greater the leverage that mayors and governors can be expected to wield—a theoretical distinction that is especially important for their ability successfully to challenge the national policy regime (subnational policy challenge no. 2). Structure matters, though not in a deterministic or mechanistic fashion. Structurally significant regions can force the center to pay attention to and to take seriously the discordant policy preferences of the officials who govern them, but structure tells us less about how exactly the center will respond. Explaining why the national government decides to accommodate these preferences, and why instead it may reject accommodation in favor of more repressive strategies (including the suspension and/or incarceration of subnational officials), requires attention to other factors beyond economic structures, such as capacity and coalitions.

The second key factor is the level of institutional capacity that can be harnessed by elected subnational officials to act on their various policy challenges, a variable that is particularly germane for their ability to build and defend policy regimes that deviate from the center's preferred model (subnational policy challenge no. 1). Capacity matters more than authority in my three cases, which can be mined for relevant insights about the forces that either promote or retard state building—a crucial question for comparative politics. For instance, in Bolivia and Ecuador it was, surprisingly, the private sector that took the lead in generating institutional capacity at the subnational level (in Santa Cruz and Guayaquil, respectively). In both cases, local economic elites directed a gradual process of capacity-building over many decades that would ultimately explain the persistence of neoliberal policy regimes in each subnational region when they came under attack from leftist presidents at the national level after 2005. In Peru, the absence of institutional capacity has doomed efforts by regional presidents to build more state-centered policy regimes, not just because the regions are new and fledgling, but because the national government has actively sought to prevent the accumulation of capacity on the part of subnational governments, thereby hobbling efforts to challenge the center.

The third variable, coalitional strength, matters critically for both types of subnational policy challenges. In their typically bilateral interactions with ideologically hostile presidents, individual mayors and governors need to make it harder and more costly for the president simply to repress the challenges they pose. Coalitions help make subnational elected officials look "bigger" in their conflicts with the center. Precisely because of the disproportionate political, fiscal, and administrative resources enjoyed by presidents at the center, building discordant subnational policy regimes requires that individual mayors and governors reach out and construct coalitions, not just on subnational legislative bodies, but with the organized civil society actors who populate their jurisdictions. Which actors are most likely to join these coalitions is, of course, strongly shaped by the ideological content of the model that the mayor or governor is trying to build and/or defend; business groups are typically key members of coalitions to sustain subnational neoliberalism, while other constituencies, including labor unions, neighborhood associations, and environmental groups, figure prominently in coalitions to support subnational statism. The key point is that the availability (or lack thereof) of local coalitional partners is a major factor shaping the success or failure of this first type of challenge. Turning to the second type of subnational policy challenge, a different type of coalition strongly conditions the ability of subnational elected officials to contest the national policy regime. Here coalitions are important not within but across particular subnational jurisdictions; subnational elected officials need to hold together as a group of peers if they hope to scale up and gain redress from the center. I argue that this theoretical framework outperforms rival explanations based on institutional authority, partisan and electoral dynamics, leadership qualities, and international factors.

The empirical core of the book—Chapters 3, 4, and 5—focuses in turn on each of my three country cases. I examine these countries in the order of increasing success, beginning with the least and ending with the most effective cases of territorial resistance. Each empirical chapter shares a common organizational logic, focusing initially on the relative success or failure of efforts to develop ideologically deviant subnational policy regimes (that is, the first type of subnational policy challenge) and subsequently on the relative success or failure of efforts to disrupt the national policy regime (that is, the second type of challenge).

Chapter 3 explains the failure of both types of subnational policy challenges in Peru. I argue that absent coalitional partners and deep capacity deficits, which have been intentionally and unintentionally worsened by the national government, have kept regional presidents who occupy a variety of positions on the left from successfully developing policy regimes that would deviate from the neoliberalism insisted upon by Lima. Structural constraints derived from the center's ownership of subsoil resources, along with the atomization of regional presidents, have hindered the second type of policy challenge as well. Chapter 4 explores the hybrid case of Ecuador, truly a case of policy regime juxtaposition. High levels of institutional capacity and effective local coalitions have enabled the right-wing mayors of Guayaquil to defend that city's unique liberal model from constant attacks by the president, but Guayaquil's waning structural power and isolation relative to other subnational spaces have limited its national leverage vis-à-vis the powerful Correa government. Chapter 5 turns to the critical Bolivian case, where both types of subnational policy challenges largely succeeded. As in Guayaquil, economic and political elites in Santa Cruz invested over time in the creation of a series of distinctly liberal local institutions, and then built a broad local coalition to defend those institutions and the liberal policy regime they sustained. Unlike their peers in Ecuador, however, these same *cruceño* elites were also able to force the national government of Evo Morales substantially to moderate its initially heavily statist orientation—an outcome I attribute to their ability to build a still broader coalition with the country's other eastern departments, as well as to Santa Cruz's significant structural leverage as a critical producer of foodstuffs.

The final chapter concludes by returning to the broader questions raised by these subnational policy challenges and by the tighter connectivity between territorial and ideological conflict that they reflect. Here I use the experience of my three country cases further to probe and to explore the three main elements of my theoretical framework: structural significance, institutional capacity, and coalitional strength. On the one hand, these three cases suggest that structural constraints powerfully shape the ability of subnational elected officials to execute policy challenges, and that countries in which many subnational regions enjoy structural leverage will be characterized by much higher levels of territorial friction in the fight over development models than countries where few or no regions outside the national capital region are structurally significant. On the other hand, my cases suggest that we need to think of structure in non-structural ways; just as presidents can and do actively try to diminish the structural weight of key subnational jurisdictions, officials in those jurisdictions can seek to reinforce, defend, and deepen their structural significance. Structure is not destiny. With respect to capacity, the three cases suggest that private-sector behavior contributes to subnational state formation in some contexts (Guayaquil and Santa Cruz) but not in others (Peru). Strong regional identities can encourage economic elites to promote rather than retard institution-building—provided they can control these institutions. Finally, my cases point to the need to broaden our understanding of coalitions to include not just their material but also their discursive dimensions. Whether subnational elected officials can tap into deep-seated territorial identities and grievances is an essential factor in explaining their ability substantially to widen defensive coalitions vis-à-vis the national government. If multilevel governance results not just from the technical considerations of "scale" as predicted by public goods theory but from deeply social considerations of "community" as well (Hooghe and Marks 2016), "community" in turn can be constructed through discursive coalitions that transform conflicts over economic ideology into conflicts over territorial attachments.

2

When do Subnational Policy Challenges Succeed?

Structure, Institutions, and Coalitions

What explains variation in the effectiveness of subnational policy challenges? Why are elected officials able to build and defend their own divergent policy regimes in some subnational regions, but not elsewhere (policy challenge no. 1)? Why are these same officials able to change national policy regimes they do not like in some cases, but not in others (policy challenge no. 2)? If the introduction of elections for subnational officials has transformed them into more important players in their countries' ideological conflicts over the market, it is essential that we develop a better understanding of why they win or lose. The theoretical framework developed in this chapter focuses on three separate causal variables—structural, institutional, and coalitional—that are critical in understanding the success or failure of these challenges. After situating my core hypotheses relative to a variety of political science literatures, the chapter then introduces Bolivia, Ecuador, and Peru as the three cases that form the empirical core of the book. The cases are characterized by significant and intriguing variation on the dependent variable: both types of subnational policy challenges have largely succeeded in Bolivia, neither has succeeded in Peru, and Ecuador experienced an intermediate outcome marked by the success of the first type of challenge (that is, the defense of a deviant, neoliberal subnational policy regime) and the failure of the second (that is, the inability to alter the statist national policy regime).

To summarize the argument up front, I argue that a subnational district's structural significance, institutional capacity, and coalitional strengths help explain the outcomes of both types of challenges examined in this book—those that seek to create and defend divergent subnational policy regimes and those that seek to contest and transform national policy regimes. The argument is depicted in schematic form in Table 2.1, which scores subnational

Table 2.1. Scoring subnational challenges on the independent (IV) and dependent (DV) variables

Country	IV1 Structural significance	IV2 Institutional capacity	IV3 Coalitional strength (internal/ external)	DV1 Defense of subnational policy regime?	DV2 Impact on national policy regime?
Peru	Medium	Low	Low/Low	No	No
Ecuador	Medium	High	High/Low	Yes	No
Bolivia	High	High	High/High	Yes	Yes

governments for each of my three cases, along with the observed outcomes. As will become clear in the discussion that follows, the first causal variable (structural significance) is especially critical for the ability to influence the national policy regime (DV2), the second causal variable (institutional capacity) is essential for the defense of subnational policy regimes (DV1), and the third causal variable (internal and external coalitional strength) matters for both types of challenges.

Theorizing Subnational Policy Challenges: Structure, Institutions, and Coalitions

Subnational chief executives occupy the center of this theoretical framework, which emphasizes the very different landscapes these individuals encounter when, as a result of their direct election, they now seek to advance subnational policy challenges. Other subnational actors, including nongovernmental organizations, neighborhood associations, and local business chambers, can certainly challenge national policy regimes; and regionalized economic elites are an especially important actor in the theory developed here because of the way they have contributed to administrative capacity and strengthened societal coalitions. But subnational elected officials deserve to be considered the analytical starting point because of the roles they play as the protagonists who are best positioned to articulate, coordinate, and maintain subnational policy challenges. These officials are much better positioned to do so than the national legislators who represent their districts (or some combination of districts) in Congress. This is because national legislators play hybrid roles as both subnational and national figures, and therefore serve less well as defenders of the subnational. Political decentralization has been a profoundly threatening phenomenon for national legislators, one that has called into question the brokerage roles between national and subnational levels they have traditionally played in most democracies. In numerous countries, decentralization has enabled subnational elected officials to supplant legislators as protagonists in their (shared or overlapping) electoral districts. While this was not the case before political decentralization, when subnational officials were appointed from the center, the introduction of direct subnational elections has given many winning candidates strong incentives to lead subnational policy challenges. My central theoretical question is what determines their success or failure in waging these challenges.

I pay special attention to subnational chief executives such as mayors and governors (though they may be given other titles, including "regional presidents" in the Peruvian case), rather than representatives in subnational legislative bodies such as city councilors or members of departmental assemblies.[1] This decision reflects the reality that, while decentralization has challenged the vertical concentration of power in national as opposed to subnational governments, it has mostly replicated the horizontal concentration of power in (subnational) executive as opposed to (subnational) legislative branches that has long characterized Latin American presidentialism (Carey and Shugart 1992). In effect, most countries in Latin America have experienced the "decentralization of hyper-presidentialism" (Eaton 2012: 39). Mayors and governors have become by far the most important protagonists within subnational political society, easily dominating their counterparts in representative bodies (for example, municipal councilors and departmental legislators). Indeed, one of the most consistent findings in the burgeoning literature on local politics in Latin America is the paramount importance of subnational chief executives, whose agency and leadership qualities have assumed special significance in the post-decentralization period. According to a number of scholars focusing on different aspects of local government, most recent municipal success stories in Latin America can be traced to the efforts of talented and entrepreneurial (and, increasingly, indigenous) mayors who are committed to changing the status quo (Grindle 2007; Wampler 2007; Van Cott 2008; Avellaneda 2009; Cameron 2009).[2] Although I focus on subnational executives rather than representatives in this book, the quality of the inter-branch relationship at the municipal or departmental/provincial level does help explain the relative success of attempts by subnational chief executives to build legislative coalitions that can defend distinctive subnational policy regimes vis-à-vis the center.

[1] Note that I do not develop a separate theoretical argument for mayors as opposed to governors or, more generally, for chief executives at the local as opposed to intermediate level of government. While scale matters for the content of the formal authorities these officials are able to draw upon in their challenges, their ability successfully to prosecute these challenges depends on the same underlying logic of structural, institutional, and coalitional power. For the outcomes I seek to explain, my claim is that we do not need a separate theory for mayors versus governors.

[2] For the more general exposition of this claim about the growing global importance of mayors, see Barber (2013).

Not only does my theoretical framework privilege subnational chief executives over both subnational civil society and subnational legislators, it also privileges these executives over the national government actors with whom they are embattled. Presidents are no less strategic than the mayors and governors they are fighting, but for a variety of reasons it makes sound theoretical sense to pay more attention to the types and levels of resources (structural, institutional, coalitional) that are available to the latter rather than the former. First, the decision to do so represents an attempt to counter the traditional and dominant scholarly bias in favor of the national government. Although comparative politics as a subfield has begun to shed its "whole nation bias" and to question whether what happens in a national capital can be taken as representative of a country's political life writ large (Snyder 2001), the temptation to begin with and thereby privilege the center remains a powerful one. Second, and more importantly, the playing field upon which subnational elected officials engage in combat with their counterparts at the national level is a profoundly uneven one. Notwithstanding important cross-national differences generated by history, institutions, and geography, the center almost everywhere enjoys extraordinary advantages as it seeks to discipline and "overawe" subnational governments (Riker 1964). In all countries, subnational chief executives confront a basic and difficult asymmetry; while the national chief executive is just one individual, they are many—and can therefore be played off against one another in the politics of divide and conquer. Furthermore, sovereignty as the dominant norm in the international state system assigns a variety of privileges to the national government that no subnational government enjoys (Murphy 1996). Precisely because the fight is such an uneven one, resources that can be leveraged by subnational actors will play a preponderant role in explaining the outcome of their uphill struggles against the center.

Third, turning to Latin America, there are regionally specific reasons to shine theoretical attention on the subnational rather than national level. Most importantly, presidentialism has functioned as a system of government in Latin America that concentrates power in the national executive rather than in the national legislature—in contrast to the greater inter-branch balancing that characterizes presidentialism in the USA. In the "hyper-presidential" systems and "delegative democracies" that continue to characterize many countries in the region—notwithstanding institutional strengthening in several noteworthy cases—presidents have enormous political, fiscal, and symbolic resources to deal with non-compliant subnational challengers, precisely because of the weakness of national-level checks and balances (O'Donnell 1994). National legislators struggle mightily to participate in the policymaking process with the president on an equal footing (Carey and Shugart 1992; Eaton 2002), and judicial institutions struggle just as dramatically to develop independence from overweening presidents (Helmke and Rios-Figueroa 2014). I argue that the persistent weakness of national-level checks and balances in Latin America has had the effect of freeing up presidents to prioritize their responses to important subnational challenges, when these emerge. The presidents in all three of my country cases, for example, faced very few constraints from actors at the national level who could challenge their preferred ideological approaches; instead, the really significant challenges all came from below.[3] This does not mean that presidents did not behave strategically vis-à-vis subnational challengers or that their response strategies were irrelevant; in the cases included in this book presidents worked aggressively to undermine their challengers' structural positions, to hinder efforts that would deepen their institutional capacity, and to keep them from forming viable coalitions amongst one another. But subnational challengers themselves deserve central billing in the theories we develop to explain the degree to which they succeed or fail.

To understand the outcome of subnational policy challenges thus requires a theoretical framework that recognizes the greater importance of subnational executives relative both to other subnational actors and to the national government. My central theoretical question is not about the origin of these executives' policy preferences but rather about the conditions (structural, institutional, coalitional) that enable them to advance these preferences, either by creating and defending their own subnational policy regimes or by influencing the content of national policy regimes. In practice, however, it can be difficult to assess the conditions that either favor or inhibit subnational challengers in the contemporary world without taking seriously the origin of their preferences and the source of their grievances. For example, while I shall argue that administrative capacity helps subnational officials succeed today in their challenges and grievances against the national government, the existence of capacity may itself reflect the outcome of earlier challenges and grievances. As demonstrated in Chapters 4 and 5, economic elites in Guayaquil and Santa Cruz began to invest in local institutions in the nineteenth century and in the 1950s, respectively, not just because they believed they could control these institutions but out of a sense of grievance vis-à-vis the neglect of the central government. Over many decades, they built capacity that could subsequently be deployed to defend local approaches in response to a much later set of grievances—namely, the left turn that took place at the start of the twenty-first century. In other words, subnational officials need capacity to challenge the national government, but capacity is partially

[3] In Peru, once President Ollanta Humala reversed the campaign promises he had made in the run-up to the first round in 2011 and opted instead to embrace (indeed to strengthen) the neoliberal model, he faced no significant national-level institutional constraints. Before this reversal, one could argue that he was strongly constrained by the financial wing of the national bureaucracy. See Vergara and Encinas (2016).

endogenous to the challenges advanced by their predecessors. Likewise, it can be easier for subnational challengers to build effective internal coalitions—my third causal variable—if they are able to draw on a history of territorial grievance against the center. By extending the time frame backwards in time, the empirical chapters that follow are able to appreciate the often important residue that is left by earlier challenges even while staying focused on the outcome of contemporary challenges.

Beginning with structure

Subnational officials are unequal in terms of the structural significance to the national economy of the jurisdictions they govern. Mayors and governors who preside over districts that are important for aggregate economic outcomes in the country should enjoy greater leverage than their counterparts in less economically important districts. This simple distinction generates substantial analytical leverage and offers an essential starting point for any sustained discussion of subnational policy challenges. But the impact of this structural variable differs depending on the type of challenge in play. With respect to the first type of policy challenge, one can hypothesize an indirect relationship between structural significance and the prospects for success; subnational officials with deviant policy preferences in structurally *insignificant* jurisdictions should be more able to pursue these preferences—precisely because they can be dismissed as irrelevant, non-threatening, or otherwise not worthy of the notice of the national government. As argued in the next section, however, in places where structural insignificance might give subnational elected officials the necessary breathing room to innovate and/or deviate, insufficient capacity is likely to operate as a drag on the construction of viable subnational policy regimes. In many developing countries, the two variables co-vary in the rural districts that make up the overwhelming majority of the national territory. Small, sparsely populated rural municipalities in lesser developed subnational regions typically lack both structural significance and institutional capacity; the latter is certainly an obstacle, but the former should be perceived as a permissive condition.

The relationship between structural significance and the success of the second type of policy challenge is more complicated, and mostly runs in the opposite direction; the greater the importance of the local or regional economy to the national economy, the more likely it is that subnational officials will matter, and that the national government will be unable to ignore attempts by these officials to contest the national policy regime. Officials who govern structurally significant regions will be more likely to influence and alter the content of the national development model, when they oppose it, than their peers who govern in less important regions. At the same time, the greater economic significance of a given subnational region does not mean that the national government will necessarily *accommodate* the discordant preferences of its elected officials. Instead, in the desire to preserve its preferred policy regime at the national level, the center may opt to devote greater time, attention, and resources to the suppression of these subnational preferences, rather than their accommodation. In other words, structure matters, but the impact of structural factors on the success of this second type of subnational policy challenge is mediated by institutional and coalitional factors. What seems clear is that, in structurally significant jurisdictions, the introduction of elections for subnational officials poses an enormous potential problem for the national government, which it can solve either through accommodation or through coercion.

In order to assess these structural arguments, I borrow from and adapt the literature on the structural power of business, which is the most useful place to look for insights into how subnational regions can leverage their structural influence (Dahl and Lindblom 1976; Lindblom 1977). For instance, once the word "sector" is replaced with "region," the following sentence by Tasha Fairfield (2015a: 43–4) offers an illuminating point of departure: "A sector [region] that constitutes a large proportion of GDP, serves as a growth engine, drives job creation, or plays a critical role in ensuring that the broader economy functions smoothly . . . has the potential to generate stronger structural power than a sector [region] lacking such characteristics." When the focus shifts to analyzing the structural influence of regions rather than businesses, additional sources of leverage become important, including (1) the ability of the region in question to tap independently into global markets and export more or less independently from the center (which increases its power), (2) the location within the subnational region of significant subsoil natural resources (which increases regional power), and (3) the region's role in producing price-sensitive agricultural goods for consumption in the domestic market (which increases its power). In other words, the sources of a region's structural leverage are multiple. As Fairfield (2015a: 48) goes on to argue, "given the specificity of structural power to particular contexts and reforms, structural power must be carefully evaluated on a case by case basis."

Significant similarities and differences characterize the study of structural power when it is exercised by regions as opposed to businesses. As in the study of business, a distinction must be drawn between anticipated reactions and ex-post behavior. While the structural power of business operates largely through the law of anticipated reactions in the sense of *preventing* governments from adopting policies disfavored by business (Lindblom 1977; Przeworski and Wallerstein 1988), business's structural power can also result in the retraction and/or moderating of policies once they are adopted (Fairfield

2015a: 45).[4] The same is true when it comes to subnational regions, whose negative reactions to various policy measures can sometimes be accurately anticipated by national policymakers unwilling to provoke those reactions. Even where national policymakers are imperceptive in anticipating these reactions, or successfully anticipate the reactions but adopt the policy in question anyway, subnational regions with structural power can still mobilize *ex post* to force retraction or moderation, just as businesses can. Likewise, the same distinction between "command" and "inducements" made by earlier theorists who were concerned about the ability of corporations as "private governments" to eschew commands from government (Dahl 1970) is also relevant for regions; the shift from appointed to elected subnational officials that took place with political decentralization can be understood as a shift from the straightforward politics of command to the more ambiguous politics of inducements.

Another important similarity is the significant role played by the credibility of threats as perceived by policymakers, which matter for the structural power of regions no less than for the structural power of businesses (Hacker and Pierson 2002: 282). National governments are often surprisingly ignorant about the subnational governments that populate the territories they govern; particularly in countries that are coming out of highly centralized pasts and/or that have only recently decentralized, it may be hard to gather and analyze high-quality information about possible subnational responses to national policy approaches. A final similarity can be seen in the inherent limitations of structural power. Vogel (1987: 394) argues that the structural power of business is "fundamentally limited by the fact that it cannot be employed without also hurting the capitalists themselves." The same is often true of regional governments, which can respond to central government policies they do not like by coordinating investment strikes with local businesses (as in Santa Cruz, Bolivia) or leading protests against mining projects (as in a variety of Peruvian regions), but not without also incurring localized costs in the form of job losses and decreased tax receipts.

At the same time, the structural power of regions is also subject to a number of crucial differences relative to the structural power that business can wield. One critical difference is that of mobility. Although capital in different business sectors varies in the degree to which it is mobile, the option of shifting investment to other territorial jurisdictions is by definition categorically undesirable to subnational regions. Mayors and governors can coordinate with local capitalists to withdraw or reduce investment to discipline the

[4] According to Fairfield (2015a: 45–6), "actual disinvestment after a reform is implemented may lead policymakers to subsequently amend or repeal the offending reform." See also Fairfield (2015b).

national government and its policymakers, but they will not coordinate with local capitalists to send investment elsewhere (as much as these capitalists themselves might be willing to pursue this "exit" option). Another key difference is the important distinction between disinvestment and disruption. Most of the literature on the structural power of business has focused on the threat of disinvestment, which can be disaggregated into the withholding threat and the exit threat (Fairfield 2015a). While regional governments can leverage only the former and not the latter (short of secession), they can leverage another kind of structural power not available to business: the threat of disruption. In addition to encouraging disinvestment as a disciplining tool, subnational elected officials can use the powers of their offices to help disrupt investment decisions by others—including both private- and public-sector actors—as a means of protest against the policies under which those decisions are taken.

As discussed in greater detail in subsequent empirical chapters, the Peruvian and Bolivian cases illustrate the important difference between the threat of disinvestment versus the threat of disruption. Peru's neoliberal economic model depends on the continued ability of transnational corporations to invest in large-scale mining operations across the country's twenty-five regions. While some regional presidents have welcomed these investments, others have adopted a much more critical or skeptical attitude and have sought to use the full range of their powers to slow down, raise questions about, or altogether halt large-scale mining and the neoliberal policies under which it occurs. These behaviors in structurally significant regions like Arequipa, Cajamarca, and Cusco have provoked an aggressive and multifaceted response on the part of the national government, which has initiated corruption investigations into and arrests of subnational officials, blocked or reduced fiscal transfers, and sought to revoke the possibility of re-election for regional presidents. However, while regional presidents have been able to stop particular mining projects, they have been wholly unable to force changes in the neoliberal economic model under which these projects take place. In Bolivia, in contrast, the credible threat of disinvestment on the part of structurally significant subnational regions was a powerful factor in forcing the national government to accommodate its subnational ideological opponents in Santa Cruz. The disproportionate role that Santa Cruz plays in supplying Bolivia's domestic market with critical products such as cooking oil, sugar, and meat, combined with the willingness of these producers to withhold supplies, gave the region's governor significant negotiating power vis-à-vis President Evo Morales, who responded with a series of policy compromises in order to dissipate the supply threat.

One critical distinction brought to light by this comparison between Peru and Bolivia is the question of who owns exportable resources and whether subnational regions can bring these resources to market without the help of extra-local actors. In the most structurally significant Peruvian regions, the important resources are subterranean and thus owned by the (national) state, and can be extracted only with the aid of technologies monopolized by transnational firms allied with the central state. In other words, Peruvian regions cannot independently access their resources and sell them in world markets because of subsoil state ownership and technological constraints. In structurally significant Bolivian departments like Santa Cruz, the key resources are agricultural and owned by private actors whose productive activities enjoy greater independence from the national government. The Peruvian and Bolivian cases suggest that the national government will sit up and take note when subnational policy challenges are backed up by structural power, but also that structure alone does not tell us everything about how it will respond. The ability of opposition-controlled subnational governments to form coalitions in Bolivia but not in Peru (discussed later in this chapter) is essential in order to explain the center's accommodating response in the former case and the center's coercive response in the latter case.

Although the structural significance of a local or regional economy may change only slowly, the Ecuadorian case shows that subnational regions can indeed lose significance over time, with important consequences for their ability to mount policy challenges. Just as the structural power of business can wax and wane, so too can the structural leverage of subnational regions change through time. Guayaquil remains Ecuador's leading city, with a privileged position as the port through which most of the country's exports have passed since the early nineteenth century, but it has lost structural power in recent decades owing to a host of factors. Most important is the discovery of oil in the country's eastern Amazonian departments in the 1970s, which is exported via pipelines that do not depend on Guayaquil's port. Subsequently, the historic run-up in oil prices in the first decade of the twenty-first century further decreased the dependence of central coffers on the export revenues that Guayaquil generates. Of equal significance is the late 1990s collapse of the city's financial sector, which served as one of the lynchpins of Guayaquil's structural power for over a century. But the Ecuadorian case also reminds us that changes in structural power are not entirely exogenous to the political process. Even as the oil boom and the financial collapse made it easier for President Rafael Correa to ignore his ideological opponents in Guayaquil city hall, he also sought further to weaken its structural position by proposing to relocate the port outside Guayaquil city limits, and by financing rival port and other infrastructural investments in neighboring, politically compliant regions. Agency matters, even for the most structural component of this theoretical framework.

Institutional capacity

Subnational officials are also unequal in the institutional capacity of the governments they command by virtue of their direct election. When countries around the world opted recently to decentralize responsibilities to subnational governments, they adopted laws reassigning authorities between levels of government that took place immediately upon passage of the legislation. Formal authority can be shifted from one day to the next, but the capacity necessary to make use of newly devolved authorities is another matter. Although administrative capacity can dissipate quite rapidly when politicians decide to use the state bureaucracy for short-term political purposes (Geddes 1996), it typically takes a long period of time for capacity to accrue and accumulate. Not unlike their counterparts at the national level, for most mayors and governors hoping to deliver on their policy mandates while in office, institutional (in)capacity is no more subject to their immediate control than the structural significance of the districts they govern. Capacity is mostly experienced as a given, and as a key constraint that is quite difficult to overcome within the short time horizons facing most politicians.[5]

Until the recent adoption of decentralization, subnational governments around the world did not need to develop much capacity because centralizing traditions in most countries denied them important governing roles. The transfer of real responsibilities, however, has exposed the problem of insufficient capacity at subnational levels, as has the widespread preference for devolution (to subnational bureaucrats) over deconcentration (which merely relocates national bureaucrats to the subnational branches of central ministries). The capacity problem, as documented by the vast literature on decentralization, takes various forms, including manifest failures in delivering more administratively challenging services, along with greater dependence on fiscal transfers owing to the inability of subnational governments to extract resources locally (Bardhan 2002; Smoke, Gomez and Peterson 2007; Mansuri and Rao 2013).

I argue that prospects for the success of subnational policy challenges are enhanced if elected officials can count on relatively capable subnational governments.[6] While institutional capacity clearly boosts the effectiveness of territorial resistance by subnational challengers, this hypothesized relationship is subject to two types of asymmetry. First, capacity levels take on different importance depending on the nature of the subnational policy challenge in question. The second type of challenge, which seeks to alter the content of

[5] For the exceptional case of the state of Ceará in Brazil, where Governor Tasso Jereissati rapidly deepened institutional capacity in the late 1980s, see Tendler (1998).

[6] Sinha (2003) also focuses on subnational capacity, but as a factor that shapes how central policy directives are differentially "translated" and unevenly implemented.

the national policy regime, requires far less subnational capacity than the first type, which seeks to construct and defend subnational policy regimes. Subnational executives may be able successfully to influence national policy regimes by using the visibility provided by their elected positions to articulate and broadcast policy critiques, and to draw media attention to the costs of the national model—either individually or in concert with other subnational challengers. One of the most effective ways that subnational executives can further this type of policy challenge is to mobilize and lead groups that have borne losses under the current national policy regime, which does not require much institutional capacity. In contrast, the first type of policy challenge requires higher levels of infrastructural power.[7] Subnational executives need to be able to design, finance, implement, and monitor their own policies more or less independently of the national government if they are going to be able to sustain discordant subnational policy regimes.

Second, although institutional capacity is necessary for the construction of any coherent subnational policy regime, it stands to reason that it is especially critical for the establishment of a statist (as opposed to neoliberal) policy regime, given the greater roles that subnational administrations are expected to play in this kind of model. As we know from the literature on the politics of liberalization as a national-level phenomenon, it is a mistake to overlook the critical forms of state capacity on which even market-centered economic models depend (Kahler 1990; Fukuyama 2004). This is true at the subnational level as well, where neoliberal mayors and governors are rarely indifferent to state capacity; indeed, they typically argue that limiting the scope of what their governments do enables them to excel at those few responsibilities deemed critical for market-driven growth, including quality infrastructure, efficient transport systems, and effective policing. And yet the kinds of professional training, technical know-how, and personnel systems that are required to build a state-centered model involve a much higher level of both complexity and flexibility. Picking winners through subnational industrial policy, running subnational banks, and guaranteeing universal coverage to social services provided by subnational governments all place serious demands on the quality of subnational bureaucracies.[8] To summarize, capacity matters more for the first type of subnational policy challenge than the second, and more for subnational statism than for subnational neoliberalism.

[7] Michael Mann (1986) defines "infrastructural power" as the capacity of the state to enforce policy throughout the national territory; I use the term interchangeably with "institutional capacity."

[8] While I argue that insufficient capacity is a more critical constraint than insufficient authority, it is also the case that subnational statists will more quickly bump up against problematic constraints on authority than is the case for subnational neoliberals. I thank Diego Díaz for helping me see this distinction.

If the institutional capacity of the subnational state matters, where does it come from? Until very recently, and despite the looming presence of Max Weber, the comparative politics literature has tended to neglect state capacity relative to other critical topics such as regime type, revolutions, party systems, and the design of political institutions.[9] In recent years, as a consensus has emerged about the responsibility of weak states for some of the world's worst problems, the questions of state capacity and state formation have begun to generate renewed scholarly interest (Herbst 2000; Centeno 2002). This new literature—much of it focused on Latin America—conceptualizes, measures, and theorizes about capacity as a national-level variable. For example, Kurtz (2013) explains the surprisingly superior performance of the state in Chile and Uruguay relative to Argentina and Peru as the result of different labor systems and patterns of class conflict. Focusing largely on the same set of countries, but differentiating more emphatically between the emergence versus success of state-building efforts, Soifer (2015) offers instead an account that emphasizes ideational and geographic factors. In Saylor's "bottom-up" account (2014), state-building outcomes depend on the participation in governing coalitions of export elites who demand public goods and stronger institutions in order to reap the benefits of boom times. Like this set of authors, Dargent (2014) keeps the focus on the national level, but explores the causes and consequences of internal variation in the capacity of the state across different sectors of the bureaucracy, contrasting the strength of financial ministries with the relative weakness of social ministries in Colombia and Peru.

Figuring out why states in some countries are so much stronger than in others will remain an important scholarly endeavor, even as greater understanding emerges of the significance of intra-country variation in the strength of the state across the national territory. The seminal contribution here is that of O'Donnell (1993), who emphasized the persistence of "brown areas" characterized by the absence of the state and the dominance of arbitrary forms of rule. More recently, Fukuyama (2004) has argued for the need to study the state in a disaggregated fashion, remaining attentive to both functional *and* territorial variation. In a direct challenge to the state capacity literature, which has emphasized the ability of the central state to control and penetrate territory, Harbers (2015: 374) argues that local governments are integral parts of state. She encourages us to ask "not so much whether the central state dominates local territories, but to what extent effective state structures exist in these areas," which leads her to focus on municipal tax collection as a key

[9] Some scholars writing on these topics sought to tie them explicitly to the question of state capacity, including Linz and Stepan (1996), who argued that consolidated democracies require "usable" states, and Skocpol (1979), who used cross-national variation in the state to explain revolutionary outcomes.

measure of local state capacity. Scholars have used intra-country variation in the strength of state to explain a range of important outcomes, including the survival of subnational undemocratic regimes (Giraudy 2015), the implementation of national social policies such as healthcare and conditional cash transfers (Niedzwiecki 2016, forthcoming), the selection of federal as opposed to unitary institutional designs (Ziblatt 2006), and the territorially uneven operation of criminal networks in the wake of liberalization (Davis 2010). Disaggregating the state along territorial lines has also enabled more enlightened approaches to the study of state–society dynamics, including the various ways that regionalized societal actors can assist capacity-building efforts within the public sector in the attempt to "mobilize the state" (Abers and Keck 2009, 2013).

Although we still know much less about why state capacity varies from one subnational unit to the next within the same country than we do about national-level variation, this too is beginning to change thanks to a new body of research. The answer, according to Singh (2011, 2015), lies in subnational identities or collective forms of "we-ness" that vary significantly across the national territory, and that can generate not just higher levels of public goods provisioning but deeper investments in subnational state capacity. Questioning demand-side explanations and arguing for a "decentralized path to infrastructural power," Ziblatt (2008: 276) emphasizes the importance of the "priorities, ambitions, and goals" of the professionals who work within the (subnational) state and who exhibit varying levels of professionalism. Others have focused on the importance of electoral competition at the subnational level. Whereas Fiszbein (1997) attributes higher levels of local capacity to more locally competitive electoral environments, Pribble (2015) adopts a more nuanced perspective, arguing that electoral competition may encourage capacity-building efforts but also compromise these efforts if competition generates high levels of turnover. Finally, other scholars adopt an approach closer to my own, emphasizing that subnational economic elites hold the keys for understanding how and why state capacity varies across territory. Boone (2003a) emphasizes the differential bargaining power of local elites as they interacted with national state builders in Ghana, Côte d'Ivoire, and Senegal,[10] whereas Montero (2002) points to the importance of competition among regional elites, which discouraged subnational governments from creating insulated public-sector agencies in select Brazilian states.

[10] In Senegal, for example, the material and spiritual authority of rural notables in the Woloff groundnut basin led the national government to rule this region "indirectly" via these notables, who received devolved powers. The absence of similar local elites in the region of Lower Casamance produced a more centralized, top-down pattern of rule. See also Boone (2003b).

Like these authors, I emphasize the importance of regionalized economic elites. According to the argument I derive from the Bolivian and Ecuadorian cases, the absence of the central state in Santa Cruz and Guayaquil respectively led local business elites to invest heavily in a series of quasi-public, privately controlled subnational institutions within their regions of influence.[11] Many subnational governments in Bolivia and Ecuador suffer from debilitating capacity deficits, but Guayaquil and Santa Cruz have built up relatively strong administrative structures over the course of several decades. What is interesting, indeed ironic, in both spaces is that it was grievance against the central state and its perceived absence from the local territory that encouraged non-governmental actors in the private sector to invest in institutional capacity. These local institutions, including the Charity Board and Transit Committee in Guayaquil and the Regional Development Corporation of Santa Cruz (*CORDECRUZ*), served as incubators for the development of public-sector local capacity.[12] Here I examine the private origins of public capacity, which in turn helps explain the ability of subnational executives to defend subnational policy regimes when they began to come under concerted attack by national-level opponents in the course of the left turn after 2005. Jaime Nebot as mayor (2000–) and Rubén Costas as governor (2005–) have benefited from advantageous institutional legacies in Guayaquil and Santa Cruz, respectively. A further point that I develop here is that, while this private-sector path to local state capacity resulted in more effective subnational administrations than elsewhere in Ecuador and Bolivia, the private-sector path also imposed relatively narrow parameters on what the local state could legitimately do.

Peru represents the opposite experience, where the absence of subnational capacity has derailed subnational policy challenges. On the one hand, insufficient capacity in Peru is to be expected, given that regional decentralization since 2002 has taken the form not merely of transferring responsibilities to existing regional governments, but of creating these governments wholesale out of the administrative units that were established under the Fujimori regime. In general, the twenty-five regional presidents elected in the four cycles conducted so far (2002, 2006, 2010, 2014) have faced deep capacity deficits, and, as I show in Chapter 3, these deficits have hindered the ability of Peru's most ambitious regional presidents to act on their non-neoliberal policy

[11] My argument is broadly compatible with Soifer's argument (2016) about regionalism, state capacity, and the provision of public goods by national-level actors. While, as Soifer argues, regionalism should depress central state capacity, I argue that it should facilitate capacity-building at the subnational level. See also Singh (2015).

[12] See Gorski (2003) and Loveman (2005) for the argument that non-state actors, including the private sector, can be critical for the administrative development of the state, especially when the state can "harness the existing organizational and symbolic resources of the local... authorities, gradually incorporating them into the state" (Loveman 2005: 1677).

preferences through the implementation of distinct approaches subnationally. One of the regional presidents I examine, César Villanueva of San Martín, is the exception that proves the rule. Villanueva invested much more heavily and creatively in administrative capacity-building efforts in San Martín—a region without mineral resources—than his peers in mineral-rich regions, and generated in turn one of the most successful governing experiences in any Peruvian region. On the other hand, the Peruvian case is important because it shows not simply that capacity is hard to come by, or that it is difficult to transfer extant capacity from the national to the subnational level. The problem is worse: national governments may actively try to undercut efforts to build up subnational capacity, leaving subnational governments intensely dependent on the temporary consultants who cannot effectively substitute for public-sector professionals. For this reason, Chapter 3 also uncovers and analyzes the variety of practices sponsored by the central government that have had the effect of undermining rather than aiding the accumulation of subnational administrative capacity—all in the service of heading off subnational policy challenges.

The coalitional imperative

If institutional capacity is especially relevant for the defense of deviant subnational policy regimes (subnational policy challenge no. 1), and structural leverage is especially critical in order to compel changes in the national policy regime (subnational policy challenge no. 2), coalitions are crucial for the success of both types of challenges. Subnational executives cannot succeed on their own, either within the borders of the districts they govern, or beyond them on the national stage. If individual mayors and governors stand alone in the policy challenges they pose to the president, they are more likely to fail. Given the tremendous advantages enjoyed by the national chief executive in terms of media attention, fiscal resources, and administrative leverage, subnational chief executives must enlist the support of political and civil society at the subnational level, and they must coordinate. To defend discordant subnational policy regimes, mayors and governors need to construct "internal" coalitions within the districts they govern, not just by mobilizing local beneficiaries but by marginalizing detractors—including those potentially activated, funded, and coordinated by the national government. To contest the national policy regime, mayors and governors need to construct "external" coalitions amongst themselves that can transcend the jurisdictional boundaries that separate them; these are critical because of the often overwhelming power asymmetries between even the most powerful subnational executives and the presidents they are confronting. Whereas my arguments about structural leverage, institutional capacity, and internal coalitions all consider subnational governments as individual units, the focus on external coalitions between subnational districts introduces a more interactive element into the theoretical framework, which could otherwise be criticized for overstating the independence of these units. Presidents strongly prefer to deal with individual subnational governments in a bilateral fashion, and they usually get away with it unless officials in different subnational governments can find a way to coalesce.

Here I draw on a long tradition of coalitional analysis within the literature on comparative political economy, according to which the content and stability of national policy regimes can be fully explained only with reference to their underlying support coalitions. This same analytical approach may hold even more promise when we shift from the national to the subnational level, given the necessarily embattled status of mayors and governors who are seeking to defend discordant local models and/or transform the national model. At any level of government, the core insight holds: no economic development model is viable in the long term without a political coalition to sustain it and to defend it from opponents. Political entrepreneurs and bureaucratic "change teams" can play important proactive roles in supplying policies that they adopt before the support coalition is in place (Waterbury 1993), but to a significant extent politicians are constrained by the availability of societal partners and by the regularity with which exogenous shocks in the global economy either empower or impoverish domestic economic groups (Gourevitch 1986). According to Gourevitch's pioneering work, coalitional arrangements are more important than any other causal factor (including institutional, ideational, and partisan) in explaining whether European countries opted for free trade or protectionism in response to major economic crises in the 1870s, 1930s, and 1970s. More recently, scholars seeking to understand the neoliberal shift that began in the 1980s and 1990s have documented the new coalitions that emerged in the developing world to sustain market-oriented economic reforms, thereby calling into question the sufficiency of technocratic insulation and bureaucratic entrepreneurship (Kaufman 1986; Kaufman and Stallings 1989; Conaghan and Malloy 1994; Schamis 1999; Roberts 2015).

I argue that three different types of coalitions are critical for the success of subnational policy challenges. First are legislative coalitions that guarantee the subnational challenger majority support in local councils and provincial/departmental assemblies, without which ideological allies of the president might be able to "challenge the challenger" from within the subnational district. Subnational legislative coalitions are important in two senses. First, they enable mayors and governors to present a united front vis-à-vis the center, whose attacks on the subnational unit look more like attacks in the case of unified (opposition) partisan control of the two subnational branches.

Second, not being able to count on majority support in local legislative bodies means that subnational chief executives have to wage war on two fronts simultaneously: one against the center and one against these local bodies. In some countries, where legislative bodies faithfully and accurately represent and give expression to societal cleavages, legislative and societal coalitions may be largely overlapping. In many contexts, however, a significant gulf exists between "state and society" at the local level no less than at the national level, and in these cases it is important to assess both legislative and societal coalitions.

Second are locally or regionally specific societal coalitions with organized interests that represent the socioeconomic groups who stand to gain from the policy model preferred by the subnational executive. These "internal" coalitions are important in part because they lengthen the time horizon of subnational officials, which is critical in the context of electoral uncertainty if they are to design, build, and nurture discrete subnational policy regimes (Grindle 2007; Van Cott 2008; Pribble 2015). The membership of these "internal" coalitions will depend on the ideological content of the subnational policy challenge in question.[13] Labor unions, NGOs, and neighborhood associations are likely to loom large in coalitions that support forms of subnational statism, the pursuit of which is complicated in the absence of these kinds of societal actors. In contrast, regionalized economic elites, business chambers, and elite-dominated civic associations are key coalition partners in the defense of subnational neoliberalism; their absence from or weakness within a given district significantly limits the prospects for policy challenges by subnational liberals. Across the board, owners of capital are more important as members of support coalitions than any other societal group. The absence of capitalist allies severely limited the success of statist challenges by subnational officials in Peru, and capitalist support instead for Peru's neoliberal national model greatly empowered the center in its repression of these challenges. In Bolivia, the presence of capitalist allies in support coalitions significantly enhanced the neoliberal challenges posed by subnational officials in Santa Cruz, and the early opposition of capitalists to Evo Morales limited his room for maneuver vis-à-vis this eastern opposition. The Ecuador case, however, cautions against overstating the ability of capital owners to dictate outcomes; *guayaquileño* capitalists contributed substantially to the defense of the neoliberal local model even as they were unable to prevent the repudiation of neoliberalism at the national level by Rafael Correa.

A particularly critical question to ask about business as a coalitional partner is the extent to which economic elites in a given country are subject or not to

[13] For a classic analysis of coalitional politics at the city level, see Stone (1989).

salient regional cleavages (Gibson 1996). In my three cases, regional cleavages among economic elites have been consistently prominent in Bolivia and Ecuador, and of decreasing significance in Peru where land reform and the civil war tended to depopulate the countryside of economic elites (Vergara 2015). As will become clear in the following three chapters, the strength of regionalized economic elites helps explain the survival of subnational neoliberalism in Guayaquil and Santa Cruz.

But I also argue that it is important to appreciate the discursive strategies that are deployed to build coalitions; subnational policy challengers can certainly broaden support coalitions by emphasizing material benefits, but they can also do this by adopting discourses designed to resonate with local identities.[14] Subnational executives have a greater shot at winning their policy struggles when they can widen their coalitions by emphasizing the territorial as opposed to purely ideological nature of their conflict with the president. When subnational chief executives can claim that important territorial prerogatives and identities beyond ideology are under threat, and that questions of "community" are at stake, their chances of enlisting the support of a larger percentage of the local population substantially increase. As Hooghe and Marks (2016: 3) argue, "territorial community is perhaps the strongest form of solidarity there is." Though subnational collective identities are real and significant (Singh 2015), my cases suggest that mayors and governors are not above manipulating these identities in the service of their economic policy battles with the national government. Here it is critical not to conflate territorial and ethnic identities. In countries where territorial boundaries between subnational districts more or less overlap with ethnic divisions, subnational policy challengers can indeed harness ethnic identities. In most of Latin America, however, territorial and ethnic boundaries do not align well (Madrid 2012), and the coalitional prospects of subnational challengers are best served when they can develop discourses that tap into pan-ethnic identities shared by all who happen to reside in the territory.

While the first two coalitional forms are internal to a specific subnational district, the third type of coalition breaches district boundaries and brings individual subnational executives together as peers in defense of a common set of policy preferences. "External" coalitions of subnational challengers that span different subnational jurisdictions are critical for subnational policy challenges that seek to scale up and influence the national policy regime, but might be irrelevant for challenges that "merely" try to defend a deviant policy regime within a particular subnational unit. A number of factors either facilitate or

[14] See Pasotti (2010) for a comparative study of how mayors use cultural politics to galvanize local societal coalitions in support of city-level reforms—often with the intent of circumventing opposition on municipal councils.

complicate the construction of these external coalitions. For example, when mayors and governors share not just their ideological opposition to the national policy regime but also membership in the same opposition party, their coalitions are easier to build and maintain. When subnational units enjoy institutional representation in national bodies, typically in Senates or upper legislative chambers that represent subnational territories, the regularized interactions that take place in these venues can also facilitate coalition-building across units. At the same time, it is important to note that subnational elected officials are increasingly taking the lead in creating their own organizations, including associations of mayors and governors' leagues, outside formal national institutional channels (Falleti 2010).[15] In addition to partisan, institutional, and organizational factors, the territorial contiguity of opposition-governed subnational units may also facilitate coalition-building, especially if contiguity means that these units share common socioeconomic, cultural, and political traits, as is in the Bolivian case discussed in Chapter 5. Finally, while external coalitions typically bring together chief executives at the same subnational level (that is, mayors with mayors, governors with governors), this does not necessarily need to be the case; coalitions of ideologically like-minded chief executives can span different subnational levels (that is, combinations of mayors and governors).[16]

Limited coalitional possibilities have severely handicapped subnational executives in Peru, in their ability both to build subnational policy regimes and to force change upon the national policy regime. With respect to the former, many regional presidents confront a difficult societal landscape marked by fluidity, fragmentation, and the absence of coherent civil society organizations. According to numerous scholars, Peru's civil society was flattened by a prolonged internal armed conflict in which the Shining Path insurgency targeted for elimination the very organizations that could have served as coalitional partners for the contemporary left. Also important are the legacies of the Fujimori regime, which closed associational space and passed market reforms that led to the relocation of industries to Lima (Gonzales de Olarte 2000; Yashar 2005). The disappearance of organized labor from numerous regional economies means that unions cannot play the coalitional roles

[15] External coalitions among subnational chief executives may be especially important for subnational chief executives on the left whose inspiration comes from socialism. As Leopold and McDonald (2012: 1847–8) argue in their analysis of the prospects for municipal socialism: "Without a national (and perhaps international) network of support, it is hard to imagine how a single municipal authority—no matter how large or well-resourced—can withstand the legislative, financial and political assaults of hostile national and supranational state agencies and private service companies."

[16] Perhaps even more daunting than the creation of domestic coalitions among mayors and governors within a given country are attempts by these same actors to build coalitions of peers that span international boundaries. A salient case in point is the C40 coalition of mayors seeking to challenge global inaction on climate change (Erickson and Tempest 2014; Gordon 2016).

that were critical in the emergence of "municipal socialism" in countries like Brazil (Baiocchi 2003; Goldfrank and Schrank 2009). Although several regional presidents have sought to foster and coordinate anti-neoliberal protests against large-scale mining, protests have been largely ephemeral and have failed to produce much of an organizational residue once protests subside (which they often do in response to promises of corporate social responsibility facilitated by the national government). Simply put, regional presidents on the left often find that there are few established groups with whom they can partner.

Not only have regional presidents in Peru been unable to build robust societal coalitions within their own districts, but coalitions have also failed to emerge among like-minded regional presidents who are displeased with the neoliberal policy regime at the national level. Many do battle with Lima on a bilateral basis in the absence of multilateral networks that would enable them to join ranks and coordinate behaviors. The 2007 elimination of the National Council for Decentralization, which was the only national level institution in Peru that allowed any formal participation by subnational governments, dimmed prospects for the emergence of coalitions among regional presidents. Even more importantly, the weakness of political parties and the failure of national parties even to compete in most regional elections means that opposition parties cannot serve as a venue through which coalitions of regional presidents might develop (Tanaka 2006; Battle 2012). Regional presidents on the left may share overlapping preferences for less neoliberal approaches and for more state intervention in the economy, but their failure to build coalitions with their peers has left them politically isolated from one another.

In Ecuador, the strength of the internal coalition constructed by León Febres Cordero and maintained by his successor Jaime Nebot—both from the conservative Social Christian Party (*Partido Social Cristiano* (*PSC*))—helps explain the survival of a neoliberal policy regime that President Rafael Correa has repeatedly criticized and sought to dismantle. As the former head of the powerful Chamber of Industries, Febres Cordero was in an ideal position as mayor to enlist the support of local business associations in his effort to remake Guayaquil in a neoliberal image, which he accomplished through privatization and the streamlining of the municipal bureaucracy. Nebot then cemented this coalition through the extensive delegation of formerly municipal responsibilities to private foundations that provided services with public monies. When the model came under attack after Correa's election in 2006, Nebot relied heavily on elite-dominated civic associations to organize and finance a major demonstration in 2008, which sought simultaneously to critique the president's statist proposals and to articulate the demand for autonomy sufficient to defend the city's distinct policy regime. In addition to societal coalitions, both Febres Cordero and Nebot also controlled the city council, thanks to legislative coalitions that effectively locked their local opponents out of city government.

The designers and defenders of the Guayaquil model, however, have been far less successful building coalitions with subnational executives in other jurisdictions, and this has limited their influence vis-à-vis Ecuador's national policy regime. Unlike in Peru, where like-minded regional presidents failed to coalesce owing to the absence of institutional and partisan channels, in Ecuador the greater problem has been the scarcity of subnational executives who share the policy preferences so forcefully articulated by Guayaquil's mayors. Unlike in the Bolivian lowland departments, no coalition has emerged in Ecuador's coastal provinces among neoliberal subnational challengers. Even as Nebot's popularity within Guayaquil shows no signs of flagging, as seen in his comfortable fourth electoral victory in 2014, the mayor is largely isolated relative to other subnational executives.

In Bolivia, we see the presence of robust coalitions of all three varieties, and the strength of these coalitional arrangements helps explain why subnational policy challenges succeeded here to a greater degree than anywhere else. First, Santa Cruz landowner and governor Rubén Costas has sustained a legislative majority in the department assembly since his election in 2005, thanks in part, ironically, to the defection of lowland indigenous representatives who joined the opposition against President Evo Morales over his proposed highway project through the *TIPNIS* (*Territorio Indígena y Parque Nacional Isiboro Sécure* (Isiboro Sécure National Park and Indigenous Territory)). Second and more importantly, the political defense of Santa Cruz's neoliberal model elicited the support of the department's most powerful and well-financed interests, including the service cooperatives for water, telecommunications, and electricity that are controlled by local elites grouped into two long-standing "lodges." Just as important is the Pro-Santa Cruz Committee, an elite-dominated organization that has roots in the 1950s movement for local control over oil revenues, and that served as an effective mobilizing structure in the struggle to defend neoliberalism in the department after the rise of Morales. Third, Santa Cruz's governor led the construction of a powerful coalition of eastern governors who opposed Morales's national "process of change" and who sought to defend the neoliberal status quo. Grouped together in the National Council for Democracy (*Consejo Nacional Democrático* (*CONALDE*)), the opposition governors coordinated a series of protest activities over the course of 2008 that, by sharply dividing the country between east and west, forced the president toward moderation, accommodation, and, ultimately, reconciliation.

To conclude this presentation of the theoretical framework, it should be apparent that the content of the ideology motivating subnational challengers is mostly irrelevant from a theoretical standpoint.[17] With the partial exception of capacity, which I deem to be especially critical for subnational statists, all kinds of subnational challengers are empowered by high scores on the same three key variables: structural significance, institutional capacity, and coalitional breadth. It is also important to note that my argument operates in a probabilistic rather than a deterministic mode. Instead of an identification of necessary and/or sufficient conditions, the core claim is that subnational policy challengers are more likely to succeed when they preside over jurisdictions that enjoy structural leverage, administrative capacity, and robust internal and external coalitions. At the same time, while I maintain that structure, capacity, and coalitions are highly useful in explaining why policy challenges met such different fates in Bolivia, Ecuador, and Peru, these three variables cannot account for all aspects of the outcomes in these cases, and there are limits to the explanatory power of my three-part causal argument in each country. For example, given the ultimate failure of Ecuadorian President Rafael Correa's attempt to remove the port from Guayaquil, long considered the lynchpin of its structural power, my theory would predict that the city should have been able to generate more policy muscle at the national level than it did. In Peru, a comparison of the regions of Cajamarca and Arequipa suggests that capacity constraints are not necessarily fatal to subnational challengers, who were able to use foreign NGOs and consultants to design a new zoning process in the former case that was as "anti-neoliberal" as in the latter, higher-capacity case. In Bolivia, while the external coalition built by eastern governors was powerful enough to force substantive policy compromises upon President Morales, it is also true that he was able individually to repress some of the governors who stitched this coalition together, which my theory cannot easily explain.

Considering Alternative Explanations

By focusing on three broad categories of analysis—structure, capacity, and coalitions—my theoretical framework opts explicitly for analytical breadth over parsimony. This does not mean, however, that there are no alternative explanations to consider. This section casts doubt on the utility of four important competing explanations for the outcomes I seek to explain in this book, based in institutional authority, partisan and electoral factors, leadership qualities, and international dynamics. Though these rival explanations have limited power in my three country cases, I anticipate that they may find

[17] I am grateful to Matthias vom Hau for helping me articulate this point.

more purchase in cases other than the three from which I have derived my theory. For instance, the formal division of authority between levels of government might loom larger as a causal variable in countries with more robust judiciaries and greater respect for the rule of law, and subnational challengers in countries with institutionalized party systems and hierarchical political parties might find that their room to maneuver is much more limited by partisan constraints than was the case in Bolivia, Ecuador, and Peru.

The first and perhaps most obvious alternative explanation would emphasize the importance of the institutional authority that is extended to subnational elected officials, rather than the institutional capacity of the offices they hold. Subnational officials around the world vary enormously in terms of the scope of authority under their control, variation that results not just from institutional choices like that between federalism and unitarism, but from a number of macro-level processes such as decentralization, liberalization, and integration. In any given country, institutional authority is specified in a range of formal documents that might include articles in the constitution; laws, codes, and statutes passed by national legislators; and decrees and regulations emitted by national executives and ministers. Authority is easier to measure than capacity, and could form the basis of a clear hypothesis vis-à-vis my dependent variables: the greater the authority under the control of subnational elected officials, the greater the chances that their subnational policy challenges will succeed. Authority would appear to be particularly germane for the first challenge—that of creating distinctive subnational policy regimes.

The main problems with this hypothesis are twofold. First, enjoying a wider range of formal authorities does not do much for subnational officials if they cannot simultaneously count on sufficient levels of administrative capacity to make use of those authorities.[18] Second, my research suggests that subnational officials can do a lot with a little; even mayors and governors without a lot of formal authority can conscientiously and concertedly use their limited authority in ways that congeal in quite distinctive and identifiable approaches, as in the cases of Guayaquil and Santa Cruz. Especially where the rule of law is weak and central states have a hard time policing and enforcing the distribution of formal authority, formal authority matters less than capacity. All things being equal, greater institutional authority can contribute to the success of subnational policy challenges and, if successful, attempts to recentralize various forms of authority in the wake of decentralization in recent years could be negative for the prospects of subnational policy challenges (Dickovick and Eaton 2013). But authority is not the crucial factor.

[18] In contrast to my distinction here between capacity and authority, see Abers and Keck (2013) for the argument that these two concepts cannot be fully separable, and should instead be considered mutually constitutive—especially in weaker states.

A second rival approach would be to place more causal weight on partisan and electoral dynamics to explain the success of subnational policy challenges. At first blush, parties are less helpful in explaining variation because, in focusing exclusively on subnational challengers, I am focusing on subnational officials who do not belong to the president's party; their similar membership in opposition rather than (nationally) governing parties therefore cannot explain their uneven successes. But other partisan hypotheses can be identified and considered. For example, given the empirical significance of cross-national and cross-party variation in the internal organization of parties, one could hypothesize that subnational officials are more likely to succeed with their policy challenges where parties are highly decentralized (rather than centralized) internally (Willis, Garman, and Haggard 1999). However, in a region like Latin America where parties are decreasingly relevant and broadly repudiated, and in a moment like the present one when new communication technologies make it possible for politicians to reach voters without parties (Levitsky, Loxton, and Van Dyck 2016), there are good reasons to question the importance of how a decreasingly relevant organization (for example, a political party) is organized internally.[19] Another, equally unsatisfying hypothesis would focus on party *system* dynamics; relative to inchoate party systems, institutionalized party systems should limit the political and electoral space that "upstart" subnational challengers might occupy (Mainwaring and Scully 1995; Flores-Macias 2012). However, traditional party systems collapsed in all three of my cases, which suggests that this variable is of limited usefulness in explaining cross-national variation in the success of subnational policy challenges. While parties do not play a central role in my theoretical framework, they are not absent from it altogether; party dynamics are important if they shape the legislative coalitions that subnational executives need to build locally, and they can either facilitate or impede coalition-building across subnational units. But coalitions offer a more useful analytical lens than parties.

In addition to partisan hypotheses, one could argue that electoral outcomes and the size of electoral victories also matter; mayors and governors who easily dominate their jurisdictions electorally (as opposed to barely winning election) should be in a stronger position to mount both types of subnational

[19] One plausible party-centered hypothesis deserves further consideration. One could argue that it was the vigorous party-building efforts championed by the national government in Bolivia under the *MAS* that encouraged *MAS* leaders to grant policy concessions to Santa Cruz as a means of enhancing the party's electoral prospects in the east. However, the national government in Ecuador under the governing party (Alianza PAIS) also aggressively promoted the territorial penetration of the party into opposition-governed jurisdictions like Guayaquil, but without compromising on policy. This comparison helps reinforce the conclusion that the dominant dynamic in Bolivia was the offering of policy concessions in response to a powerful oppositional coalition with serious structural leverage.

policy challenges. In practice, however, the possibility of split-ticket voting (where this is allowed) probably reduces the importance of this consideration. It may indeed be harder for the president to attack hugely popular mayors or governors for fear of antagonizing their voters, who might as a result feel compelled to choose between supporting their local officials and supporting the president, but these voters can and often do split their votes. More generally, that subnational officials are popular enough to win re-election does not mean that they can necessarily advance and defend distinctive policy regimes or alter the national regime. Re-election and re-re-election have definitely augmented the challenges posed by the two key protagonists in Bolivia and Ecuador (Santa Cruz Governor Rubén Costas and Guayaquil Mayor Jaime Nebot), but all four of the regional presidents I survey in the Peruvian case won re-election and also failed as policy challengers. Subnational officials need to win in order to succeed as challengers, but coalitional strength matters more than partisan or electoral strength.

A third type of explanation would underscore the importance of the individual leadership qualities that mayors and governors bring to their subnational offices and that may explain their ability to succeed as policy challengers. This is a particularly important hypothesis to explore, given that I have put subnational elected officials at the center of my theoretical framework. Modern political science has done a notably poor job assessing and accounting for the role of leadership, although the recent literature on the consequences of decentralization for a range of good governance outcomes has pointed to the paramount importance of strong leadership at the mayoral level (Grindle 2007; Wampler 2007; Van Cott 2008).[20] Whereas these authors have emphasized some of the more positive traits of successful leaders, one could argue that less positive traits are just as or more important in helping mayors and governors succeed as policy challengers. For example, numerous interviewees in all three of my cases argued that their subnational leaders were essentially *caudillos*, an infamous term in Latin America that refers to nineteenth-century leaders who, through force of personality and through the militias they commanded, were able to challenge the center and exert strong-arm control over subnational territories. Much as they resist the center, subnational officials in Bolivia, Ecuador, and Peru have often adopted highly centralizing behaviors *within* their districts, at both the local and the intermediate levels of governments. Additionally in all three cases, critics accuse subnational leaders of authoritarian and populist leadership styles, which could be hypothesized to enhance their ability to prosecute subnational policy challenges vis-à-vis the center. While leadership talent, charisma, and

[20] See also Leopold and MacDonald (2012: 1841) for the argument that municipal socialism depends on "charismatic socialist mayors."

strong oratorical skills all help subnational officials, the critical factor is whether the necessary building blocks are available to form support coalitions. I see my argument as roughly compatible with that of Gourevitch: Bismarck loomed large in the construction of Germany's historic "iron and rye" coalition, but what mattered more was the existence of the requisite support groups to sustain this coalition in the nineteenth century (Gourevitch 1986). Even the most charismatic subnational challenger will find that he or she can do very little in the absence of structural leverage, coalitional opportunities, and institutional capacity. Gregorio Santos, Regional President of Cajamarca in Peru, is a case in point, as demonstrated by his inability successfully to challenge Lima despite deep reserves of charisma.

The final alternative explanation is perhaps the easiest to dismiss; subnational challengers should have a greater chance of success when they can leverage support either from external actors outside the country or from transnational allies who have a presence within the country. This type of international explanation is less persuasive in part because policy disputes between national and subnational levels are usually seen as quintessentially domestic conflicts, well protected by dominant norms of state sovereignty. On several occasions in Bolivia and Peru (but not in Ecuador), subnational policy challenges have produced important episodes of political violence and small numbers of casualties; in the former case this was sufficient to trigger the involvement of the Union of South American Nations (*Unión de Naciones Suramericanas* (*UNASUR*)), which sent a negotiating team to Bolivia in 2008 to encourage dialogue between the national and subnational governments. While the Bolivian case would appear to support the importance of external actors, *UNASUR* intervened only because—as I show in Chapter 5—the structural and coalitional power of the east had brought the country to the brink of civil war. Likewise, although one could argue that other external actors, including the US Ambassador and USAID, sought to support the subnational opposition in Bolivia, both were expelled by the national government, thereby isolating subnational policy challengers from their erstwhile external allies. With respect to non-governmental rather than governmental external allies, the Peruvian case indicates that subnational challengers can and indeed do receive important forms of support from transnational partners like environmental NGOs. This support has been more than cancelled out, however, by the transnational mining companies that are allied with the national government against subnational governments. Furthermore, in all three of my cases irrespective of ideological orientation, national governments have cracked down aggressively in recent years on the operations of all foreign NGOs, which sharply limits their availability as possible allies for subnational challengers (Carothers and Brechenmacher 2014).

Introducing the Cases

Adopting a small-N, comparative historical approach, the core empirical chapters of this book apply the theoretical framework to three countries in the central Andes: Bolivia, Ecuador, and Peru. As described in this section, these three countries share a remarkable number of similarities that facilitate their comparison—similarities that other scholars have used to gain analytical traction vis-à-vis many other important substantive questions, including the emergence of indigenous mobilization (Yashar 2005), the role of business groups in economic reform (Conaghan and Malloy 1994), and the performance of ethnic parties (Madrid 2012). Consider the following commonalities that make these three countries a particularly fruitful setting for the comparative study of subnational policy challenges.

First, all three countries are characterized by highly incomplete processes of state formation, and some of the lowest levels of central state capacity in all South America. Along with Colombia, these three countries face the most challenging topographies anywhere in the continent, with the Andean mountain chain dividing national territory into distinct and remote geographical regions. Regardless of where the state is centered, mountainous terrain has raised the costs of transport and communication with far-flung regions, and made it difficult to project power either downward from Andean capitals (for example, La Paz in Bolivia and Quito in Ecuador) or upwards from a coastal capital (Lima in Peru). In all three countries, the central state struggled unsuccessfully to develop capacity vis-à-vis its most urgent tasks, including not just the ability to extract resources from powerful societal actors but even more fundamentally to defend national borders from external threats. If Latin America has experienced far fewer inter-state conflicts than other world regions, a disproportionate number of the conflicts that have occurred over the last two centuries have involved these three countries as the main combatants—and yet war-making has not generated the predicted effect on state-making (Centeno 2002). Bolivia and Peru suffered devastating territorial losses at the hands of Chile in the War of the Pacific (1879–83), Bolivia lost additional territory to Paraguay in the Chaco War (1932–5), and Ecuador lost a third of its territory to Peru in 1941. Territorial dismemberment serves as a stark, painful, and persistent reminder of state weakness in all three cases. While the deficient capacity of the central state can be considered a permissive condition for the emergence of subnational policy challenges in all three countries, levels of *subnational* state capacity vary considerably, with important consequences for the outcome of these challenges.

A further similarity, which can be considered both cause and consequence of incomplete state formation, is the presence of deep ethnic and regional cleavages in all three countries. Population densities made the central Andes, along with Mesoamerica, an especially important site for the Spanish colonial project, which designed and implanted a series of institutional practices based on ethnic domination, imposing coercive labor systems on indigenous communities and concentrating landownership among whites and mestizos. Although comparatively high levels of miscegenation (relative to other world regions) might account for the relative absence of exclusionary ethnic appeals in these three countries (Madrid 2012), persistent and pervasive forms of ethnic discrimination served to constrain both state-building and nation-building in Bolivia, Ecuador, and Peru. This constraint was far less pronounced in southern cone cases such as Argentina and Chile, which are characterized by higher levels of ethnic homogeneity—at least in part owing to outright campaigns of extermination in the nineteenth century.

Deep regional cleavages within each of these three countries, which overlap with and reinforce ethnic cleavages far less perfectly than in other highly ethnically diverse societies, are another important commonality. Regionalism has long been and today remains a core political dynamic in each country. For example, according to historian José Luis Roca (2001), the history of Bolivia can best be understood as the history of regional (and not class) struggle, though the axis of conflict shifted from the struggle in the highlands between La Paz in the north and Sucre in the south in the nineteenth century, to the more recent struggle between the eastern lowlands and western highlands (Roca 2001). Peru likewise has experienced a number of regional cleavages; southern regions led by Arequipa articulated defiant challenges against the center in the first half of the twentieth century, after which the economic and demographic decline of regions like Arequipa has led to more generalized grievances between the country's poorer departments in the Andean and Amazonian interiors against the more prosperous regions on the coast, especially Lima (Cotler 1978; Vergara 2015). In Ecuador, the persistent regional conflict between Quito in the Sierra and Guayaquil on the coast has been at the epicenter of political life since Independence (Quintero and Silva 1991). These regional cleavages are important because, as I argue in subsequent chapters, regional identities can offer one of the most effective building blocks for the construction of the type of broad coalitions that are necessary to defend deviant subnational policy regimes.

In addition to weak states and deep ethnic and regional divisions, Bolivia, Ecuador, and Peru face serious economic development challenges, as reflected in Table 2.2. Although the World Bank classifies Bolivia as a lower-middle-income country and Ecuador and Peru as upper-middle-income countries, the economies of these three countries reflect common dynamics and weaknesses. Each suffered the effects of enclave economies in the nineteenth century, along with forms of structural heterogeneity and pre-modern labor practices that persisted well into the twentieth century. All three countries are highly

Table 2.2. Bolivia, Ecuador, and Peru in comparative perspective (2013 data)

Indicator	Bolivia	Ecuador	Peru	Latin America	High-income OECD	World
Population	10.5 million	15.5 million	30.5 million	620 million	1.1 billion	7.2 billion
Urban population (% of total)	67.7	63.3	77.9	79.3	80.5	52.9
Land area (sq. km.)	1,083,300	248,360	1,280,000	20,041,653	31,627,835	129,735,257
GDP per capita (constant 2005 US$)	1,083.74	3,017.34	2,892.34	5,188.84	33,816.20	7,093.35
Government expenditure (% of GDP)	13.87	14.09	11.19	15.32	18.51	17.59
Industry, value added (% of GDP)	33.42	32.99	35.18	33.45	25.39	28.23
Mineral rents (% of GDP)	1.64	0.03	4.68	1.40	0.18	0.38
Oil rents (% of GDP)	4.90	15.14	1.58	4.25	0.48	2.13
GINI index (World Bank estimate)	48.06	47.29	44.73	49.41	32.04	N/A
Poverty headcount $1.90 per day (2011 PPP, % of population)	7.7	4.43	3.7	9.11	0.41	12.73
Infant mortality rate (per 1,000 live births)	32.80	19.50	14.20	15.92	4.34	33.70

Notes: *Latin America*: figures include Caribbean countries. *High-income OECD* refers to all member countries of the OECD apart from Mexico and Turkey. All figures for the last three columns are averages. Figures for GDP per capita, industry, and mineral/oil rents are all averages for 1996–2013. PPP stands for Purchasing Power Parity.

Sources: *Population*: United Nations (2015). *Urban population*: United Nations (2014). *Land area* (sq. km): Food and Agriculture Organization, electronic files and website. Data from World Development Indicators, last updated October 14, 2015 (accessed November 5, 2015). *GDP per capita, Government expenditure*, and *Industry, value added*: World Bank national accounts data, and OECD national accounts data files. *Mineral and oil rents*: Estimates based on sources and methods described in World Bank (2011). *GINI index* and *Poverty headcount at $1.90 a day*: World Bank, Development Research Group. Data are based on primary household survey data obtained from government statistical agencies and World Bank country departments. Data for high-income economies are from the Luxembourg Income Study database. *Infant mortality rate*: Estimates developed by the UN Inter-Agency Group for Child Mortality Estimation at <www.childmortality.org>.

dependent on their natural resource endowments (minerals in Peru, hydrocarbons in Ecuador, and both minerals and hydrocarbons in Bolivia), and each has struggled unsuccessfully to diversify its economy and to generate higher levels of value added. As a result, this vulnerable set of countries has been persistently buffeted by the destabilizing cycles of commodity booms and busts. All three countries exhibit lower levels of industrialization and urbanization relative to larger and more diversified Latin American economies such as Argentina, Brazil, and Mexico. Despite recent improvements, each country has large percentages of the population living below the poverty line—a problem that is especially acute among indigenous communities—along with some of the highest levels of infant mortality in the continent. The inability to overcome these deep-seated obstacles to economic development and to produce sustainable and broad-based economic growth has heightened the stakes surrounding the ideological debate over rival economic development models, and in turn the significance of subnational policy challenges.

Perhaps the most striking commonality across these three cases can be seen in the similar evolution that took place in each country's national economic policy regime over the course of the twentieth century. As Conaghan and Malloy argue (1994), these three countries followed a clear sequence that differentiates them from other, more developed and industrialized countries in the region. First, traditional landed elites retained their political hegemony well into the 1950s, 1960s, and 1970s in Bolivia, Peru, and Ecuador, respectively—decades after their counterparts were first displaced from power in countries such as Argentina, Brazil, and Chile. The ability of these elites to veto, delay, and/or weaken socioeconomic reforms, including policies of state-led industrialization, meant that each country's liberal policy coalition was abandoned comparatively late within Latin America (Thorp and Bertram 1978; Conaghan 1988; Klein 2003). Second, in strong contrast to the southern cone, when military officers subsequently took power in the 1960s and 1970s, reformist elements within the armed forces used their control of government to shift the national policy regime in a statist direction. Although this phenomenon was particularly pronounced in the Velasco Alvarado government in Peru (1968–75) and the Rodríguez Lara administration in Ecuador (1972–6), nationalist military presidents also introduced statist reforms in Bolivia in the 1960s and 1970s. Third, given the nature of the threat it posed to economic elites, military rule in each case subsequently encouraged the private sector to lead the movement pressing for a return to democracy in the 1980s. Emphasizing the unpredictable and arbitrary nature of military rule, business emerged as a critical pro-democratization force in all three countries—again in contrast to other cases where business worried about and often worked to prevent the restoration of democracy (Conaghan and Malloy 1994).

In each country, the return to civilian rule brought to power elected presidents in the 1980s and 1990s who proposed sweeping neoliberal transformations. In Bolivia, President Víctor Paz Estenssoro of the *Movimiento Nacionalista Revolucionario* (*MNR*) (Nationalist Revolutionary Movement) responded to the country's deep hyperinflationary crisis in 1985 by introducing a draconian set of fiscal cuts and pro-market measures. In the 1990s, Gonzalo Sánchez de Losada as president then consolidated neoliberal reforms by implementing an innovative approach to privatization (the so-called capitalization program). In Peru, President Alberto Fujimori over the course of his decade in power (1990–2000) introduced and defended an equally ambitious set of neoliberal measures, including deregulation, tariff reduction, the removal of constraints on direct foreign investment, and a new constitution in 1993 that enshrines and protects the role of the market. Neoliberals encountered more effective resistance on the part of societal and congressional opponents in Ecuador, but Presidents León Febres Cordero (1984–8) and Sixto Durán (1992–6) were nevertheless able to advance important pro-market policies in a number of sectors, including banking, labor rights, and land tenure in the countryside.

Although each country experienced qualitatively similar neoliberal reforms at roughly the same moment in time, and although these reforms can be seen as reintroducing the liberal approaches that had been abandoned in the 1950s and 1960s, neoliberalism did not meet the same fate in these three countries. While the neoliberal transformation of Peru's national policy regime has proved to be extraordinarily resilient, elections in Bolivia and Ecuador in the 2000s brought to power presidents on the left who have sought to reverse and replace the neoliberal reforms of the 1980s and 1990s, prompting advocates of neoliberal ideas to find refuge in subnational governments. The different fate of neoliberalism in my three countries presents a research opportunity because it has led to variation in terms of where the leading advocates of neoliberalism and statism are located territorially within each country. The persistence of neoliberalism at the national level in Peru and its subnational retreat in Bolivia and Ecuador have produced opposing configurations of territorial and ideological conflict, making it possible to study subnational statism in the Peruvian case and subnational neoliberalism in Bolivia and Ecuador.

The last important similarity has to do with the common adoption of decentralizing changes in all three cases since the 1990s. Although I argue that the decentralization of authority matters less than the capacity to make use of this authority in explaining my outcomes of interest, the reality that subnational governments in each country gained new forms of authority has made it possible for their elected officials to try to challenge the center. Bolivia experienced one of the most radical and daring decentralization programs in the developing world when the national government in 1994 decided not just to create 300 new municipal governments, but to share 20 percent of the center's tax revenues with municipalities and to institute oversight of municipal officials by local civil society groups (Zuazo, Faguet, and Bonifaz 2012; Faguet 2013). One decade later, the focus shifted from the municipal to the departmental level with the introduction of direct elections for governors and the sharing of resources from Bolivia's new tax on hydrocarbons in 2005, followed by the creation of departmental assemblies in 2009. Decentralization in Peru has also empowered both municipal and regional governments, shifting administrative responsibilities to each and adopting new rules that devolve revenues from income taxes on mineral production to subnational units in the so-called canon system (Zas Friz 2004). In Ecuador, decentralization has privileged the municipal sphere, chiefly through the "Law of the 15%" in 1997, which gave municipal governments a much greater degree of independence from the center by introducing the institution of automatic revenue-sharing (Carrión 2003). While the scope of decentralized authority varies across the three countries, and while each country has also experienced episodes of recentralization in the aftermath of decentralization, in each case enough decentralization occurred to facilitate the subnational policy challenges that are examined in the following chapters.

Scoring the Dependent Variable

Vigorous policy challenges from subnational governments have emerged in all three of my cases, but these challenges have not been equally successful in terms of their ability to generate effective territorial resistance. This section describes unevenness in the effectiveness of territorial resistance across the three country cases, presenting these cases from least to most effective. In Peru, neither of the two main types of subnational policy challenges already discussed has experienced much success. Despite significant opposition to the national government's neoliberal policy regime on the part of left-of-center regional officials, these officials have failed to force the center to introduce any significant adjustments in that regime, just as they have been unable to build their own distinctive policy regimes. In Ecuador, in contrast, one of the two main types of subnational policy challenges has largely succeeded. Since 2000, Guayaquil's pro-market mayor has managed to defend the core elements of that city's neoliberal policy regime from attacks by the national government, though he and his local allies have been powerless to influence President Correa's national-level policy regime. In Bolivia, both types of subnational policy challenges have achieved noteworthy successes. Not only have subnational neoliberals managed to defend the central components of Santa Cruz's neoliberal policy regime, but they were also able to moderate the national policy regime by leveraging their influence at the national level as well.

As this section and the following empirical chapters make clear, the outcome of subnational policy challenges should be conceptualized as a continuous rather than discrete (dependent) variable. Subnational officials are more or less able to build and defend deviant local models, just as they are more or less able to shape the national model. For example, even though subnational policy challenges have mostly foundered in Peru, some left-leaning regional officials have been able to engage in planning processes that impose limits on mining. On the opposite end of the spectrum, even though challengers in Santa Cruz managed to defend that department's uniquely liberal institutions, many officials in the departmental government complain that heightened oversight from La Paz since 2006 has limited their traditional scope of action.

As the least effective case of territorial resistance on my three-country continuum, Peru stands out for the striking depth and persistence of its neoliberal model, which has experienced no major modifications since its introduction by Fujimori beginning in the 1990s. Centered on privatization, deregulation, and generous tax incentives for foreign investors, Peru's neoliberal model has dramatically shrunk the scope for state intervention in the economy, heightened the country's dependence on investments by transnational mining corporations, and produced one of Latin America's fastest-growing economies. When economic liberalization in the early 1990s was followed by decentralization in the early 2000s, brand new regional governments came into existence under the control of elected regional presidents, many on the left who have won election on the basis of a variety of anti-market and non-neoliberal appeals. Regional presidents and municipal mayors have offered critical support for widespread protests against the dominant economic model, but none has been able to establish truly alternative subnational models that deviate from neoliberalism in meaningful ways. Nor have they been able to moderate the radically neoliberal approach favored by Lima. Instead, the national government has responded to subnational policy challenges by "doubling down" on neoliberalism, adopting ever more draconian pro-market approaches that raise serious questions about the (political and environmental) sustainability of its neoliberal model in the medium to long term. Hence, though Peru is my least effective case of territorial resistance, even here subnational policy challenges are still having an impact in the sense that they have pushed the center to adopt highly reactionary, and often quite authoritarian, behaviors.

Subnational policy challenges have been more consequential in Ecuador, where the left turn at the national level since 2006 has thrown into stark relief a neoliberal policy model in the country's most populous and economically powerful municipality: Guayaquil. The roots of this model reach way back into the nineteenth century, when the city's private sector took the lead in service provision by fashioning a series of *sui generis* local institutions under the control of commercial and financial elites. While the model built by economic elites clashed with the populist mayors who governed Guayaquil from the 1950s through the 1980s, the right-wing mayors who have consistently governed the city since 1992 have successfully extended, deepened, and consolidated this neoliberal policy regime. Stung by the failure of his neoliberal project when president of Ecuador (1984–8), León Febres Cordero initiated the neoliberal transformation of the municipal government in his two terms as mayor (1992–2000), which his successor Jaime Nebot (2000–) has sought to defend vis-à-vis the national government. Though the Correa government has chipped away at the city's neoliberal policy regime, its core elements remain in place along with the right's continued electoral dominance in the municipality of Guayaquil. Advocates of neoliberalism in Guayaquil, however, have had little success moderating the statist policy regime that President Correa has designed and implemented since 2006, and through which he has sought to end Ecuador's "long dark night of neoliberalism."

Bolivia since 2005 has witnessed the most momentous subnational policy challenges in this set of countries, indeed in all Latin America. As in Ecuador, the left turn at the national level brought to power political actors who have sought to construct a much more statist policy regime that would reverse the neoliberal approaches of the 1980s and 1990s. Also like Ecuador, this attempted transition at the national level brought into sharper relief the existence of a neoliberal policy regime in the department of Santa Cruz, whose capital city now ranks as Bolivia's largest and most economically dynamic. Beginning in the 1950s and in response to the similar neglect of the central government that motivated their peers in Guayaquil, emerging private-sector actors in Santa Cruz took the lead in designing and financing a constellation of regional institutions under the control of regional economic elites. While Santa Cruz's subnational policy regime aligned neatly with the neoliberal policy regime in place at the national level from 1985 to 2005, the collapse of the national party system and the rise to power of the leftist *MAS* opened up a period of profound territorial conflict over development models, culminating in the 2008 sacking of national government institutions by President Evo Morales's opponents in Santa Cruz. After several years of polarization, however, the president largely reconciled with the Santa Cruz opposition. Not only did Santa Cruz's neoliberal policy regime survive the conflict with the president relatively unscathed, but its defenders also managed to exert real influence vis-à-vis the moderation of the President's initially much more radical proposals for a statist policy regime at the national level.

Conclusion

Moving from theory to cases, the following chapters examine in depth the emergence and success or failure of subnational policy challenges in the three countries introduced in this chapter. The case material analyzed in these chapters was collected over the course of a decade of field research that took the form of nine approximately month-long trips between October 2005 and September 2015. For each of the three countries, taking this relatively long view proved to be critical in order to develop more sound and accurate judgments about the outcomes of these various policy struggles. In Bolivia, for example, the success of Santa Cruz's policy challenge and the extent of the national policy alignment that it forced upon the center became fully apparent only in the years after 2010. In Ecuador, this longer time frame makes it possible to state with confidence that Guayaquil Mayor Jaime Nebot, re-elected in 2010 and again in 2014, has indeed been able to defend the core elements of that city's neoliberal model—against nearly a decade of attacks from President Rafael Correa. For Peru, extending the time frame of the research was necessary because regional governments were introduced only in 2002; while elected regional presidents may still emerge as more robust policy challengers in the future, it can safely be concluded that they failed to do so in their first decade of existence.

As seen in the chapters that follow, the book relies on a variety of sources of information. First, the analysis makes extensive use of secondary sources in order historically to situate the contemporary policy challenges that I analyze. This was particularly essential in documenting the deep roots of deviant subnational policy regimes and the gradual accumulation of subnational state capacity that has occurred over time. Second, I was able to draw upon the research and position papers produced by independent NGOs and think tanks, many of whom have well-developed opinions about the relative appeal of the ideological models that are in conflict in all three countries. Newspaper analysis offered a third important source of information, and it proved especially illuminating to compare not just how newspapers with different ideological sympathies covered the same news, but how national and local newspapers report differently on similar issues. Fourth, I developed relationships with Bolivian, Ecuadorian, and Peruvian academics, who were very generous both with their own insights and with contacts and logistical help. Fifth and most importantly, the case studies depend heavily on over 200 interviews that I conducted with a broad range of politicians, bureaucrats, and business leaders—at both national and subnational levels. Especially useful were those interviewees who granted multiple interview requests over time. This gave me the opportunity to see how these stakeholders might have changed the views they earlier expressed to me about past events, while also hearing them articulate positions on more recent manifestations of the important policy challenges that are now emerging from subnational governments.

3

Subnational Contention in Neoliberal Peru

Beginning in 1990, ideological struggles over the content of Peru's economic development model have increasingly taken on a territorial logic. At the national level, a succession of governments since 1990 have designed and defended a policy regime that is remarkable both for its profoundly neoliberal orientation and its resilience vis-à-vis critics and opponents. At a time when most governments in Latin America have questioned, substantially amended, or abandoned outright the neoliberal models implemented across the region in the 1990s, in Peru all four successors of President Alberto Fujimori (1990–2000) have upheld and in some respects even deepened the neoliberal reforms that he introduced. According to its supporters, the market-oriented policy regime initiated by Fujimori has generated enormous benefits for Peru, including a record period of macroeconomic stability, a historic drop in the level of poverty, and a doubling in the size of the economy between 2004 and 2014. Detractors of neoliberalism, in contrast, attribute GDP growth to a prolonged period of unusually high prices for Peru's exports and argue that neoliberalism has dramatically worsened inequality; while Lima and the coast have prospered, the rest of the country has been left further behind.

Critics on the left have been unable to dethrone neoliberalism as the dominant model at the national level, but they have been swept into office at the subnational level across Peru, taking control of both regional and municipal governments.[1] Three decades after the implosion of the United Left party (*Izquierda Unida* (*IU*)) in the early 1980s, which devastated the left's chances of winning office nationally (Roberts 1996), the *IU*'s successor parties and a variety of other left movements have managed to penetrate deep into Peru's interior. In other words, while it has been frustrated at the national level, opposition to neoliberalism has found echo in Peru at the subnational level, where it has been channeled into impressive regional and local victories.

[1] According to Carrión (2015: 41), a higher percentage of citizens live in cities governed by the left in Peru than in all other Latin American countries with the exception of Brazil and Mexico.

Drawing on diverse backgrounds in NGOs, universities, *rondas campesinas* (peasant patrols), and even guerrilla insurgencies, leaders who come from the left have tried to use their subnational victories both to create alternatives to neoliberalism and to contest the persistent neoliberalism on offer from the center. This political development is all the more significant because of a series of decentralizing reforms adopted in the aftermath of Fujimori's fall from power in 2000, including the wholesale creation of new regional governments in 2002. Decentralization has significantly expanded the authority and resources under the control of these now left-of-center subnational governments.

Peru's newly empowered subnational governments have clearly become more important spaces for critics of neoliberalism, who have mostly failed to gain any traction within national institutions. Furthermore, conflict over the market in Peru is now unfolding along a core territorial axis; just as neoliberals have consolidated a stranglehold on the national government, the most important and influential political critics of neoliberalism now have subnational identities. Nevertheless, territorial resistance to neoliberalism in Peru has been ineffective in the two dimensions emphasized in this book. As I argue in the first half of this chapter, attempts to build subnational policy regimes that would deviate from neoliberalism have foundered owing to a combination of capacity and coalitional constraints. The lack of institutional capacity, which is to be expected in brand new regional governments but which also results from explicit strategic choices and behaviors by the national government, has been fatal for the ability to build distinct subnational models, as seen most clearly in the struggles over territorial regulation (*ordenamiento territorial* (*OT*)). But subnational executives have also failed to build the kinds of local coalitions with civil society actors that would be necessary to sustain deviant subnational models, not because they have chosen not to, but rather because of an exceptionally thin civil society landscape. Because of the absence of any fully formed subnational policy regime in Peru, I focus in this chapter on the general constraints that have impeded these regimes from taking shape, in contrast to the subsequent chapters on Ecuador and Bolivia, where I examine in depth the vibrant policy regimes that have emerged in specific subnational spaces: Guayaquil and Santa Cruz.

In the second half of the chapter, I show how a different set of constraints—structural and coalitional—have shaped the second type of subnational policy challenge in Peru, which has sought to contest neoliberalism as the dominant national policy regime. Subnational officials at the regional, provincial, and municipal levels have provided critical support for protests against neoliberal mining policies and the extractive projects they have incentivized. While these protests have succeeded in delaying, suspending, and altering some of the most important projects in the country, subnational officials are undercut by a key structural constraint, which is their inability independently to access and control the resources in question. In the meantime, the national government has been able to deal with non-compliant subnational officials on a bilateral basis because of the absence of effective coalitions between individual regional presidents (as distinct from the coalitions between regional presidents and regional societal partners that are critical for the first type of subnational policy challenge). The difficulty of collective action among subnational officials has weakened their ability to leverage policy influence at the national level.

While the primary goal of this chapter is to explain the lack of effective territorial resistance to neoliberalism in Peru as a negative case, the chapter also demonstrates that, even when subnational policy challenges do not succeed, they can still achieve great political significance. Subnational policy challengers have failed to build distinctive local models and they have failed to introduce meaningful changes in the national policy regime, but they are nevertheless now shaping politics in Peru in momentous ways. First, these challengers have succeeded in derailing and/or delaying some of the most important large-scale mining projects in the country—even if they have not been able to alter the neoliberal policies under which the national government has pursued these investments. Second, the disruptive (as opposed to constructive) tactics of subnational challengers have forced the national government to adopt increasingly radical and often repressive behaviors to defend its preferred policy regime, harsh tactics that have widened the already considerable gulf between state and society in Peru. Through a range of measures examined in this chapter, the national government has defended neoliberalism by engaging in additional neoliberal policy experimentation that goes even further in questioning the very existence of representative government at the local level.

Subnational Policy Regimes in Peru: Motivations and Constraints

In order to explain the limited development of subnational policy regimes in Peru, this section proceeds in three parts. The first part shows how economic liberalization and decentralization in Peru provided the motivation for elected leaders to pursue subnational policy regimes that would deviate from the national policy regime. I argue that the particular combination of liberalization with decentralization created fertile terrain for the emergence of subnational policy challenges in Peru, even if other constraints have reduced the effectiveness of these challenges. The second part describes various "flavors" of the subnational left by providing a brief survey of four regional presidents from distinct left origins who have governed recently in four different regions in Peru. These illustrative examples differ in the position each regional president occupied on the ideological spectrum, and in the degree to which they deviated from neoliberalism, but each subnational leader supported substantially more scope for governmental action than is currently allowed in Peru's national policy regime, which makes them important subnational reference points. The third part then presents my argument about how capacity and coalitional constraints have prevented elected officials from developing viable subnational policy regimes.

Liberalization and decentralization in Peru

Peru in the early 1990s experienced one of the most thoroughgoing neoliberal reform processes anywhere in Latin America under the presidency of Alberto Fujimori (1990–2000). One critical factor in explaining both the depth and the persistence of the neoliberalism that took root in Peru in the early 1990s is that it was adopted against the backdrop of a decade of civil war between Shining Path insurgents and the Peruvian state. The armed conflict sharply exposed the state's lack of territorial presence in much of the country (Burt 2010); nowhere else in Latin America did neoliberals have to overcome such a negative investment climate or such high levels of country risk. While the armed conflict in this sense created a problem for those who sought to attract foreign investors to Peru and to shift from state-led to market-oriented development, it also created an opportunity since it gave President Fujimori the pretext to close Congress in the *autogolpe* (self-coup) of 1992 (Mauceri 1995; Conaghan 2006).

Neoliberal reform certainly preceded the self-coup, as in the 1991 Law to Promote Foreign Investment, which opened up all sectors of the economy to direct foreign investment, eliminated restrictions on profit repatriation, and guaranteed equal treatment of foreign and national capitalists (Cameron 1994; Kenney 2004). But the coup was important, as Moises Arce (2005: 38) argues, because it "provided technocrats the political space in which to consolidate the ongoing process of market restructuring." Fujimori used the coup to implement a development model that would depend overwhelmingly on large-scale investments in mining by transnational corporations, overturning the statist model introduced under military rule (1968–80) and returning to the liberal mining code of 1950 (Bebbington 2011). Critical changes under Fujimori include the privatization of 200 mining operations, the ratification of bilateral and multilateral investment treaties, the passage of a National Mining Cadastre that guarantees mining companies exclusive land rights, and, perhaps most consequentially, the offer of tax stability contracts to protect investors from any changes in tax treatment (Bury 2007). Especially important is the law in 1995 (26505) that gave the national government the right to expropriate land for mining companies and that eliminated prohibitions on the sale or mortgage of communally held land (Ponce and McClintock 2014). The decision to lock in low tax rates became highly advantageous for transnational mining companies when global commodity prices spiked in the decade after 2002. Thanks to the generous treatment of foreign capital and the granting of concessions to private mining firms that by 2013 covered over 20 percent of the national territory (de Echave and Diez 2013: 7), Peru's liberalization process triggered a boom in what became Latin America's fastest-growing economy. Advocates of neoliberalism today can contrast the growth and stability of the contemporary period with the economic chaos and armed conflict of the period before Fujimori, and it is no coincidence that detractors of neoliberalism in Peru are sometimes dismissed as terrorists and/or guerrilla sympathizers.[2]

Within Latin America, Peru's neoliberal model is as remarkable for its persistence as its depth; whereas equally sweeping neoliberal reforms in Argentina and Bolivia were called into question by the left turn in the last decade, neoliberalism in Peru has proven to be far more resilient. In part this is due to Fujimori's decision to embed neoliberalism into the new constitution that his supporters designed and adopted in the wake of the 1992 coup, most concretely in the form of Article 60, which sharply restricts public participation in the economy.[3] According to Vergara and Encinas (2016: 5), Article 60 is "the cornerstone of the neoliberal citizenship regime and its derived policies that have progressively taken root in Peru." When Fujimori's regime ended in 2000 in the midst of a widespread corruption scandal, interim President Valentín Paniagua ruled out constitutional reform as a destabilizing move that would complicate redemocratization, thereby limiting the possibility of a serious revision of the neoliberal model at the moment of the transition. Subsequently, the election of Alejandro Toledo in 2001 and Alán García in 2006 brought to the presidency leaders who came to defend the neoliberal model introduced by Fujimori. Given the statist and heterodox course García set as president in the 1980s, his embrace of the neoliberal model was especially significant when he returned to the presidency, culminating in the 2009 Free Trade Agreement with the USA further to lock in the national policy regime, along with the heavy use of repression in response to increasingly widespread subnational protests against further liberalization (Cameron 2011).

[2] "Terrorismo antiminero: Otra burda mentira," Noticias SER, April 22, 2015.

[3] Interview with a top official in the National Confederation of Private Business Institutions (*Confederación Nacional de Instituciones Empresariales Privadas* (*CONFIEP*)), May 7, 2014, Lima (Interview P1).

The persistence of neoliberalism after 2011 is even more striking. Many in the private sector feared the election that year of Ollanta Humala, a nationalist who promised a Great Transformation (*Gran Transformación*) away from neoliberalism, but who after his inauguration upheld the neoliberal course set by Fujimori and affirmed by Toledo and García. Fundamental continuity can be seen in a number of dimensions. For example, while Humala did introduce a new tax on mining companies, along with a new "duty" (*gravamen*) on companies protected by tax stability contracts, he agreed to let them deduct these payments as operational costs in computing income tax payments, which has dramatically reduced the positive net effect on fiscal revenue (Monge 2012: 65).[4] Likewise, Humala endorsed a feckless "prior consultation" law that denies indigenous communities meaningful authority to influence investment decisions, and failed to remove control over Environmental Impact Assessments from the Ministry of Energy and Mines (Gamboa and Snoeck 2012).[5] Through sweeping investment-promotion legislation passed in 2014 (law 30230), Humala also weakened the already-anemic Environment Ministry by restricting its authority to set clean water and air standards, by taking away its right to set aside zones for conservation, by cutting in half the fines it can impose on extractive firms, and by extending Fujimori-era tax stability contracts (Durand 2016).[6] In sharp contrast to his counterparts in Bolivia and Ecuador, Humala has at every turn opposed efforts to increase the state's presence in the hydrocarbons sector, ultimately opting not to buy Repsol from Spanish investors, not to take public ownership over the oilfields in La Talara, and not to develop petrochemical activities in connection with the new gas pipeline in the south of the country.[7] Perhaps most meaningful as a sign of neoliberal continuity was Humala's decision to appoint high-level figures from the García administration, including Economy and Finance Minister Miguel Castilla and Central Bank President Julio Velarde (Schuldt 2012; Rodríguez and Bueno Hansen, forthcoming).[8] In 2016, Peruvians elected to the presidency former World Bank economist and Minister of Economy and Finance Pedro-Pablo Kuczynski, one of the leading architects and defenders of Peru's neoliberal model.

Explanations vary of neoliberalism's unusual endurance in Peru. Some explain the resilience of Peruvian neoliberalism as the result of the capture

[4] Since income-tax revenues are shared with regions via the canon system while the new *gravamen* is not, this change also decreases fiscal transfers to subnational governments. Interview with a former Secretary of Decentralization, May 8, 2014, Lima (Interview P2).

[5] See Orijuela (2014) for the argument that neoliberal ideology in Peru has generated an "unfriendly arena for environmental regulation."

[6] "Paquete reactivador sí viola acuerdos internacionales," *La República*, July 7, 2014.

[7] Interview with a former Head Staffer of the Congressional Committee on Decentralization, May 6, 2014, Lima (Interview P3). See also Vergara and Encinas 2016.

[8] Interview with a high-level official in *CEPLAN*, April 30, 2014, Lima (Interview P4).

of the state by business interests, particularly the financial sector (Durand 2010). Others attribute this persistence not to the private sector but to the public sector—namely, entrenched technocrats in key bureaucracies such as the *Ministerio de Economía y Finanzas* (*MEF*) (Ministry of Economy and Finances) and the Central Bank whose expertise and mastery of administrative procedure has enabled them to shield the neoliberal policy regime from political interference (Dargent 2011, 2014; Vergara and Encinas 2016). Bureaucratic actors who might favor a revision of neoliberalism are unable to do battle with the *MEF* or the Central Bank, including not just the social and environmental ministries but also a new planning agency (*Centro Nacional de Planeamiento Estratégico* (*CEPLAN*) (National Center for Strategic Planning)) that has carefully avoided conflict with the pro-market voices that dominate within the cabinet.[9] Whatever the cause of this persistence, the inability of opponents of neoliberalism to generate even a serious debate about the neoliberal model contrasts strongly with other countries in Latin America, where neoliberalism has been seriously questioned (for example, Argentina, Bolivia, Ecuador, Venezuela) or complemented with important new forms of state-financed social protection (for example, Brazil and Chile) (Levitsky and Roberts 2011; Garay 2016).

The persistence of neoliberalism in Peru takes on special political significance in light of the territorially uneven distribution of the costs and benefits arising from the model. This is most acute vis-à-vis the neoliberal mining policies that are at the center of Peru's model. On the one hand, all Peruvians benefit from the foreign-exchange earnings and fiscal revenues generated by transnational mining companies, which have made possible a record period of macroeconomic stability and low inflation. On the other hand, economic growth since 1990 has disproportionately benefited (and accelerated migration to) Peru's wealthier and more urban coastal regions, rather than the rural highland and Amazonian regions where most natural resources are located. For example, although the mining boom is credited with reducing poverty in Peru, the national figures mask significant regional variation (Ghezzi and Gallardo 2013). In 2010, poverty affected only 20 percent of the urban population but 61 percent of the rural population (Remy 2013: 135). While regional inequality certainly pre-dates both neoliberalism and the mining boom that began after 2000, there is a pervasive sense that, as María Isabel Remy argues, "not all regions have been invited to the party in Peru."

In addition to not sharing equally in the gains, Peruvians who live near the mines disproportionately pay the costs associated with neoliberal mining policies. These include displacement of peasant communities from lands

[9] Interview P4.

sold to the companies at below-market value, a tendency by mining companies to meet their labor needs extra-locally, and negative impacts on the quality and quantity of water owing to the prevalence of water-intensive forms of mining (Bury 2007; Gil 2009; Grompone and Tanaka 2009). Although mining has been important in Peru since the colonial period, new technologies since 2000 have significantly extended the mining frontier, vastly multiplying the number of regions affected by mining and threatening the viability of non-mining productive activities in territories that have never had mines (Bebbington 2007; Sanborn and Dammert 2013). As evidenced in the thousands of lethal mining protests that have engulfed Peru during the mining boom, the country is experiencing an acute territorial conflict between regional winners (metropolitan Lima and the coast) and losers (the rest of the country).[10]

While the regional losers who disproportionately bear the costs of neoliberalism in Peru have been unable to exert much leverage in national institutions since 1990, thanks to decentralization these institutions are no longer "the only game in town." Important new governing spaces have emerged at the subnational level owing to the decentralizing reforms that accompanied redemocratization in the early 2000s (Arce 2008, 2014). In the attempt to distinguish himself from his authoritarian predecessor, whose economic policy preferences he mostly shared, President Toledo (2001–6) adopted a series of decentralizing measures that contrasted directly with those of Fujimori, who had cancelled regional elections, manipulated municipal governments, and brought centralism in Peru to new heights (Gonzales de Olarte 2000; Zas Friz 2004). Toledo opted for decentralization as a democratizing move that would help undo the legacies of Fujimori's highly centralizing regime (McNulty 2011). Less than a year into his administration, Congress approved constitutional reforms in March 2002 that identified decentralization as a permanent and irreversible policy of the state, followed in July 2002 by a framework law for decentralization (*Ley de Bases de la Descentralización*). In addition to creating the National Council of Decentralization (*Consejo Nacional de Descentralización* (*CND*)), which was identified as the lead agency that would push the decentralization process forward, the framework law eschewed the simultaneous adoption of decentralizing changes in all three dimensions (political, fiscal, and administrative) and established instead a gradual and explicitly sequenced approach to decentralization. All three

[10] While the interior has gained far less than coastal Lima from the resource boom of the early twenty-first century, it is also important to note the highly unequal treatment of interior regions in the canon system of revenue-sharing, which rewards producing regions in the highlands while neglecting neighboring, non-producing regions. This makes it harder for jurisdictions in the interior to come together and challenge the dominant model.

Map 3.1. Peru: Administrative Divisions
Source: Perry-Castañeda Library Map Collection at the University of Texas.

dimensions matter for the fate of the subnational policy challenges that are discussed later in this chapter.

First, according to the 2002 framework law, decentralization would begin in the political sphere with the creation of regional governments on the basis of Peru's twenty-five existing administrative departments, as seen in Map 3.1. The law stipulated that the first elections for regional presidents were to be held before the end of the year (2002), and that regional officials were to assume their duties in January 2003. Reflecting the rushed nature of decentralization, it was only the day before regional elections were held on November 20, 2002 that Congress actually passed the Organic Law of Regional Governments, thereby specifying the legal prerogatives and responsibilities of the governments that were politically constituted the following day. In addition to regional elections, the framework law also introduced participatory reforms by stipulating the mandatory creation of Regional Coordination Councils (*Consejos de Coordinación Regional* (*CCRs*)) through which civil society groups would help shape regional budgets (McNulty 2011). Ultimately, the newly constituted regional governments were to be replaced by the formation of larger and more viable "macro-regions" based on the fusion of two or more regional governments. Despite the passage in 2004 of an ancillary Law of Incentives for the Integration of Regions, however, voters rejected all five proposals to amalgamate regions in a 2005 referendum, and the question of "macro-regions" has been sidelined ever since. Adopted as a fiscally cheap, technically quick, and broadly popular way to mark the end of the Fujimori regime, political decentralization produced a sea change in Peruvian politics by institutionalizing the election of regional governments that Lima cannot easily control. If a profound disconnect between national and subnational political spheres is one of the defining features of contemporary politics in Peru (Arce 2014; Battle 2012; Panfichi 2011; Tanaka 2005; Vergara 2011), Toledo's precipitate decision to decentralize in 2002 contributed significantly to this outcome.

Second, fiscal decentralization in Peru was intended to follow directly upon political decentralization. The 2004 Law of Fiscal Decentralization adopted a two-phased approach to fiscal transfers. In the first phase, fiscal revenues would be transferred to subnational governments as a function of the specific administrative responsibilities assumed by these governments. In the second phase, revenue sharing (*coparticipación*) would be introduced once macro-regions had been created via referendum; the law did not contemplate the possibility of fiscal transfers to municipalities.[11] In practice, fiscal decentralization has not really occurred in Peru, in part because voters rejected the formation of macro-regions, without which revenue sharing cannot occur under the 2002 legislation, and in part because of steadfast *MEF* concerns that it would threaten the country's newfound fiscal balance.

While fiscal decentralization as such has not taken place, it is important to emphasize that the national government in 2002 increased revenue-sharing with regions that produce natural resources in the so-called canon system (*canon minero*). Adopted before the mining boom began with the uptick in

[11] Interview with a former Head of the Cabinet of Advisors in the *MEF*, September 13, 2007, Lima (Interview P5).

international mineral prices after 2002, the canon system has had an unexpected, positive, though highly unequal impact on regional finances (Crabtree 2014). According to this system, 50 percent of the national income tax revenues paid by extractive industries are shared with the district, provincial, and regional governments where the resource is located (Bland and Chirinos 2014). For my purposes, the canon system cuts both ways with respect to the likelihood of effective subnational policy challenges. On the one hand, the canon inhibits these challenges. This is because revenue flows to subnational units depend on continued investment by private mining companies who are attracted to Peru by its neoliberal policies; mayors and regional presidents currently have virtually no hopes of securing sizable revenue flows without productive mines in their jurisdictions. On the other hand, for the subnational districts lucky enough to receive them, canon transfers mean that mayors and regional presidents in Peru finally have the resources to finance alternative local policy regimes and forms of governmental action that are more vigorous than anything allowed in the national neoliberal model.[12]

Finally, Peru's staged decentralization process was meant to culminate with administrative transfers. During this third stage of decentralization, the national government would transfer functions to local and regional governments in all sectors except education and health, which would be transferred only in the fourth and final stage of decentralization (Conterno 2007). Transfers of functions were governed by a 2004 law that established a system of accreditation according to which functions could be transferred only to subnational governments whose sufficient capacity had been verified in advance by the national government.[13] Neither the 2002 framework law nor the 2004 law established a great deal of clarity about the exact division of responsibilities between different levels of government (national, regional, provincial, municipal), just as the 2002 Organic Law of Regional Governments had assigned national and subnational governments overlapping responsibilities. While ambiguous and overlapping authorities create challenges of their own, it is important to note that administrative decentralization has indeed given entrepreneurial subnational officials considerable authority to innovate, if they so choose. Insufficient administrative authority has been far less of a problem than insufficient administrative capacity.

To summarize this section, Post-Fujimori Peru has experienced rapid and meaningful decentralization, even as it has maintained continuity with respect to Fujimori's liberal economic model. Although the decentralization

[12] The onset of the canon system also appears to be responsible for a sharp increase in the number of candidates for subnational office. Interview with a former President of the Zoning and Territorial Regulation Committee in the National Society of Mining, Petroleum and Energy (*Sociedad Nacional de Minería, Petróleo y Energía* (*SNMPE*)), May 12, 2014, Lima (Interview P6).

[13] Interview with a decentralization expert in PRODES, September 21, 2007, Lima (Interview P7).

process has not conformed to the highly sequenced course set out in 2002, it has altered Peru's political landscape by giving regions the right to elect their own chief executives—a right that has become increasingly institutionalized over the past four electoral cycles (2002, 2006, 2010, 2014). In addition to their direct sources of democratic legitimacy, regional presidents also now often have significantly greater access to fiscal revenues and important expenditure responsibilities. Simultaneously, they are facing regional electorates dominated by the very groups who have borne the negative impacts of neoliberalism, but who have been powerless to affect policy change through their participation in national level elections.

Four flavors of the subnational left in Peru

The mix of liberalization and decentralization already described has resulted in the election of a number of regional presidents who hail from different points of origin on the left, and whose administrations have explored a number of alternatives to neoliberalism. To demonstrate the range of the challenges they represent, this section briefly sketches profiles of four important regional presidents: Juan Manuel Guillén of Arequipa, Gregorio Santos of Cajamarca, Yehude Simon of Lambayeque, and César Villanueva of San Martín. Each of these regional presidents rose to prominence out of a different history of left political activism and from different launching pads, including regional universities, *rondas campesinas*, guerrilla insurgencies, and environmental NGOs, respectively. Each has governed in a different part of Peru, exposing them to an array of distinct socioeconomic challenges: Arequipa in the south, Cajamarca in the northern highlands, Lambayeque on the coast, and San Martín in the Amazon. As a reflection of their popularity, and in a context in which few regional presidents have been re-elected since the introduction of elections for these offices in 2002, all four of these regional presidents were re-elected by their constituents (Simon in 2006, Guillén and Villanueva in 2010, and Santos in 2014, albeit from a jail cell).

By introducing Guillén, Santos, Simon, and Villanueva into the analysis, I do not mean to suggest that all regional presidents have innovated in ways that implicitly or explicitly critique neoliberalism; indeed several on the right have sought to build policy regimes at the regional level that merely replicate the national policy regime (examples include César Acuña in La Libertad, Javier Atkins in Piura, and Tito Chocano in Tacna).[14] Nor is it to suggest that all four profiled here pose equal threats to the neoliberal order; indeed, as a reflection of

[14] Interviews with a high-level analyst in Asociación SER, September 14, 2007 and April 29, 2014, Lima (Interview P8); and with an expert on regional development in Grupo Propuesta Ciudadana, May 13, 2014, Lima (Interview P9).

their status as moderates who have moved from the left to the center of the political spectrum, Simon and Villanueva were actually appointed prime ministers (premiers) by presidents who have reinforced the neoliberal policy regime (García and Humala). Instead, I merely hope to show that regional governments have become an important space for the articulation of projects that would offer meaningful alternatives to the draconian version of neoliberalism defended by the *MEF* in Lima, even if these projects have largely failed in the face of the constraints that are discussed in the next section.

Juan Manuel Guillén of Arequipa transformed himself into a politician on the basis of a successful public university career. Guillén graduated from the National University of San Agustín (*Universidad Nacional de San Agustín* (*UNSA*)), chaired its philosophy department, and then modernized the university in a lengthy and distinguished tenure as rector between 1989 and 1998.[15] The Fujimori years (1990–2000) were difficult for Arequipa, which had formerly developed important industries but which rapidly deindustrialized in the wake of tariff liberalization (Vergara 2015).[16] With the relocation of industries to Lima, the *UNSA* under Guillén became an important pillar of support for regional planning and public investment in research and development, and of opposition to neoliberalism. This culminated in a controversial visit to the *UNSA* in 1998 by Fujimori himself, when thousands of residents who had gathered in the new university stadium built by Guillén humiliated the president by whistling at him in a show of opposition. Guillén leveraged his protagonism and visibility as rector into a successful bid for mayor of Arequipa in 1998. As mayor, Guillén captured national attention in the so-called Arequipazo when he led a broad movement against privatization that was opposed to President Toledo's attempt to sell two local electricity plants (EGASA and EGESUR) to a Belgian utility giant (Tractabel).[17] Arguing that the privatization of state-owned enterprises should require regional approval, Guillén offered critical material and symbolic support for five strikes from February to June of 2002 (including a hunger strike in which he himself participated), and ultimately forced the Toledo government to surrender (Arce 2008; Eaton 2010). Guillén thus played a key role not just in stopping privatization in Arequipa, but in paralyzing privatizations for the remaining four years of Toledo's presidency.[18]

[15] Interview with a former Vice President of the Region of Arequipa, September 20, 2007, Arequipa (Interview P10).

[16] Interview with a Congressman from Arequipa, September 12, 2007, Lima (Interview P11).

[17] Interview with one of the leaders of the *Frente Amplio Cívico de Arequipa*, September 20, 2007, Arequipa (Interview P12).

[18] Interview with the former President of the Arequipa Chamber of Commerce, September 18, 2007, Arequipa (Interview P13).

As regional president of Arequipa (2006–14), Guillén showed his frustration with the inflexibility of the neoliberal model inherited from the Fujimori era, along with his support for more vigorous governmental action, in a number of policy disputes. For example, in his first term he led the Committee to Fight Cerro Verde, which challenged the Cerro Verde company's continued use of its tax stability contract to reduce tax payments when it sought to expand the footprint of mining activity beyond its initial investment.[19] In 2011, Guillén played an important role in the suspension of one of Peru's largest mining projects, the proposed Tía María copper mine by the Southern Peruvian Mining Corporation. Another instructive case is the controversy surrounding the licensing of a new fish processing plant in the municipality of Camaná. According to the governmental minister who was sent to resolve the conflict, while the local mayor favored the project, Guillén worked actively to foment opposition to the project and to demand stricter environmental regulations.[20] Finally, over the course of his eight years as regional president, Guillén sought to use his authority over public lands owned by the regional government to promote the second phase of the large-scale Majes Siguas irrigation project that had been initiated by Peru's statist military regime in the 1970s.

Gregorio Santos of Cajamarca pursued a rural rather than an urban path to the regional presidency, one that began as a peasant leader with extensive ties to the patrols (*rondas campesinas*) organized initially to defend peasants from cattle-rustling. In the wake of land reform in the 1970s, which created a power vacuum by eliminating the regional landed elites (or *gamonales*) who had long dominated the countryside, the *rondas* emerged as important civil society actors and political players (Degregori 1996). Santos also became a member of Patria Roja, a far left party with approximately 30,000 members and a lineage that can be traced back to the *IU* in the 1980s. Santos captured national attention in 2011 as the leader of a movement that opposed the $5 billion Conga gold mining project proposed by the Yanacocha company. Not only did Santos's leadership lead to the suspension of the project and the freezing of a number of other projects in the region; it also triggered a national political crisis that caused the collapse of three cabinets. Santos used his position not just to bring attention to the potentially devastating impacts of the project on water access and local livelihoods, but to critique the neoliberal policies under which the project was authorized without meaningful environmental oversight. Santos also articulated a sharp personal attack on Humala, whose candidacy he had supported in 2011 and whose transformation from neoliberal critic to defender was attacked by Santos as a major

[19] Interview with an employee in the Public Affairs Unit of the Cerro Verde Mining Company, September 18, 2007, Arequipa (Interview P14).
[20] Interview with the former Minister of Production, May 2, 2014, Lima (Interview P15).

betrayal of the left. Santos is considered by the conservative Lima daily *La República* to be the regional leader in Peru who most closely approximates the figure of Evo Morales in Bolivia.[21]

Though he is often dismissed as more of a critic than an innovator or administrator, Santos has been aggressive in pushing to transform Cajamarca into a region that would be governed by a model different from the neoliberal one Humala has come to defend in Lima. For example, in seeking to prevent Conga, Santos issued a regional ordinance declaring the project ecologically unviable and claiming that the 2009 Law of Hydraulic Resources enables the designation of watersheds as "intangible" zones. Although the Constitutional Tribunal ruled against Santos, arguing that regional governments have authority only over small-scale and artisanal mining and not over large-scale projects like Conga, other subnational officials in other regions have since issued similar ordinances, which have had significant political consequences despite their questionable legality. Just as importantly, in the *OT* process that is discussed in greater detail later in this chapter, Santos presided over one of the most aggressive attempts in Peru to use regulatory authority vis-à-vis zoning to impose governmental limits on where and how mining can occur.[22] Specifically, Santos resisted using data supplied by national agencies like the National Water Authority, whose objectivity he questioned, and directed bureaucrats in his regional government to collect data of their own.[23]

Yehude Simon of Lambayeque embodies a not uncommon trajectory within the Latin American left, marked by a lengthy prison sentence that led him to repudiate the legacies of the violent left in favor of a more participatory approach. After representing Lambayeque in Congress in the 1980s as a member of the *IU*, Simon founded the Movimiento Patria Libre in 1991, widely alleged to be the political wing of Peru's second most important guerrilla insurgency, the Tumac Amaru Revolutionary Movement. In the aftermath of the 1992 *autogolpe*, Simon was tried and found guilty for the offense of "apology for terrorism." Although sentenced to twenty years in prison, Simon was released after the fall of Fujimori in 2000 and subsequently pardoned by President Toledo in 2002. Later that year, having written extensively in prison about his conversion experience, when fellow prisoners from subaltern groups led him to question the traditional vanguard approach of the Peruvian left, Simon founded a new moderate left Humanist Party to contest regional elections (Simon 2011). Despite predictions that Peru's historic *APRA* party (*Alianza Popular Revolucionaria Americana* or American Popular

[21] "Gregorio Santos: Presidente Regional juega al todo o nada," *La República*, December 1, 2011.

[22] Interview with a former Director of Territorial Regulation in the Ministry of the Environment, May 2, 2014, Lima (Interview P16).

[23] Interview with a Senior Specialist in Environmental Affairs, *SNMPE*, May 12, 2014, Lima (Interview P17).

Revolutionary Alliance) would maintain its traditional dominance in the departments of the northern coast, Simon produced a historic upset by defeating the *APRA* in elections for regional president in 2002, and again in 2006.

Simon's governing record as regional president offers further evidence of a leader who has shifted from the radical left, and from a position of apparent support for insurgent methods, to one of deep commitment to participatory democracy and civil society empowerment. According to Stephanie McNulty's comparative study (2011) of the participatory institutions that were established across Peruvian regions in the aftermath of decentralization in 2002, Lambayeque outperformed other regions, largely thanks to Simon's leadership and commitment. Simon personally attended the participatory budgeting process, accepted substantive changes proposed by the region's coordinating council (*CCR*), and gave civil society members of the *CCR* office space within the regional government buildings (McNulty 2011: 130). McNulty credits Simon's successful promotion of and identification with participatory governance for the fact that he increased his margin of victory over the *APRA* in the 2006 regional elections by more than 20 percentage points relative to the 2002 elections (132). In addition to seeking to promote a more participatory model of governance at the regional level, Simon as regional president bristled under the spending constraints imposed by the *MEF*, which he saw as obsessed with fiscal austerity. As one example, Simon flouted *MEF* rules that require regional authorities to rent rather than buy equipment in the attempt to provide a more rapid and vigorous response to a flooding disaster he faced as regional president.[24] More generally, in support of a more interventionist government, Simon has argued that "the state in Peru must invest in those areas like highways and infrastructure that are uninteresting to the private sector, otherwise the poor will remain marginalized."[25]

César Villanueva of San Martín illustrates a fourth pathway on the left as an environmental leader who leveraged his extensive experience in the NGO world into a successful bid for regional president in 2006. Although he began his political career in the early 1980s as a member of *Vanguardia Revolucionaria* (Revolutionary Vanguard), one of the radical parties allied with the *IU* for which he ran (unsuccessfully) for Congress in 1983, Villanueva subsequently abandoned politics. Over the course of the following two decades, he developed substantial technocratic expertise as the director of a number of important environmental NGOs, including the *Centro de Desarrollo e Investigación de la Selva Alta* (*CEDISA*) (Center for Development and Research on the Highland Jungle) and *Concertación y Competitividad Amazónica*

[24] Interview with a top official in the Regional Government of Lambayeque, May 13, 2014, Lima (Interview P18).

[25] Ivan Hinojosa, "El golpe estoico de Yehude Simon," *Caretas*, March 4, 2004.

(Amazonian Concertation and Competitiveness). Villanueva emerged as a consistent advocate for sustainable development, environmental protection, and conservation—all values that clash with the ethos of the neoliberal model imposed from Lima, with its heavy dependence on large-scale mining by private investors and hostility to environmental regulation.

Widely viewed as one of the most successful regional politicians in Peru, Villanueva delivered an energetic and innovative performance as regional president of San Martín, coming closer than any of his peers to the actual creation of an identifiable subnational policy regime. Most importantly, in response to the relative absence of large-scale extractive and agricultural activities in the region, Villanueva branded San Martín as a "Green Region" (*Región Verde*) and privileged the pursuit of ecotourism. Inspired by the successful experience of Costa Rica, where he sent a team of experts on a two-month study trip, Villanueva drew heavily upon environmental NGOs in staffing the regional bureaucracy, and was the first regional president to create a separate environmental department.[26] Along with the much more radical Santos in Cajamarca, Villanueva presided over one of the most restrictive territorial regulation processes anywhere in Peru, including the requirement that private investors must abide by the zoning restrictions adopted by the regional government.[27] Faced with limited revenues and little in the way of canon transfers, Villanueva also showed great entrepreneurialism in generating the revenues he would need to pursue the kinds of public investments in infrastructure, education, and coca-crop substitution that he advocated for the region. Specifically, Villanueva convinced the national government to eliminate long-standing tax incentives for residents of San Martín and other Amazonian regions, and to place the additional revenues thereby collected in a special fiduciary fund under the control of the regional government.[28] Like that of Simon in 2008, Villanueva's selection as prime minister in 2013 reflects his moderate (as opposed to radical) ideological position, and yet "neoliberal" is not an accurate label for the forceful vision of governmental action that he pursued as regional president.

Insufficient capacity and weak coalitions as impediments to subnational policy regimes

In response to liberalization and decentralization, regional presidents like the four described in the previous section have tried to build local models in Peru that deviate from neoliberalism in a variety of significant ways. Nevertheless,

[26] Interviews P2 and P9.

[27] Interview with a former Director of Conservation in the Sociedad Peruana de Defensa Ambiental, May 9, 2014, Lima (Interview P19).

[28] Interview P9.

they have failed to construct coherent and viable subnational policy regimes—in contrast to some of their peers in Ecuador and Bolivia. In this section, I attribute their failure to do so to the absence of institutional capacity and support coalitions. Regional presidents do not lack the motivation to deviate, but they do lack the requisite administrative capacity to act on non-neoliberal visions and the necessary societal partners to sustain these attempted transformations. Insufficient administrative capacity at the subnational level is especially problematic for officials who are trying to expand—rather than reduce—the role of the state, and it has created a particularly uneven playing field considering the successful experience with capacity-building that has taken place since 1990 within the select national ministries that police the neoliberal model, including the *MEF*, *Ministerio de Energía y Minas* (*MINEM*) (Ministry of Energy and Mines), and Central Bank (Dargent 2014). In addition to institutional capacity, subnational officials must be able to depend on effective coalitions with civil society partners; here I examine a series of changes beginning with the agrarian reform in the late 1960s that have sharply limited the possibility of these partnerships, and argue that local and foreign NGOs are ultimately poor substitutes for the trade unions and regional elites that have mostly disappeared from Peru's regional landscape.

Insufficient Capacity. Concerned that capacity issues would be particularly acute in regional governments that did not exist as such before 2002, designers of the decentralization process in Peru endorsed a gradual process of accreditation by which the national government would transfer responsibilities only once it had verified sufficient capacity.[29] This design choice was an explicit response to the growing evidence elsewhere in Latin America that many subnational governments were simply not prepared to act on the new authorities assigned to them as part of decentralization.[30] Five years into this often protracted process of capacity-building, however, and deeply frustrated with the slowness of administrative decentralization, President García implemented a "decentralizing shock" in 2007 that finalized the administrative transfers by rapidly shifting responsibilities without capacity-building, thereby circumventing the accreditation process (Ballon 2011).

In addition to abandoning explicit capacity-building, the national government has imposed a series of exacting rules on subnational hiring and spending that have crippled attempts by regional government to deepen capacity on their own.[31] Many of these rules reflect overriding *MEF* fears of the possible

[29] Interviews P2 and P5.

[30] Interview with a former Secretary of Decentralization in the Council of Ministers, September 12, 2007, Lima (Interview P20).

[31] Though I focus here on the regional level, similar capacity problems loomed large in the failure of Lima Mayor Susana Villarán (2010–14), who followed upon a series of right-wing mayors

threats posed by subnational governments to macro-level fiscal stability. Most important is the National System of Public Investment (*Sistema Nacional de Inversión Pública* (*SNIP*)), which requires national government approval of subnational spending on projects above a very low threshold. If subnational officials are to have any hope of receiving "on the job training," the *SNIP* limits these opportunities by delaying if not paralyzing subnational spending. Critics note that the same inflexible rules that govern public entities with thousands of employees like the national tax agency (*Superintendencia Nacional de Administración Tributaria* (*SUNAT*)) or the interior ministry also govern municipalities with only four or five employees (República del Perú 2013: 20).[32] Thanks to tight *MEF* controls on salary, regional bureaucrats who run multi-million dollar projects earn salaries that top out at 3,500 soles (roughly $1,500 a month).[33] Low salaries lead to high turnover, and the difficulty of hiring permanent staff generates an overreliance on consultants. Both of these dynamics reinforce the dependence of regional governments on local NGOs, which often try to substitute for missing administrative capacity.[34] Complicating matters is the stipulation that canon monies to subnational governments can be used only for capital expenditure and cannot be used to hire employees, which means that many regional governments finally have fiscal resources but cannot employ sufficient staff actually to spend these resources (Ponce and McClintock 2014).[35] As complained by former mayor Carlos López Jiménez, "the canon cannot be used to contract staff, but existing staff cannot pull off the bigger projects that are theoretically now possible because of the canon."[36] As a result of these various constraints, according to *CEPLAN*, subnational governments on average are able to spend only 50 percent of their revenues in Peru—a clear sign of limited administrative

who had systematically underinvested in the city's public administration. Interview with an urban planning expert in the Citizen Security Committee of the Metropolitan Municipality of Lima, May 12, 2014, Lima (Interview P21).

[32] The difficulty of spending also leads would-be suppliers of subnational governments to prefer to work with the private sector instead (República del Perú 2013: 20).

[33] Interview P2.

[34] Interestingly, progressive NGOs and mining companies—which are typically on the opposite side of social conflicts in Peru—both complain that high levels of staff turnover (especially in the aftermath of regional elections) make it nearly impossible to work with regional governments. Interview P19 and interviews with the Corporate Social Responsibility Manager (Interview P22) and Director of Corporate Affairs (Interview P23) of a mid-size Peruvian-owned mining company, May 9, 2014, Lima.

[35] As an example, some regional governments have experienced a 1200% increase in capital expenditure and only a 60% increase in current expenditure. Interview with the former Technical Secretary of the National Association of Regional Governments, April 30, 2014, Lima (Interview P24).

[36] Interview with a top-level official in the Network of Urban and Rural Peruvian Municipalities (*Red de Municipalidades Urbanas y Rurales del Perú* (*REMURPE*)) May 6, 2014, Lima (Interview P25).

capacity.[37] While canon monies at least stay in local accounts, other funds not spent by the end of the year must be returned to Lima.

In addition to sharp constraints on hiring and spending, the national government has also experimented aggressively with a number of other, often less obvious, mechanisms that inhibit the development of subnational capacity and prevent alternatives to neoliberalism from emerging. Thus, while national officials complain of "African levels of public administration in Peru's regions—even as the country is booming," it is important to emphasize the complicity of the national government in this outcome.[38] Here I emphasize three national strategies that have inhibited subnational capacity-building: infiltration, marginalization, and displacement.

Infiltration refers to the ability of Peru's neoliberal nucleus within the *MEF*, *MINEM*, and Central Bank to penetrate other parts of the government and thereby check ideological deviations. While Vergara and Encinas (2016) argue that the infiltration strategy has unfolded across the national cabinet, this same strategy has also affected regional governments. According to one former Secretary of Decentralization, the national government can still often control regional governments—despite decentralization—through a few well-placed emissaries in regional departments (*direcciones*).[39] For example, rather than collaborate with mining departments established by regional governments, the *MINEM* has set up sectoral offices in the regions that are staffed by bureaucrats who answer to Lima (Congreso de la República del Perú 2013: 14). While this preference for deconcentration improves the capacity of the national government, it does little to improve the capacity of regional bureaucrats to act independently of the center. The same suspicions that have led the national government to infiltrate regional governments have led it to oppose as illegal the creation by regional governments of new departments other than the five contemplated in the original 2002 legislation.[40]

Turning from infiltration to marginalization strategies, the administrative capacity of subnational governments in Peru has also suffered from the intensive and extensive encouragement of corporate social responsibility (CSR) on the part of the national government. Especially in Peru's lesser-developed regions, CSR undoubtedly has financed the kinds of much-needed and valuable goods and services that are not being provided by subnational

[37] Interview with the former Coordinator of Strategic Planning, *CEPLAN*, April 30, 2014, Lima (Interview P26).

[38] Interview with the former National Director of Monitoring and Evaluation, *CEPLAN*, April 30, 2014, Lima (Interview P27).

[39] Interview P3.

[40] At the same time, some regions, like Arequipa, have successfully defended the proliferation of new agencies on the grounds that regional governments are autonomous. Interview with a decentralization expert and professor in the School of Government, Catholic University, April 29, 2014, Lima (Interview P28).

governments, including road construction, health clinics, and a host of infrastructure projects. Furthermore, CSR is particularly welcome as a partial offset to the light tax burden that was guaranteed to mining companies at the time of Peru's turn toward neoliberalism in the 1990s. At the same time, CSR should be seen as a phenomenon that has had the effect of marginalizing subnational governments and attenuating citizen demands for better governmental performance, which is one of the classic sources of pressure on these governments to deepen capacity.

Over the course of the post-2002 mining boom in Peru, the national government became increasingly sophisticated and coordinated in its promotion of CSR, initially to respond to local conflicts over mining and eventually in a more preventative mode to inhibit the onset of these conflicts.[41] Under the auspices of García's Social Conflict Unit (*Unidad de Conflicto Social* (*UCS*) and Humala's National Office for Dialogue and Sustainability (*Oficina Nacional de Diálogo y Sostenibilidad* (*ONDS*)), the national government has privileged the use of "dialogue round tables" (*mesas de diálogo*), which bring together representatives of the *MINEM*, mining companies, and local community leaders, and which identify priority local needs that the company can meet.[42] In remote regions, these round tables have encouraged Peruvians to develop a quite expansive view of the powers of mining companies, as reflected in the perhaps apocryphal story of one community, whose demands on the mining company included even the extradition of Fujimori from Chile.[43] While CSR has been functional to the national neoliberal model by undermining the capacity of subnational governments that could otherwise potentially deviate from neoliberalism, it is also important to note that these governments themselves often welcome CSR.[44] Indeed, when facing the sharp constraints on hiring and spending just described, it can be very tempting for regional officials simply to let companies step in and provide goods and services directly through CSR, which in effect lets subnational governments "off the hook." Regional President Guillén, for instance, welcomed the construction of a sewage treatment plant in Arequipa by the Cerro Verde company, even as he led the fight to get the company to assume a greater tax burden.[45]

[41] Interviews with two regional coordinators (for Southern Peru and Central Peru) in the *ONDS*, May 8, 2014, Lima (Interviews P29 and P30).

[42] Interview P23. 3). See also Oficina Nacional de Diálogo y Sostenibilidad (2013).

[43] Interview with a Minister in the Ollanta Humala cabinet, May 6, 2014, Lima (Interview P31).

[44] It is also important to note that, while many companies have sought to displace the state, other, newer and more "modern" companies see themselves as trying to "bring the state" to the regions where they operate. Interview P22.

[45] Interviews with a leader in the Committee to Fight Cerro Verde, September 19, 2007, Arequipa (Interview P32); and with a former Director of the Centro de Estudios Cristianos y Capacitación Popular, September 19, 2007, Arequipa (Interview P33).

The accumulation of institutional capacity in subnational governments has also been challenged by even bolder attempts not just to marginalize but to displace these governments altogether. Since 2006, the national government has begun two radical experiments with tax policy: (1) the Voluntary Contributions (*Aportes Voluntarios*) approach of President García (2006–11) and (2) the Works for Taxes (*Obras por Impuestos*) modality developed under President Humala since 2011. In different ways, each of these programs represents a major departure from traditional arrangements in which the private sector pays taxes to the state, which then engages in political processes (democratic or not) to determine where and how those public revenues are spent. Increasingly in Peru, businesses are being invited to circumvent the state entirely and directly to spend revenues on projects of their own choosing *in lieu of* tax payments (rather than, as is the case with the CSR model, *in addition* to these tax payments). In contrast to the dialogue round tables already discussed, through which the state tries to leverage and direct CSR in dialogue with local communities, the logic of these new tax policies is to remove subnational governments from the equation all together, with dire consequences for capacity-building.

The Voluntary Contributions program arose in response to growing outrage among the Peruvian population at the amount of public revenues being generated by extractive industries under the tax stability contracts offered by Fujimori (Bebbington 2007; Arellano-Yanguas 2011). According to the national government's own figures, thanks to stability contracts only half of the country's mineral exports in 2012 were subject to royalty payments (de Echave 2012). In response to broad public support for an increased tax burden on mining, Alán García campaigned in the 2006 presidential election on a promise that he would introduce a tax on windfall profits if elected. Subsequent to his victory, however, pressure from the mining lobby and threats of lawsuits encouraged García to propose an alternative according to which mining companies would voluntarily contribute revenues to finance spending projects in the regions where they are invested. Specifically, companies were asked to contribute 3.75 percent of their profits if prices stayed above a certain level. In the four years between 2007 and 2010, mining companies' net profits amounted to $17 billion, of which they voluntarily contributed $640 million (Campodónico 2011). What is critical is that companies were largely able to act unilaterally in deciding how to spend their contributions, privileging the company's own needs in identifying projects, circumventing regional governments, and ignoring their plans (Grupo Propuesta Ciudadana 2011).[46]

[46] Interview P8.

While Voluntary Contributions ended along with the García administration in 2011, another innovative tax program has emerged with equally dire consequences for subnational government capacity. According to the Works for Taxes program, which is available to mining and non-mining enterprises alike, participating companies can finance and execute local spending projects and deduct the cost of those projects from the income taxes that they owe the national government, after which the national government reduces its revenue transfers to the subnational government by the amount equal to the project cost.[47] Companies can pay up to 50 percent of their taxes through the program. Initially limited to infrastructure projects, Works for Taxes was subsequently broadened to include any type of project; likewise companies can deduct not just construction costs but also the costs of maintaining or operating projects, including roads. Participating companies use their own contractors, which promoters of the program celebrate as a way to prevent local governments from soliciting kickbacks from construction companies.[48] According to Pro-Inversión, a national government agency charged with facilitating connections between interested companies and local governments, the program is a win–win; communities like it because the private sector can act much more quickly than the local government, and companies like it "not only because they can control territorially where their taxes are going, but because they can use their taxes to improve their local brand."[49]

If, as this section has argued, a number of factors explain the problem of insufficient subnational capacity in Peru, the critical importance of this problem can be most readily seen in attempts by regional governments to engage in territorial regulation (*OT*), an authority that was decentralized in 2002.[50] *OT* is now considered a shared competency between subnational and national governments (Azpur 2012: 16), and regional officials since 2012 have sought to use these new powers in the attempt to exert greater influence over which types of investments should be allowed in which parts of their territory.[51] More specifically, thirteen of twenty-five regions (as of September 2016) have completed the Ecological and Economic Zoning exercise (*Zonificación Ecológica Económica* (*ZEE*)), a diagnostic instrument that is designed as an input in the broader regulatory process, and that produces an integrated picture of a given region with technical information about the aptitude of particular territories for various uses (for example, mining, agriculture, urban

[47] Interview with a technical specialist in Pro-Inversión, May 13, 2014, Lima (Interview P34).
[48] Interview P6. [49] Interview P34.
[50] See Gustafsson (2016: 102) for the argument that territorial zoning can "be a way of pursuing regional or local interests in contradiction to national policies."
[51] The relevant decree is DS No. 087-2004-PCM, which defines the *ZEE* as a "participatory, concerted, dynamic and flexible process aimed at identifying different alternatives for the sustainable use of a specific territory."

development, conservation).[52] By synthesizing, and making public, up-to-date information about current territorial uses, the *ZEE* represents a potentially powerful instrument for regional governments that have long been disadvantaged by the superior mapping capabilities of mining companies.[53] Regional presidents decide whom to invite to the meetings at which decisions are made about the priorities that should govern the use of various territories. According to the pro-mining National Society for Mining, Petroleum, and Energy (*Sociedad Nacional de Minería, Petróleo y Energía* (*SNMPE*)), many regional presidents have used their convening powers to over-represent anti-mining groups and critics of neoliberalism, and to limit the representation of the mining industry by giving the private sector a single seat at the table.[54] In regions where the anti-mining thrust of the exercise has become increasingly clear, the private sector has in some cases decided to boycott the *ZEE–OT* altogether.[55] Not only are regional governments trying to use regulations to restrict where mining can occur, but this process itself reflects a more fundamental challenge to the neoliberal model through which the national government has let market forces alone dictate how territory is used, and where mining should take place.

In 2007, an important decree (DS 087) required national ministries to respect the outcomes of the zoning process in the regions, though this requirement was subsequently eliminated in 2014 with the passage of law 30230 (Article 22), which stipulated that the national government has no obligation to take into account territorial plans elaborated by regional governments.[56] In the seven-year period when regional governments enjoyed this formally binding authority, what they lacked was capacity. The technical demands posed by the *ZEE–OT* exercise often exceed the skill level found in many regional governments, with poorer regions such as Apurímac and Pasco employing only one staff member in charge of the *ZEE–OT*.[57] National rules that prevent subnational governments from using canon monies to hire permanent new staff mean that regional governments have largely had to rely on consultants in order to conduct the *ZEE–OT* exercises.[58] This does little to build up regional capacity and raises questions about the ownership of the process once the consultants have completed their work and moved on to the next

[52] Interview with a research analyst in MINAM, May 2, 2014, Lima (Interview P35).

[53] Interview P19.

[54] Interview P6.

[55] The reaction of the private sector to zoning initiatives, however, has not been uniform across regions, as seen in Maria-Therese Gustafsson's comparative work on variation in the regional *ZEE–OT* process. According to Gustafsson, extractive companies in Puno, for example, do not see the ZEE-OT as a threat. Personal communication with Gustafsson. See also Gustafsson (2016).

[56] These changes were implemented as a result of strong pressure from *MEF*, *SNMPE*, and *MINEM*, along with threats that the responsibility over *ZEE* would be withdrawn altogether from *MINAM*. Personal communication with Maria-Therese Gustafsson.

[57] Interview P16.

[58] Interview P24.

region.[59] Regional governments remain heavily reliant on domestic and foreign donors, including the Japanese government, which recently donated high-quality satellite images at the 5-meter level for the use of all regional governments.[60] With its forty staff members, the Office of Territorial Regulation of the Ministry of the Environment (*Ministerio del Ambiente* (*MINAM*)) attempts to support *OT* activities by regional governments, but is itself embattled with other national ministries such as *MEF* and *MINEM* that are fundamentally opposed to territorial regulation by regional governments.

Weak Coalitions. Despite significant electoral support across Peru for left-of-center regional officials and their non-neoliberal visions, when these officials confront the hostility of the national government described above, they typically and very quickly find themselves quite isolated. This is because Peru's notably flat civil society, which scholars have attributed to the devastating twin legacies of the Shining Path insurgency and Fujimori's authoritarian response (Yashar 2005; Burt 2010), is even flatter at the subnational level. In the words of one cabinet member in the Humala administration, "regional presidents simply do not have civil society counterparts in Peru."[61] Especially significant is the absence of the type of organized counterparts who would benefit from, and therefore presumably provide political support for, departures from neoliberalism.

Among the most consequential missing counterparts are the regional elites who have largely disappeared in Peru as a result of agrarian reform. Peru under military rule in the 1970s experienced one of most radical land reforms anywhere in Latin America, characterized by the expropriation not just of traditional haciendas in the sierra that produced for the domestic market, but large-scale, agro-exporting businesses on the coast as well (Stepan 1978; McClintock 1981). Faced with political tumult and rancor in the countryside, along with the insurgent violence of the following decade, most former landed elites used the compensation bonds they received as part of the reform to transform themselves into commercial and financial elites in Lima (Meyer 2009). This exodus by formerly regionalized elites is a critically important political development in Peru's recent history, one that helps explain both the absence of territorially-organized national political parties (Tanaka 2002) and the de-activation of a regional cleavage that powerfully shaped political competition as recently as the 1950s (Vergara 2015). For my purposes, agrarian reform and its effects have deprived left-of-center regional officials of the kind of regionalized industrial bourgeoisie that might have favored the construction of state-centered subnational policy regimes (Gonzales de Olarte 1982). If

59 Interview P8.

60 Interview with a zoning specialist in the *MINAM*, May 2, 2014, Lima (Interview P36).

61 Interview P31.

regional elites had survived agrarian reform, nothing guarantees that their descendants would have opposed neoliberalism today, and yet, if they existed, regional elites in both agricultural and industrial sectors alike would have cause to resist the privileged position of mining within the current neoliberal model.[62] In a more concrete organizational sense, the dissipation of regional elites has inhibited investments in regionally specific business chambers of the sort that have proved to be so important in the construction and defense of discordant subnational policy regimes in Bolivia and Ecuador.

Also missing from the regional landscape in Peru are possible trade union partners. Elsewhere in Latin America, according to Goldfrank and Schrank (2009), local unions have played a critical role in the emergence of "municipal socialism." In Uruguay, Venezuela, and especially in Brazil, local unions in the 1980s and 1990s proved to be the critical anchor for a "set of policies designed to expand and improve municipal services, engage in redistributive spending, increase taxes, facilitate popular participation and generally strengthen the role of the local state" (Goldfrank and Schrank 2009: 451–2)—all at a time when national governments were pursuing market-oriented stabilization and adjustment. Unions mostly cannot play an equivalent role in Peru, and for a variety of reasons. First, the same forces that encouraged regional elites to abandon the regions in the 1970s—namely, agrarian reform—constrained the development of unionized jobs in the regions. Most private-sector union workers live and work in Lima. Subsequently, neoliberalism led to deindustrialization and a shrinking population of unionized workers, including in Lima. Finally, while deindustrialization means that unions in the public sector have become increasingly important as the position of unions in the private sector has weakened further, public-sector unions in Peru remain highly centralized. Thanks to administrative decentralization, the salaries of teachers and doctors are now paid by regional governments, but these employees belong to unions that are still controlled nationally and that are beset by deep-seated internal conflicts between rival left parties. Union organizations such as the *Confederación General de Trabajdores del Perú* (*CGTP*) (General Confederation of Workers of Peru), and the *Sindicato Único de Trabajadores de la Educación del Perú* (*SUTEP*) (Unified Union of Education Workers of Peru) occasionally do flex their muscles, as in the coordinated strikes that took place across Peru's main cities in June 2009 to protest against the García administration's repression of anti-neoliberal protestors in Bagua, but they cannot and do not offer significant coalitional support at the regional level.

[62] Eduardo Dargent (2013) argues that the growing strength of agro-exporters in northern regions such as Piura and La Libertad could lead to more effective resistance against Lima's mining policies in the future.

Against the backdrop of this quite flat civil society terrain, one new type of potentially significant counterpart for subnational officials has emerged in the form of the hundreds of local defense fronts (*frentes de defensa*) that have emerged across Peru since 2000. These defense fronts, which are made up of a heterogeneous mix of local groups that might include neighborhood associations (*juntas de vecinos*), peasant formations (*rondas campesinas*), women's organizations, and student groups, typically come together to contest large-scale mining projects. The strategies of these defense fronts vary significantly, ranging from non-violent participation in the Environmental Impact Assessment process to physical attempts to sabotage extractive projects (Bebbington 2007; Jaskoski 2014). Local defense fronts were critical in the struggles in Arequipa, where they mobilized against the privatization of state-owned enterprises, and in Cajamarca, where they effectively blocked the Conga project from going forward. More generally, most successful attempts to block, suspend, or delay extractive projects in Peru since 2000 (including Tambogrande, Tía María, Tintaya, Santa Ana, Cerro Quilish, Río Branco, and Pucamarca) can all be traced back to the mobilizing capacity of local defense fronts. However, while defense fronts are important, they tend to be ephemeral in ways that render them less effective as medium- or long-range coalition partners (Meléndez 2009). According to the large literature on anti-mining protest in Peru, local defense fronts have succeeded in coordinating protest and short-term demand-making, but have struggled mightily to sustain these mobilizations (Panfichi 2011; Arce 2014). Especially as the national government has gotten better at preventing protests altogether (through such practices as CSR and "dialogue roundtables"), rather than extinguishing them through a mix of repression and co-optation once they have emerged, it seems unlikely that local defense fronts could serve as the necessary organizational pillar for subnational policy regimes.

If regional elites and unions are mostly missing, and local defense fronts are frequently fleeting, the result is that regional presidents often develop an overreliance on domestic and foreign NGOs as governing partners. On the one hand, NGOs have been a valuable resource for subnational officials in Peru, especially considering the serious capacity challenges these officials face. Consider the case of *OT*, which is designed as both a technical exercise and a participatory process in which regional presidents identify and invite civil society participation. The expertise of regional NGOs, including *CEDISA* in San Martín and *Grupo de Formación e Intervención para el Desarrollo* (*GRUFIDES*) (Group for Interventions in Development) in Cajamarca, is a critical factor in explaining why the *OT* process in both regions culminated in meaningful governmental restrictions on the mining industry.[63] Across

[63] Interviews P16, P19, and P35.

Peru, foreign NGOs have also contributed important resources and networking opportunities to Peruvian NGOs, which in turn partner with subnational officials who favor more vigorous environmental regulations.[64] On the other hand, heavy reliance on NGOs is subject to all the inherent risks and dangers that have been identified in the development literature. NGOs organized at the regional or local level are not evenly distributed across subnational governments in Peru. NGOs organized at the national level tend to concentrate on specific, high-profile regions, and to shift their focus as protests wax and wane. Furthermore, the prominence of national NGOs raises concerns about the extent to which they (consciously or not) impose national priorities on local or regional demand-making. Foreign NGOs are subject to similar critiques, and have the additional challenge of trying to operate in Peru at a time when the national government (especially under García) has sought to crack down on, limit, and otherwise control their activities as a threat to the country's sovereignty. Reliance on foreign NGOs has rendered regional presidents vulnerable to the charges of "undue external influence."[65]

As a final point, it is important to note that the limited coalitional opportunities available to most regional presidents in Peru are probably reflected in their very low re-election rates. Notwithstanding the fact that the four regional leaders described in the previous section were all re-elected, the re-election of regional presidents is in fact rare in Peru, in part owing to the difficulty of creating stable coalitions with societal partners. Coalitional failures are not the only cause of infrequent re-election, which has also been attributed to the proliferation of candidates for subnational office, the tendency of canon monies to heighten political competition at the subnational level, and corruption charges against many subnational officials (Arce 2014; Seifert Bonifaz 2014). But effective coalitions would help to lengthen the time frame available to subnational officials seeking to build distinct policy models. Short time horizons in Peru contrast with the lengthier time frames that facilitated the development of coherent subnational policy regimes in Ecuador and Bolivia (analyzed in Chapters 4 and 5).

[64] For example, the Blue Moon Fund and the Moore Foundation (in addition to USAID) fund the *Sociedad Peruana de Derecho Ambiental* (*SPDA*) (Peruvian Society for Environmental Law), which works with a number of regional governments in the Amazon. Interview P19.

[65] A common allegation, according to one consultant for the mining industry, is that corrupt regional presidents use their relations with foreign donors to hide acts of corruption, since their contracts with these donors are less subject to oversight by the national government. Interview with a mining consultant, May 5, 2014, Lima (Interview P37).

Failed Efforts to Change Peru's National Policy Regime

If subnational officials have failed to create their own policy regimes that deviate from neoliberalism, neither have they enjoyed much success in their efforts to change the neoliberal content of Peru's national policy regime. Successfully challenging this national policy regime could be another way of pleasing constituents or responding to voters who oppose neoliberalism, and who have been vexed by the continued support that it has found since 1990 within the executive and legislative branches of the national government. Why have subnational officials not been able to force any significant national policy compromises upon Lima? This section proposes an answer to the question by emphasizing the structural and coalitional constraints that have prevented subnational officials—both regional and municipal—from transforming the protests they have led against neoliberalism into meaningful national policy changes. Administrative capacity, the absence of which is critical in explaining the inability to build subnational policy regimes, is less important in explaining the outcome of this second type of subnational policy challenge. Insufficient capacity has not prevented subnational leaders from using their offices to promote, finance, and coordinate powerful protests. Doing more than protest, however, has been difficult given the structural obstacles and coalitional challenges faced by subnational officials.

Structural obstacles and policy continuity

Owing to Peru's recent mining boom, which forms the backdrop against which subnational elected officials have challenged the country's neoliberal policy regime, these officials have focused their critiques on the mining policies that are at the center of this regime. Seldom do subnational officials express opposition to all forms of mining, especially given the fiscal incentives created by the canon system. More common is opposition to the national government's neoliberal approach to mining, which is characterized by (1) limited environmental and regulatory protections, (2) the absence of serious attempts to generate greater value added and employment opportunities through the refining and/or industrializing of minerals (rather than just their export as primary commodities), and (3) resistance to more robust taxation of extractive industries (which denies resources for public infrastructure projects that could promote more sustainable alternatives to mining). Given the heavy dependence of Peru's neoliberal model on resource extraction through large-scale mining projects by private firms in a lax regulatory environment, the most effective way that subnational officials can challenge neoliberalism is to challenge these mining projects.[66]

In recent years, an important literature has emerged on the increasingly pervasive mining protests in Peru that have pitted societal actors like peasant communities and local defense fronts against representatives of the state who are committed to large-scale mining under neoliberal auspices (Bebbington 2007; Arce 2008, 2014; Grompone and Tanaka 2009; Meléndez 2009). It is important, however, not to overlook the key coordinating roles often played by subnational officials, whose material and symbolic support and even direct leadership of protests have deepened their impact.[67] Protest behaviors by subnational elected officials convert what would otherwise be contention between state and society into a conflict that is increasingly unfolding within the state itself, between officials at national and subnational levels.[68] As illustration, consider the following three prominent cases where elected officials engaged in protest activity at each of Peru's three subnational levels of government: district, province, and region.

As an example at the district level, mayors of six municipalities in the region of Puno (Huacullani, Pomata, Yunguyo, Desaguadero, Zepita, and Chucuito) emerged as critical actors in the 2011 protest against Bear Creek Mining Company, one of Peru's most significant social conflicts of the last decade. In 2007, Bear Creek was granted a concession to develop the Santa Ana silver project, an open pit mine estimated to contain over 500 million ounces of silver. Owing to the mine's location within 80 kilometers of the Bolivian border, a supreme decree from the executive branch was required for the project to advance. In opposition not just to Bear Creek but also to petroleum concessions in Lake Titicaca, a local defense front organized a strike that brought the region to a standstill and blockaded the international bridge between Bolivia and Peru. The scope and duration of the strike, upheld by 12,000 protestors over a six-week period, would have been impossible to sustain without the financial and logistical support of the mayors, even though they received far less attention in the press than the leader of the local defense front, Walter Aduviri. For example, the mayors used municipal funds to pay the costs of transporting local residents from their six remote districts to the capital of Puno, and solicited in kind contributions to facilitate the communal kitchens set up to feed strikers (Quinones

[66] As Martin Scurrah argues (2008: 318), "Because the success of the model depends on the maintenance of a strategic alliance with extractive industries, the government has been reluctant to consider reforms in the norms that govern these activities."

[67] For the argument that subnational officials have used their leadership of protests as electoral catapults, see Revesz and Díaz 2006.

[68] As Bebbington and Scurrah (2013) show in their work on resistance to Peru's extractivist model on the part of the Ombudsmen's office, this conflict within the state is also playing out within the national level of government, and not simply between national and subnational levels.

2013: 25).[69] Although the strike was initially met with police repression and the death of six protestors, the national government eventually backed down, not just retracting the decree that granted Bear Creek its concession but, in a major setback for the mining industry, suspending all concessions in Puno for a three-year period.

One of the most important examples at the provincial level is that of Oscar Mollohuanca of the province of Espinar in Cuzco, site of the Tintaya copper mine under the ownership of the Swiss corporation Xtrata. Whereas his predecessors supported the mine and worked closely with the foundation that Xtrata established to identify and fund local development projects, Mollohuanca won election by criticizing Xtrata and by asserting the provincial government's right to articulate developmental goals through participatory mechanisms (Cáceres and Rojas Huerta 2013: 71). Central to Mollohuanca's 2010 campaign for office was the promise to strengthen the province's institutional capacity by directly executing projects through its administrative departments rather than bidding them out to the private sector (Cáceres and Rojas Huerta 2013: 162). In response to Xtrata's proposed \$1.5 billion expansion of the mine in 2012, Mollohuanca led protests in May that drew attention to the company's environmental impact and hiring practices, and that blocked all access to the mine for a period of several weeks. When protests continued despite the declaration of a state of emergency, a national judge ordered the detention of Mollohuanca, who was arrested by police officers in the city hall of Espinar and held in preventative detention for five months. Further to discipline the province, the national government also froze revenue transfers to Espinar (Cáceres and Rojas Huerta 2013: 162).

The most salient example at the regional level can be seen in the case of Gregorio Santos, regional president of Cajamarca and critic of Yanacocha's Conga project. In addition to issuing the anti-Conga regional ordinance discussed earlier in this chapter, Santos coordinated and financed the protests that led to the suspension of the project in October 2011.[70] More generally, Santos used his role as leader of the anti-Conga protest to emerge as Peru's most high-profile critic of neoliberalism, especially after it became clear in the second half of 2011 that the neoliberal model would be sustained by President Humala, whom Santos had supported in the 2011 election. While Santos's successful protest record animated his candidacy for re-election as regional president, it also accelerated a variety of investigations against him by the national government, which arrested Santos on June 25, 2014 for a fourteen-month period (until after the 2014 regional elections). In October 2014,

[69] "Alcaldes promovieron marchas anti-mineras en Puno," *El Comercio*, May 21, 2011.

[70] Santos also used canon revenues to provide financial support for anti-mining actions in other regions, including against Minsur's gold project in the region of Tacna (Santillana 2013).

Santos won re-election from prison, defeating two Fujimorista candidates who campaigned in favor of the Conga project.

Examining protest activity by subnational officials across these three levels of government (that is, district, provincial, and regional) suggests that they have been particularly effective when they are able to channel protests in two specific ways. First is the targeting of protest to disrupt the Environmental Impact Assessment (EIA) process.[71] Subnational governments have little formal opportunity to shape the EIA documents that mining companies are required to file and that they themselves are in charge of drafting (by the firms they contract for this purpose). Furthermore, until 2013 *MINEM* retained the right to approve these assessments, despite the conflict of interest this created given the ministry's stake in the promotion of mining, and despite the creation in 2009 of *MINAM*, which would logically control EIA approvals.[72] Although EIA rules merely require mining companies to inform local communities about the project in an official public hearing (*audiencia pública*), if the company is unable actually to hold the hearing, the EIA process cannot go forward. While the rules initially required this hearing to be held at *MINEM* headquarters in Lima, Jaskoski (2014: 874) emphasizes the significance of the fact that "it was later moved to the project zone to include affected communities." Though only a minor change in what remains a biased regulatory process, the physical relocation has enabled mayors to coordinate protestors who attend the hearing but then disrupt it from within so that it cannot be successfully concluded. More generally, protests surrounding the EIA process have led to significant delays in project approval.[73]

Second is the strategy of channeling protest activity into local referenda and popular consultations, which subnational officials are uniquely well positioned to coordinate.[74] These mechanisms are of dubious legality, but can succeed in denying mining companies the informal "social license" they increasingly need to go forward. The first local referendum on mining—not just in Peru but in the world—was organized by Mayor Francisco Ojeda of Tambogrande in 2002, in which 98 percent of voters voted against the gold mine proposed by Manhattan Minerals (Paredes 2008; Revesz 2009). Other mayors mimicked this strategy in the subsequent decade. In 2007, for example, three mayors in the region of Piura financed the holding of

[71] Interviews P29 and P30.

[72] Interview with a former Vice Minister of the Environment, May 12, 2014, Lima (Interview P38). Although authority to approve EIAs shifted from *MINEM* to the multi-sectoral National Service for Environmental Certification (SENACE) in 2013, the president can exempt specific projects from the EIA at the request of any ministry.

[73] Interview with the former Chief of Electric and Hydrocarbon Projects at Pro-Inversión, September 10, 2007, Lima (Interview P39).

[74] Interview with the former Director of Communications at Pro-Inversión, September 10, 2007, Lima (Interview P40).

non-binding referenda in which over 90 percent of those who voted opposed Minera Majaz's Río Blanco mining project. Although *MINEM* and the National Electoral Board questioned the legality of the referenda, the demonstration of local opposition led to the suspension of the project in 2007. Likewise, in March 2013 over 98 percent of voters rejected Minsur's Pucamarca project in a referendum in Ciudad Nueva (in the region of Tacna). Regional presidents have also pursued this option. For example, as already discussed, Arequipa Regional President Juan Manuel Guillén decided in 2011 that a popular consultation must be held before the Southern Peruvian Mining Company could go forward with its Tía María copper project owing to concerns it would deplete water aquifers (even after Southern had amended its EIA to clarify that it would use desalinated ocean water). What is clear is that subnational officials have contributed directly to the suspension of some of the largest mining projects in Peruvian history, including the names that have dominated Peruvian headlines: Conga, Santa Ana, Tambogrande, and Tía María.

The impact of these protests suggests that subnational officials wield an undeniable defensive power in their ability to obstruct the high-profile, privately operated mining projects that are so essential for the continued operation of Peru's neoliberal model. Nevertheless, this apparent structural power is more than offset by a considerable structural weakness: all subsoil resources are owned by the (central) state, which limits the ability of subnational officials to behave in a proactive fashion. They can, for some period of time and with varying degrees of success, create problems for the projects that have been authorized by the national government, but they cannot independently establish alternative policies to extract these resources on more state-centered or less neoliberal terms. This structural aspect of natural resource extraction sharply limits the roles these officials can play—unlike in other sectors of the economy, where subnational officials might pursue alliances with local agricultural, industrial, or financial elites against the national government. Thus, while protests sponsored by subnational governments can become too important for Lima to ignore, Lima's position is bolstered by the structural reality that these governments cannot independently access, extract, or exploit the resources in question. Confident that subnational governments cannot act independently, the national government has only to find a way to end the protests (through repression or some form of compensation) rather than offer substantive policy concessions.

In seeking to end protests that threaten to paralyze the neoliberal model, the national government has demonstrated a willingness to use the full powers of the state.[75] Complaining that regional presidents had required

[75] Interview with a high-level official in the conflict prevention unit of the Defensoría del Pueblo, May 9, 2014, Lima (Interview P41).

government employees to attend rallies and used government cars to help organize protests, President García pushed through a new anti-strike law in July 2007 that specifically forbids the involvement of subnational officials in strike activity.[76] The national government has subsequently used this authority to arrest mayors on many occasions, as already discussed in the case of Oscar Mollohuanca.[77] Other subnational officials have been arrested on other pretexts, including charges against Cajamarca's Santos for his alleged involvement in a 2005 kidnapping (of which he was absolved in 2015).[78] Another important tool is the freezing of canon transfers, which can serve as a powerful form of discipline. The case of Cajamarca is once again instructive. The arrest of Santos by national prosecutors did not prevent his re-election in 2014 from prison, but cuts in revenue transfers did produce a significant economic downturn in Cajamarca, which advocates of neoliberalism have attributed to the region's erroneous opposition to Conga.[79] According to one conflict prevention expert, "the economic difficulties that Cajamarca has faced after it dared to veto Conga have served as an important cautionary tale for other regions."[80]

Coalitional challenges and the absence of collective action

The national policy leverage of subnational elected officials is also limited by the infrequency of collective action among these officials, who have not been able to form the type of horizontal coalitions that would be hard for Lima to ignore. As with the problem of insufficient subnational capacity, this obstacle is not entirely or even largely exogenous to the national government, which has worked assiduously and effectively to prevent these coalitions from emerging in the aftermath of decentralization.[81] Given the failure of regional presidents at the regional level and mayors at the municipal level to band together as peers, individual subnational chief executives are forced

[76] "Autoridades de Arequipa piden derogatoria de DL 982," *La República*, July 27, 2007.

[77] Further to strengthen the hand of the national government in forcibly extinguishing subnational protests, another new law in 2014 (30151) frees members of the police and armed forces from responsibility for deaths that occur in the line of duty, which is likely to encourage even more lethal responses by Lima to anti-mining protests when they erupt. "Defensoría afirma que ley 30151 'pone en riesgo la vida'," *El Comercio*, January 15, 2014.

[78] "Absuelven a Gregorio Santos por acusación de secuestro," *El Comercio*, March 13, 2015.

[79] "Quieres ser Cusco o Cajamarca?," *El Comercio*, May 6, 2014.

[80] Interview with a conflict prevention expert in the UNDP, May 12, 2014, Lima (Interview P42).

[81] Although I emphasize attempts by the national government to "divide and conquer" subnational officials, a number of other constraints have impeded coordination. One particularly important constraint in Peru results from the serious border demarcation conflicts that pit subnational districts against each other. This issue dominated the Decentralization Committee hearing in Congress that I attended on May 6, 2014. According to *CEPLAN* official Carlos Cabrera, 95% of Peru's subnational districts are affected by these conflicts. Interview P26.

to interact with the national government on an ad hoc and mostly bilateral basis. The weakness of collective action is not surprising in the highly atomized context of Peruvian politics, but it is a critical part of the explanation for why subnational elected officials have been unable to transform widespread protests and deep regional grievances over neoliberalism into even modest policy changes.[82] In this section I emphasize the absence or weakness of subnational associations in Peru, which might otherwise serve as the organizational basis for a sharper articulation of subnational opposition.

At the regional level, regional presidents have suffered from the absence of an effective pan-regional venue in which they could come together as regional presidents. The absence of such a venue is especially critical in Peru, considering that since 1993 it has lacked an upper legislative chamber, which can often serve either *de jure* or *de facto* as a space for the representation of territorial demands and grievances within the national government—even in unitary countries. Neither does Peru have the type of nationally organized political parties that could coordinate the actions of like-minded regional presidents, who instead typically compete for office as the heads of regionally specific movements (Seifert Bonifaz 2014; Dargent and Muñoz 2016). The absence of both political parties and an upper chamber increased the potential significance of the *CND*, which was created in 2002 and endowed with cabinet-level representation, and which operated as the only national venue in which subnational voices could be officially raised. With formal representation assigned to regional, provincial, and municipal governments, the *CND* briefly functioned as an important space for dialogue among subnational officials, and regularly waged cabinet-level resistance against the *MEF*'s focus on fiscal austerity and centralized governance.[83] Unwilling to negotiate collectively with subnational officials, however, García eliminated the *CND* in 2007 and transferred its responsibilities to a new Secretariat for Decentralization, which was assigned only one-third of the staff that the *CND* had employed and included no regularized role for any representatives of subnational governments (Conterno 2007).[84] Although a 2007 law (*Ley Orgánica del Poder Ejecutivo*) called for the creation of an Inter-Governmental Coordination Council (*Consejo de Coordinación Inter-Gubernamental* (*CCI*)) for formal

[82] On political fragmentation across Peruvian regions, see Muñoz and García (2011).

[83] For example, in debating the 2004 Law of Incentives for the Integration of Regions, representatives of subnational governments on the *CND* wanted the national government to pledge as an incentive that macro-regions would receive not just revenue transfers but their own tax bases as well. The *MEF*, in contrast, argued that macro-regions could receive either tax bases or revenue transfers, but not both. Interview P5.

[84] The elimination of the *CND* also enabled García to accelerate and finalize administrative decentralization and to discard the emphasis on subnational capacity-building. Interview P28.

dialogue between national and subnational governments, as of 2016 this council had yet to be constituted.[85]

Faced with national government opposition to any formal coordination with subnational governments, regional presidents have sought to build their own unofficial body to facilitate collective action: the National Association of Regional Governments (*Asociación Nacional de Gobiernos Regionales* (*ANGR*)). Established by regional presidents in 2007 as a direct response to the elimination of the *CND*, *ANGR* has achieved some degree of institutionalization and has emerged as an occasionally important organizational player. For instance, *ANGR* has been allowed to participate in multi-sectoral committees established by the national government to study fiscal decentralization, and it is even mentioned in some national laws.[86] The organization has been hobbled, however, by significant legal and financial limitations. The national government has opposed a bill that would give *ANGR* the official legal status enjoyed by its municipal counterpart. According to one former Secretary of Decentralization, regional presidents have declined to offer funding for *ANGR* out of regional budgets for fear of antagonizing the *MEF*.[87] The head of *ANGR*, a position that rotates on an annual basis among the regional presidents, is expected to pay out of pocket the rent for the Lima headquarters of the organization. As a result of these limitations, *ANGR* remains highly dependent for funding on external donors like the US Agency for International Development. While *ANGR* cannot be dismissed as insignificant, it also clearly has not functioned as a space for the emergence of robust policy positions vis-à-vis the national neoliberal model or its consequences for Peru's regions.

Coordination among mayors at the municipal level has also been fraught, but for different reasons, including the significant tensions that have emerged between rival organizations that seek to represent municipalities. Founded in 1963, the Association of Peruvian Municipalities (*Asociación de Municipalidades del Perú* (*AMPE*)) is the official and formally non-partisan body to which all municipalities belong. *AMPE*, however, was penetrated by the Fujimori regime and lost much of its legitimacy in the aftermath of his fall from power and the return to democracy in 2000. In response, the Network of Urban and Rural Peruvian Municipalities (*Red de Municipalidades Urbanas y Rurales del Perú* (*REMURPE*)) was formed in 2000 as an alternative to *AMPE*. *REMURPE* has sought to achieve legitimacy by insisting on non-partisanship; while the president of the organization emerged out of the left, for example, its vice president represents the right. In contrast, *AMPE* has come to operate virtually as a component organization of a new political party (Alliance for Progress) formed by its executive director, Piura Regional President (and

[85] Interview P28. [86] Interview P24. [87] Interview P2.

private university entrepreneur) César Acuña (Levitsky and Zavaleta 2016). While *REMURPE* has emerged as an important actor in the struggle to defend subnational prerogatives, including the *OT* processes already described, its effectiveness is undercut by its non-official status. Ironically, *AMPE* remains the official body despite its more partisan orientation, while *REMURPE* is denied official status despite its insistence on non-partisanship.

Fragmentation among subnational governments and their associational bodies is an outcome that favors the national government in the defense of its preferred policies; isolated subnational governments are simply much easier for Lima to dominate through a mix of coercion and compensation. In addition to "divide and conquer" strategies, two other recent dynamics at the regional level have made it difficult for subnational officials to form policy coalitions in opposition to neoliberalism. First is a series of recentralizing moves that have put regional presidents on the defensive as they scramble to defend the prerogatives and resources that were devolved in 2002. Under the Humala administration, for example, the Decentralization Committee in Congress has complained of a *de facto* "invasion" by the central government vis-à-vis authorities that are now formally under the control of subnational governments (*invasión de competencias*).[88] Likewise, the *MEF* successfully recentralized a sizable portion of canon funds in 2011 by deciding to deduct the *gravamen minero* (mining tax) from the pool of funds subject to revenue-sharing.[89] Second is a concerted anti-corruption campaign targeted against regional presidents. In May 2014, the attorney general's office announced investigations into corruption allegations against nineteen of the country's twenty-five regional presidents and arrested three such presidents.[90] Notwithstanding overwhelming evidence of corruption against several individual presidents, the scale and timing of the charges suggest a campaign to discredit regional presidents as a class of actor. The belief that most regional presidents are corrupt also fueled passage in 2014 of legislation that would bar regional presidents from running for re-election.[91] Rather than focus on contesting national economic policies, the reality is that regional presidents have had to focus on defending their fiscal transfers, fighting for their right to run for re-election, and trying to stay out of jail.

[88] Interview P3. [89] Interview P2.

[90] "19 presidentes regionales deben responder por 158 casos de corrupción," *La República*, May 28, 2014. Another important element in the campaign to discredit subnational electoral processes can be seen in the announcement issued by ONPE/JNE in the run-up to the October 2014 elections, which warned Peruvians about the prevalence of candidates in those elections with ties to the mafia.

[91] Interview P3.

Conclusion

Peru's deep and uninterrupted experience with neoliberalism since 1990 has produced equally deep territorial grievances over the uneven distribution of costs and benefits associated with this national policy regime. At the same time, various forms of decentralization—political, administrative, and fiscal—have created important new spaces that opponents of neoliberalism have tried to use both to formulate alternative subnational models and to challenge the content of the national model. Both types of subnational policy challenges have largely failed for reasons that I attribute in this chapter to a combination of capacity, structural, and coalitional constraints. Despite the significant increase in subnational authority generated by decentralization, subnational governments simply do not have the capacity to transform non-neoliberal preferences into actual outcomes at the subnational level, thanks in no small measure to a range of actions taken by the national government that hinder subnational capacity-building. Meanwhile, successfully challenging the national policy regime, along with the neoliberal mining policies that define it, has been undercut by a key structural vulnerability: subnational officials can protest the neoliberal terms of extraction, but they cannot independently access the resources in question. Finally, I have argued that coalitions matter for the fate of both types of challenges. A mostly flattened civil society has denied regional presidents the building blocs for coalitions they would need to create and sustain deviant regional models, and the absence of effective coalitions between subnational officials has undermined the national policy leverage they might otherwise wield together.

Although subnational challengers have failed both to create their own policy regimes and to alter the national policy regime, they have nevertheless succeeded in profoundly shaping Peruvian politics—no less perhaps than their counterparts in Bolivia and Ecuador. The national government in Peru has managed to prevent subnational deviations and avoid policy compromises, and yet it would be a mistake to see this as the perpetuation of the status quo. As this chapter demonstrates, subnational challengers have forced the national government to adopt increasingly radical measures. Some of these measures are reactive, including the use of repression to end protests organized by subnational officials, the arrest of these officials, the freezing of canon transfers, the targeting of corruption charges against subnational officialdom, the imposition of subnational term limits, and the pursuit of a variety of recentralizing changes. Other, perhaps more creative and enduring, measures are proactive in nature. Whether in the guise of corporate social responsibility, Voluntary Contributions, or Works for Taxes, the national government has invited private companies to play expansive new roles that marginalize and displace subnational governments altogether, and that encourage Peruvians to look to the private rather than public sector to provide them with basic goods and services. Rather than repress and recentralize in order to undercut subnational challengers, here the approach has been to call into question the very need for subnational government by transferring its prerogatives to the private sector, thereby inculcating neoliberal values across Peru's subnational landscapes.

4

Policy Regime Juxtaposition in Ecuador

Ecuador represents an especially useful case for the study of subnational policy challenges because the two main types of challenges that are examined in this book met very different fates in this country. Unlike in Peru, where neither type of challenge succeeded, and Bolivia, where both have succeeded, mixed results obtained in the Ecuadorian case. With respect to the first type of challenge, two dynamic mayors on the right of the political spectrum—León Febres Cordero (1992–2000) and Jaime Nebot (2000–)—were able to design, build, and consolidate a distinctly neoliberal model in the critical port city of Guayaquil, Ecuador's largest city and home to the country's most powerful firms. The architects of this model subsequently managed to defend its core features in the face of repeated and direct assaults after 2006 by leftist President Rafael Correa, who was born in Guayaquil but who has dismissed its market-centered approach as an oligarchic anachronism that is incompatible with the "twenty-first century socialism" he hoped to construct. Though certainly beleaguered and in some respects diminished, Guayaquil's liberal local model survived—a survival that represents a rare and important exception to Correa's otherwise remarkably successful record in eliminating political obstacles and monopolizing government institutions (Conaghan 2011; Montúfar 2013).[1]

However, while the mayor of Guayaquil has managed to consolidate and defend its neoliberal policy regime, he and his allies within the city have been unable to exert meaningful policy influence in the national government, or to operate as a moderating force relative to the president's statist project. Despite his own past as a two-time presidential candidate in the 1990s and leading figure in the national Social Christian Party (*Partido Social Cristiano* (*PSC*)), Nebot's attempt to lead this second type of subnational policy challenge vis-à-vis Ecuador's national policy regime has largely failed. Nebot has consistently

[1] At the subnational level, Correa's party controlled 17 of 23 prefectures and 180 of 200 municipalities in the 2009–13 electoral period (de la Torre 2015).

used his perch as mayor of Guayaquil to articulate ideological critiques of Correa's policies, including by presiding over a demonstration of thousands of protestors on June 25, 2015 against proposed increases in estate and inheritance taxes, but he has not been able to force compromise upon the president.[2] The result is a situation of juxtaposed policy regimes and political deadlock: Correa has constructed a statist model at the national level on top of the liberal model that Nebot has maintained at the local level. This is where the Bolivian and Ecuadorian cases diverge. Although Correa in Ecuador and Morales in Bolivia were both forced to accept neoliberal models in each country's most dynamic subnational jurisdiction, subnational liberals in Ecuador enjoyed far less influence nationally than their counterparts in Bolivia. How was Nebot able to defend liberal principles within Ecuador's most important subnational district, and yet enjoy so little leverage beyond the confines of this district?

In the first half of this chapter, I attribute the resilience of the embattled neoliberal model in Guayaquil to a series of institutional and coalitional factors. The institutional foundations of this local model have a long history, originating in the nineteenth century when liberal agricultural and commercial elites took responsibility for service provision in the growing city in response to the neglect of the central government in Quito. For decades, healthcare, education, and infrastructure were all provided by vibrant quasi-public institutions that were under the direct control of the private sector and that existed nowhere else in Ecuador. When elites lost control of the municipality with the rise of populist mayors after 1950, their response was to expand and strengthen still further these privately controlled institutions, which are collectively referred to as the *voluntariado* or "voluntariat" to capture the volunteer nature of the work dedicated to the maintenance of these institutions by their elite patrons. After forty years in which these institutions developed in opposition to the populism of the municipal government, liberals retook city hall in 1992 with the victory of León Febres Cordero, who had tried but failed to introduce lasting neoliberal reforms during his term as President of Ecuador (1984–8). Unsuccessful on the national stage, Febres Cordero then set his sights on a neoliberal makeover of Guayaquil's municipal institutions, now fully aligned with the logic of the "voluntariat" institutions. After two terms in office, Febres Cordero was succeeded in 2000 by his co-partisan Jaime Nebot, who deepened the model by delegating services to functionally specific "foundations" (*fundaciones*), which operate as part of the private sector but with public monies. As described in greater detail in this chapter, Febres Cordero and Nebot together embody the territorial retreat of neoliberalism in Ecuador from the national to subnational spheres.

[2] "La marcha convocada por Jaime Nebot copa toda la Av. 9 de Octubre," *El Comercio*, June 25, 2015.

This neoliberal transformation of Guayaquil proceeded in a largely unimpeded fashion in the long decade that began in 1997, when the onset of political turbulence at the national level in Ecuador led to a succession of weak presidents who were unable to finish their elected terms—in strong contrast to the uninterrupted process unfolding in Guayaquil under the continuous conservative leadership of Febres Cordero and Nebot. But the rise of Correa to the presidency in 2007 triggered a new and more threatening political environment for Nebot, who could no longer count on a feckless national government, and who in response engaged in a wide-ranging and ultimately successful process of coalition-building in defense of Guayaquil's policy regime. Nebot cemented alliances with private-sector elites, who benefited directly from the many lucrative opportunities that were created by his privatization of service provision, and partnered with the many philanthropic institutions that were managed by these elites. But the mayor also sought substantially to broaden his support base through new housing, security, and social action policies designed to placate the demands of working and middle-class constituents. Like his counterparts in Santa Cruz discussed in the next chapter, Nebot also sought to portray Correa's ideological attacks against the liberal model as an attack against the city, and increasingly shed his partisan profile in order to articulate a civic demand for autonomy from the national government (Burbano de Lara 2009a, b). In addition to expanding societal coalitions, Nebot also carefully maintained his legislative coalition on the city council, which could otherwise have emerged as a source of internal opposition within the city to be exploited by Correa.

The second half of the chapter turns to the second type of subnational policy challenge and the failure of neoliberals in Guayaquil to effect meaningful change in Correa's preferred national policy regime. Here I emphasize structural and coalitional weaknesses that enabled the president to disregard the national policy preferences of subnational neoliberals concentrated in Guayaquil. For example, despite continuities in the importance of Guayaquil to the national economy that date back to the nineteenth century, a number of developments have reduced its structural leverage and hindered the ability of its political leadership to project power nationally. If, as generations of historians have maintained, the secret to Guayaquil's extensive influence was the strength of its financial sector and the dependence of the national government on Guayaquil banks (Hurtado 1977; Quintero and Silva 1991; Maiguashca 1994), this sector has faced important setbacks. The discovery of oil in the eastern Amazonian region of Ecuador in the 1970s, along with the country's emergence as an oil exporter, have buoyed fiscal resources and increased the national government's autonomy from Guayaquil financiers. While Guayaquil's influence has waxed and waned with the price of oil, historically high oil prices during most of the Correa presidency made it easier for him to tune out the voices of neoliberal critics in Guayaquil. In addition to financial challenges that have shaken a core pillar of Guayaquil's structural power, Correa has also actively sought to weaken its structural position still further by threatening its continued status as the country's most significant port, and by systematically favoring other coastal provinces through massive infrastructural projects financed by the center.

I describe a similar dynamic with respect to the type of coalition-building beyond Guayaquil that might have served to check Correa. The prospects for an oppositional coalition on Ecuador's coast were dim before the rise of Correa, and the president has brilliantly exploited opportunities to keep such a coalition from emerging. The contrast with Bolivia is instructive, where Santa Cruz leaders were able to knit together a cross-departmental coalition with ideologically and territorially proximate governors in the east. A number of factors worked against the creation of a similarly effective coalition among the opposition in Ecuador, starting with decades of grievances on the part of political actors in other subnational districts who resented Guayaquil's economic dominance as much as they did Quito's political hegemony. Although nearly all coastal provinces supported autonomy referenda in 2000 at the nadir of Ecuador's national political crisis, this push for autonomy from the national government masked significant ideological diversity. Furthermore, after Correa's rise to power, Nebot lost important provincial allies in neighboring Manabí, where the prefect defected from the *PSC* to support Correa, and in Guayas, where the newly elected prefect in 2009 likewise switched his allegiance to Correa. As a result of these many coalitional challenges, Nebot has remained strong and dominant within Guayaquil, but weak and isolated beyond his city.

The Construction and Preservation of Guayaquil's Liberal Policy Regime

At the time of independence from Spain, "Guayaquil" referred to one of only three provinces in Ecuador and included most of the country's Pacific coast. Through time, Guayaquil was subdivided into numerous provinces and its core territory was renamed "Guayas." Meanwhile "Guayaquil" came to refer only to the city that now serves as the capital of the province of Guayas, as seen in Map 4.1, and as the home of the port that has monopolized the country's foreign trade. From its beginnings, Guayaquil has faced significant advantages and disadvantages. Strategically situated where the Babahoyo and Daule rivers join to form the mighty Guayas river, and at the edge of the largest estuary ecosystem on the Pacific coast of South America, Guayaquil as a port enjoyed tremendous access through the coastal river system to the country's

Map 4.1. Ecuador: Administrative Divisions

Source: Perry-Castañeda Library Map Collection at the University of Texas.

hinterland, and benefited directly from a sequence of commodity booms beginning in the 1850s, from cacao to coffee to bananas (Pineo 1994). Despite its advantageous position, Guayaquil was also plagued by tropical diseases such as yellow fever and malaria that for decades depressed population growth, and chronic fires that repeatedly destroyed infrastructure in a city heavily reliant on wooden constructions (Rodríguez 1985). The discussion that follows describes the liberal development model that emerged in this important setting, examines the coalitions later constructed to defend it, and evaluates evidence as to the model's survival in the wake of the national left turn after 2006.

Creating the Guayaquil model: Liberal institutionalism at the local level

The long-standing importance of Guayaquil as a productive and commercial center in Ecuador contrasts sharply with the case of Santa Cruz in Bolivia, which emerged as an important economic player only in the 1970s, as discussed in the next chapter. As a result, agricultural and financial elites based in Guayaquil have enjoyed much greater leverage at the national level than their peers in Santa Cruz, particularly after Ecuador's Liberal Revolution in 1895, which brought representatives of the Guayaquil oligarchy directly into the national government and introduced deep-seated liberal reforms (Guerrero 1980, 1994). Nearly an entire century would pass before a similar development favored economic elites in Santa Cruz, with the passage of neoliberal reforms in Bolivia after 1985. Despite different levels of national influence, however, in both localities economic elites took the lead in creating, financing, and controlling a series of local quasi-public institutions whose accumulation of significant levels of administrative capacity through time bolstered the strength of this fundamentally liberal model. Local institutions in Guayaquil, as in Santa Cruz, were designed to provide critical services neglected by a national government that was centered in a faraway, Andean capital (Kasza 1981; Soifer 2016). These institutions, which had a public purpose but were under the control of the local private sector, are important today not just because they have survived and continue to provide key services, but because they set the stage for the development after 1992 of privatized models of governance within Guayaquil's city hall.

The most emblematic local institution is the Guayaquil Charity Board (*Junta de Beneficiencia de Guayaquil* (*JBG*)), founded in 1888 by leading members of the cacao oligarchy and the banks that they established, including most importantly the Commercial Agricultural Bank of Guayaquil. Financed with resources from a lottery that the national government gave it exclusive rights to manage in 1893, the *JBG* has offered free and subsidized social services at a wide range of high-quality private facilities.[3] Triggered initially by threats posed from infectious diseases, these services eventually covered all major phases of the life cycle from birth to death, including maternity and children's hospitals, schools and nutritional programs, housing for the elderly, insane asylums, and the cemetery.[4] Although the municipal government has formally recognized it from the beginning, the *JBG* is governed autonomously by a board of thirty-five "Notables" who are selected from the ranks of the local private sector. According to Patricia de la Torre, just five interconnected elite families have dominated the board (Arosemena, Azpiazu, Illingworth, Vernaza, and Ycaza), and the board has achieved a remarkable degree of stability, with "Notables" typically serving lifelong terms and executive directors holding this position on average for nearly a decade (de la Torre 2004: 95, 293). Run by elite patrons rather than health professionals, the *JBG* successfully fought off no fewer than four separate attempts to make it public, surviving the elimination of private charity boards everywhere else in Ecuador in 1906 and resisting incorporation into the new National Health Ministry in 1967.[5] Outside the purview of the *JBG*, a number of other privately run health institutes have flourished, including a leading cancer center, the Ecuadorian Society to Fight Cancer (*Sociedad de Lucha Contra el Cáncer del Ecuador* (*SOLCA*)), which is financed by a 1 percent tax on bank transactions.

In addition to devising this fundamentally liberal approach to social policy, Guayaquil elites established a number of other local institutions to accommodate the reality of deficient service provision by the national government. Given the threat that devastating fires posed to the development of the city, one of the most important and celebrated of these institutions is the Corps of Firefighters (*Cuerpo de Bomberos*), which operated autonomously from the city and through in-kind contributions by *guayaquileños* in the form of volunteer labor. Service in the Corps, which remains an active firefighting force across the city, emerged as an important rite of passage for male members of the elite, who serve as volunteer firefighters in addition to their work in the private sector.[6] Other significant and *sui generis* local institutions emerged in the area of transportation and infrastructure. Founded in 1948 by Carlos Julio Arosemena (son of the founder of the *JBG*) and financed by a local tax surcharge, the

[3] In addition to lottery monies, the *JBG* derives resources from its ownership of ten of the largest commercial centers in Guayaquil (de la Torre 2004: 93).

[4] See Ziblatt (2008: 273) for the argument that public health threats "might serve as a crucial trigger for the development of local capacity and hence state infrastructural power more broadly."

[5] Reflecting the degree of elite dominance of healthcare and the importance of these private institutions, the national government did not establish a public hospital in Guayaquil until the late date of 1970 (de la Torre 2004). Interview with a former director of the *Archivo Histórico de Guayas*, January 13, 2014, Guayaquil (Interview E1).

[6] Interview with a former President of the Junta Cívica de Guayaquil, June 3, 2008, Guayaquil (Interview E2).

Transit Committee of Guayas (*Comité de Transito de Guayas* (*CTG*)) built roads and regulated traffic (a role provided by the national police everywhere else in Ecuador). Although a representative of the municipality sat on the board, the *CTG* was dominated by local elites and enjoyed significant autonomy from the municipal government.[7] When the national government in the 1960s refused to pay for a modern bridge connecting Guayaquil with the rest of the country to the east, local elites responded by constituting a separate Roads Committee (*Comité de Vialidad*), which in 1970 completed the Bridge of National Unity (*Puente de Unidad Nacional*) with resources collected through extra fees on gas and soft drinks sold in Guayaquil.[8]

Alone in Ecuador, Guayaquil witnessed the development of a vibrant institutional model that was inspired by liberalism and that was characterized by public-service provision under the control of agro-exporting elites acting in their private capacity. But, if Guayaquil was a privileged site for liberalism, the same was true for populism—a new political force that emerged among the working classes of Guayaquil and that swept representatives of the oligarchy from city hall in 1950.[9] Under the leadership of Carlos Guevara Moreno and Assad Bucaram, the Concentration of Popular Forces (*Concentración de Fuerzas Populares* (*CFP*)) came to dominate the municipal government, where *CFP* mayors engaged in decades of conflict with landowners by championing land invasions on behalf of squatters and migrants then arriving in Guayaquil in growing numbers (Guerrero 1994). The Bucaram dynasty was particularly important; Assad was elected mayor on two occasions (1962–3 and 1968–70) and his nephew Abdala and niece Elsa served as mayor in the 1980s, though both were forced out of office on corruption charges. Under the Bucarams, the quality of public services such as water and sewerage worsened—offering a strong contrast with consistently capable service provision by the elite "voluntariat"—and public space in Guayaquil deteriorated sharply. This disastrous performance would later help explain lower- and middle-class support for the resurgent neoliberals who reimposed order in the city after 1992 (Burbano de Lara 2014).[10] It is also important to note that, although agro-exporting elites were locked out of city hall, the banana boom of the 1950s and 1960s preserved their influence at the national level (Burbano de Lara 2014)—a situation that reversed the contemporary dynamic under Correa and

[7] Interview with a prominent historian of Guayaquil, January 11, 2014, Guayaquil (Interview E3).

[8] Interview with a former General Manager of the Roads Committee, January 10, 2014, Guayaquil (Interview E4).

[9] As Burbano de Lara (2014) observes, all the oligarchy's economic and social capital was insufficient to prevent the rise of the populist *CFP*, which quickly became the chief political force on the coast.

[10] As of 1992, 1 million residents in Guayaquil received no trash collection services, 46% lacked sewerage connections, and 40% were missing from the official city registry (*catastro*).

Nebot in which economic elites in Guayaquil have enjoyed influence locally but not nationally.

Already displaced from city hall in 1950, economic elites in Guayaquil suffered a further setback in the 1970s with the onset of national governments controlled by the armed forces, a profoundly Andean institution in which Guayaquil elites were poorly represented—even in the navy.[11] Not only did the military preside over the discovery of a resource—petroleum—that undermined the influence of Guayaquil banks, but the military used these resources to build an interventionist state and to advance the first truly state-centered economic development model in Ecuador's history—the precursor in many ways to Rafael Correa's contemporary effort (Conaghan 1988). As part of its centralizing mission, for instance, the military sought to suppress several of Guayaquil's autonomous local institutions, successfully in the case of the Roads Committee but unsuccessfully in the case of the Transit Committee (Frank 2004: 141). Out of power locally and nationally, economic elites in Guayaquil rallied around León Febres Cordero, who emerged as the most vociferous critic of the military's statism and as the most articulate advocate for neoliberalism (Conaghan and Malloy 1995). Febres Cordero used his position as president of the powerful Chamber of Industries in Guayaquil to position himself as the leader of the opposition to military rule. Five years after the generals had withdrawn from power, and in the throes of the 1982 debt crisis, Febres Cordero was elected president of Ecuador in 1984 and sought to implement a sweeping program of economic stabilization and liberalization, including fiscal austerity, tariff reduction, and privatization.[12] But the neoliberal project was adopted in Ecuador only in limited measure—in contrast to the more sweeping reforms of Bolivia and Peru, and almost every other South American country (Grindle and Thoumi 1993; Corrales 2003; Pachano 2007; Andrade 2009).[13] Stung by defeat in the 1986 mid-term elections, and briefly kidnapped by members of the Air Force in 1987, Febres Cordero withdrew to Guayaquil at the end of his presidential term in 1988.

As a prominent representative of the traditional economic elites who dominated municipal politics before 1950, Febres Cordero as mayor (1992–2000) implemented a neoliberal program that both harkened back to the earlier liberal model established by his elite predecessors, and introduced considerable

[11] Interview with a former President of the National Council on Modernization (*Consejo Nacional de Modernización* (*CONAM*)), June 5, 2008, Guayaquil (Interview E5).

[12] As president, Febres Cordero strengthened autonomous institutions like the *CTG* and *JBG* and used them to compete with Abdala Bucaram as mayor of Guayaquil. While the Tribunal of Constitutional Guarantees ruled in 1988 that these autonomous agencies were unconstitutional, the decision was never implemented (Frank 2004: 182, 183).

[13] As Pachano (2007) argues, all presidents from Osvaldo Hurtado to Lucio Gutiérrez tried to introduce economic adjustment reforms in Ecuador, but all failed owing to a mix of political fragmentation, short-term calculations, and electoral incentives.

innovations in terms of expanding, financing, and formalizing this local model. Supporters and detractors alike are agreed that Febres Cordero was far more successful as mayor than as president in advancing his fundamentally liberal policy preferences. Upon his electoral victory as mayor in 1992, Febres Cordero convened a small working group of allies from the private sector ("*la escuelita*") who met at his home to plan their transformation of the city in the months leading up to his inauguration.[14] In response to the chaotic state of Guayaquil, characterized by inadequate trash collection, abysmal record-keeping, and a rat infestation on the riverside waterfront (*malécon*) that operates as the city's main public space, the new mayor closed the belle époque city hall for three months of renovations, fired over 4,000 municipal workers accused of being *pipones* (receiving salary but not working), and introduced results-based management practices. In the words of one assistant who joined the municipal administration with Febres Cordero in 1992, "our goal was to create a private enterprise within the city government."[15] With savings from his purging of the municipal bureaucracy, Febres Cordero set out to repair the city's basic infrastructure and to build overpasses that helped resolve the city's infamous traffic problems. As Freidenberg and Alcantara (2001: 52) argue, "Febres Cordero reestablished order in a conflict-ridden political space."

Beyond cutting the size of the bloated local government and immediately privatizing trash collection, Febres Cordero's real innovation came in pioneering new forms of collaboration between the private and public sectors that delegated significant governance functions to the former. Hoping quickly and visibly to transform the city, "the mayor invited each banking institution to take responsibility for maintaining a public space or park, which both lightened the financial burden on the municipality and directly integrated the private sector into the city's development" (Wong 2005: 60). Most importantly, given its symbolic value as a sign of the city's resurgence, Febres Cordero established a private foundation (*Fundación Malecón*) that would direct the process of reclaiming the waterfront as the city's premier public space (though now as a semi-privatized space).[16] Arguing for the greater speed, agility, and flexibility of the private sector vis-à-vis contracting processes, feasibility studies, and decision-making, Febres Cordero succeeded in using the foundation to modernize the waterfront. More striking still was the mayor's

[14] Interview with a high-level assistant to the mayor and participant in these meetings, January 13, 2014, Guayaquil (Interview E6).

[15] Interview E6.

[16] In designing this innovation, the mayor worked closely with the owners of Banco La Previsora, whose landmark building had eroded in value as a result of the disastrous state of the waterfront. Interview with a former Director of the Department of Tourism in the Municipal Government of Guayaquil, June 13, 2008, Guayaquil (Interview E7).

success in forcing the national legislature to adopt a bill in 1997 (law 26) that gave residents of Guayaquil the option of "donating" up to 25 percent of their national income-tax payments to the private Malecón Foundation. Though Febres Cordero had failed as president, he maintained considerable networks of influence at the national level throughout the 1990s, and used these networks on behalf of the neoliberal model under construction in Guayaquil.[17] In addition to the "donations" law, Febres Cordero used his control of the Social Christian Party, which remained the largest party in the legislature in the 1990s, to secure passage of a landmark decentralization law that substantially boosted fiscal transfers to municipalities (Muñoz 1999: 25).

While Febres Cordero laid the foundations for Guayaquil's neoliberal makeover, his co-partisan and successor as mayor, Jaime Nebot, considerably extended and deepened the model through three main instruments: foundations, concessions, and corporations. First, inspired by the success of the Malecón Foundation, Nebot presided over the proliferation of additional foundations, establishing eight new foundations focused on specific functions.[18] Rather than directly provide services through existing departments in the municipal government, which would have required adding to the payroll, Nebot opted to delegate service provision to private foundations governed by boards on which he himself (or an appointed representative) participated (Girolami 2006).[19] The foundations received free land from the municipality in addition to tax exemptions. By replacing public employees of the municipality with private employees of the foundations, critics charged that "Nebot in effect created lucrative jobs for the sons and daughters of the oligarchy."[20] Building on the experience of the waterfront renovation, the 21st Century Foundation (*Fundación Siglo 21*) executed "urban regeneration" projects in the city center and in middle-class neighborhoods, funded in part by business fees and in part by tax "donations."[21] Another important foundation was the Metrovía, a mass-transit company that introduced dedicated bus lanes for high-speed travel along three main transit routes within the city (Aguirre 2007). Nebot also put the city's important bus terminal (*Terminal*

[17] Interview with the political editor of a leading Ecuadorian newspaper, June 5, 2008, Guayaquil (Interview E8).

[18] Febres Cordero himself criticized the proliferation of foundations, arguing that Nebot was creating a parallel municipality. According to Silva (2013), Nebot needed the foundations to build the kinds of connections to traditional elite interests that Febres Cordero could take for granted, given his family status.

[19] According to Silva (2016: 97): "The physical restoration of many deteriorated areas, such as the Malecón, the municipal building, the international airport, the bus terminal, the port, and the civil registry, and investment in programs for public safety, health, and education were linked to a private administration in which the citizen had no participation of any kind."

[20] Interview E8.

[21] Interview with a former General Manager of Fundación Siglo 21, June 11, 2008, Guayaquil (Interview E9).

Terrestre) under the control of a foundation directed by Guillermo Lasso, head of the Banco de Guayaquil and presidential candidate against Correa in 2013. Another example is the *Fundación Edúcate* under the leadership of Marcia Gilbert, a descendent of one of the most socially prominent Guayaquil families who introduced a TV program ("*Aprendamos*") that touted Nebot's urban regeneration projects (Gilbert de Babra 2006). To publicize the transformation produced by his eight new foundations, Nebot in 2007 took out a major advertising supplement in *Foreign Affairs* and in the *New York Times Magazine* announcing that Guayaquil was once again "open for business."[22] Nebot's mission has been to restore Guayaquil's status as a city of services in support of the agro-export economy.[23]

The second main instrument that Nebot used to expand the neoliberal policy regime in Guayaquil was made possible by the new constitution Ecuador adopted in 1998, which introduced the possibility of granting private concessions over public utilities and infrastructure. Under the prior 1979 constitution, which reflected the statist orientation of the outgoing military regime and which operated as a major constraint on the Febres Cordero presidency in the 1980s, the role of the private sector in these areas was tightly proscribed. In the constituent assembly that produced the 1998 constitution, representatives belonging to the *PSC* pushed to relax these constraints and to delegate to subnational governments the right to grant private concessions. The 1998 constitution also endorsed an à la carte approach to decentralization according to which subnational governments could petition for the transfer of authority over various types of services, as opposed to the mandatory devolution of a set of responsibilities to all subnational governments simultaneously (Carrión 2003; Van Cott 2008). Guayaquil under Nebot actively responded to the joint liberalizing and decentralizing opportunities established in the 1998 constitution, petitioning for the transfer of services and then granting concessions to the private sector to provide these services. For example, Nebot petitioned for authority over the port and airport in Guayaquil, and then granted concessions to private companies to operate both, including a twenty-year lease to ICTSI in 2006 to develop the port's container terminal, and an agreement with the airport concessionaire to place 50 percent of its profits in a trust for the construction of a new international airport at no cost to the state (Delgado 2013). But the most controversial use of a concession was in the water and sewage sector. After a call for bids in December 1998 that failed to elicit any proposals, the municipal government relaxed regulatory constraints and minimum investment requirements and in 2001 signed a thirty-year contract with Interagua, a private company controlled by Bechtel

22 "Guayaquil: A New Page in the Evolution of a City," *New York Times Magazine*, July 1, 2007.
23 Interview with a business reporter, January 13, 2014, Guayaquil (Interview E10).

(Swyngedouw 2004; Joiner 2007: 39). This strong interest in pursuing the use of concessions in Guayaquil contrasted sharply with the disinterest in concessions on the part of subnational officials elsewhere in Ecuador (Noboa 2004: 140).

The third instrument used by Nebot to build out his neoliberal policy regime was the city-chartered corporation. Two corporations have been especially prominent. First, in 2006 Nebot signed an agreement with President Alfredo Palacios to turn over the civil registry office in the city to a private corporation. Henceforth, the *Corporación Registro Civil*, whose mission statement includes the promotion of "love for an independent Guayaquil," would provide identification documents to the residents of Guayaquil. Second, and more controversially, Nebot established a Citizen Security Corporation (*Corporación de Seguridad Ciudadana* (*CSC*)) in the attempt to enhance the role of the private sector in ensuring public safety in the city. Funded in part by an agreement with the Palacios administration and centered in a bunker-like building with sophisticated surveillance technology, the idea behind the *CSC* was to expand the number of private security officers who would act in concert with the metropolitan police in maintaining order.[24] In addition to furthering his goal of improving business perceptions of Guayaquil as a safe environment, the *CSC* played an important part in Nebot's zero-tolerance policies vis-à-vis the informal sector. In a highly visible campaign designed to protect the property rights of formal business owners, the mayor used both the *CSC* and the metropolitan police force to concentrate and confine informal venders in three specific market locations (Mascote, Pedro Pablo Gómez, and Sur). In this sense, "urban regeneration" involved not just asking businesses to pay to keep public spaces clean, but using private security forces to remove members of the informal sector from these same spaces (Andrade 2004; Aguirre 2007). Altogether, the trifecta of foundations, concessions, and corporations constitute the heart of the Guayaquil model, which sees the mayor as a manager whose chief role is to "develop the city of the market [*la ciudad del Mercado*] as an alternative to the city of chaos" (Carrión 2003: 36).

Coalition-building to defend Guayaquil's subnational policy regime

According to the argument developed in the previous section, Jaime Nebot as mayor of Guayaquil worked consistently to extend and consolidate the neoliberal policy regime he inherited from his predecessor, León Febres Cordero. Despite the intellectual coherence of the model they built over more than two decades in power, the two mayors faced very different dynamics in terms of

[24] In 2004, Minister of Government Jaime Damerval claimed that Nebot used the *CSC* to further the economic interests of his private-sector allies. Interview E4.

their relationships with the national government. Whereas Febres Cordero. maintained a great deal of national influence within legislative and judicial institutions, which he leveraged to pull down additional resources for his preferred local model, Nebot enjoyed far less political influence at the national level, especially with the collapse of the traditional party system in the 2000s and the demotion of his once powerful party (the *PSC*) to mere subnational status. Furthermore, Nebot encountered a much more challenging environment at the national level, and for two very different reasons. First, the extensive political chaos that was triggered by the country's economic collapse in 1999 and 2000, and that persisted until the rise of Correa in 2006, provided the backdrop against which Nebot tried to consolidate Guayaquil's business-friendly, market-oriented model. Second, high levels of political uncertainty before 2006 then gave way to the certainty of a committed and politically talented ideological foe in the presidency after 2006, one who cruised to re-election in 2009 and again in 2013.

In response to this much more threatening set of challenges, Nebot set out to expand and strengthen the coalition to defend Guayaquil's distinctive policy regime in ways that would not overly compromise the logic or content of that regime. As examined here, his coalition-building strategies included mobilizing *guayaquileños* around the demand for autonomy, downplaying partisan in favor of civic identities, and enlisting the support of a range of elite and non-elite societal and legislative allies.

The centerpiece of Nebot's defensive coalition-building strategy has been to emphasize not the ideological dimensions of the model that he has built as mayor, but rather the right of subnational territories to generate their own models, whatever their content. The idea here is that, while only the beneficiaries of a particular economic model might turn out to defend it in the streets, potentially all residents of Guayaquil could feel implicated in a struggle that has been reframed as a defense of territorial prerogatives against the center.[25] Characterizing Correa's behavior as an attack on the city and not on the market has been complicated by the fact of his (Correa's) birth in Guayaquil, and by the skill with which Correa has carefully targeted his attacks against traditional economic elites, whom he disparages as *pelucones* (a term that refers to "wig-wearing" elites who built the local institutions described earlier in this chapter). Nebot has nevertheless been able to tap into deeply held grievances about the realities of centralism and Guayaquil's historical role in generating wealth that is spent disproportionately in the

[25] As Quintero and Silva (1991: 53) concluded in their study of earlier regional conflicts in Ecuador, "regionalism is a historical tendency fomented by dominant economic interests, but conflicts between dominant regional classes produced inter-class articulations in each region between local level dominant and subordinate classes."

national capital region surrounding Quito (Kasza 1981). While there is nothing new about these grievances, Nebot innovated by articulating a new and specific demand for formal autonomy so that Guayaquil could enjoy the freedom necessary to develop and preserve its own model (in contrast to León Febres Cordero, who opposed the idea of autonomy for Guayaquil, perhaps because his tremendous influence in Quito rendered it unnecessary).

Autonomy as a demand was functional for Nebot in both of the challenging national environments that he faced; before 2006 autonomy was conceptualized as necessary to protect the local model from national chaos, whereas after 2006 it would serve to protect the local model from the perils of statism. In the midst of the economic crisis in 2000, for example, and in response to the national government's decision to close Guayaquil's *Banco del Progreso*, Nebot aggressively supported a successful referendum on autonomy coordinated by his political ally and prefect of Guayas, Nicolás Lapentti. Nebot interpreted the closure as yet another aggression against Guayaquil by the national government (Burbano de Lara 2009a). In one of his first speeches as mayor on October 19, 2000, he explicitly defended autonomy as an alternative to the apparent "return to Tahuantinsuyo" (the highly centralized Incan empire) that was taking place at the national level, a reference to the emergence that year of the indigenous organization *CONAIE* (*Confederación de Nacionalidades Indígenas del Ecuador* (Confederation of Indigenous Nationalities of Ecuador)) as a national power broker (Pallares 2003).[26] Although 81 percent of those who voted in the 2000 referendum supported language calling for autonomy from Quito, the push for autonomy stalled out later that year when the military opposed Nebot's call for a nationwide referendum on autonomy, fearing the country's disintegration.[27]

Nebot later reignited the autonomy movement when Correa began the process of constitutional reform in 2007. Now autonomy was necessary as a protection not against economic crisis, but rather against the new president's economic agenda. Concerned that the new constitution would enshrine statism, Nebot presided over a demonstration of over 200,000 *guayaquileños* on January 24, 2008 who rallied in favor of the mayor's "Mandate of Guayaquil." Along with demands for liberty, democracy, and the rule of law, Article 4 of the mandate stipulated: "There is no employment without places of employment, and these are not established or consolidated without confidence, juridical security, only taxes that are indispensable, private property, the dollar as currency, investment, production, competitiveness, exports and liberty of choice in terms of social security." In the end, the 2008 constitution

[26] Ramírez Gallegos (2012) also sees the regional autonomy rhetoric that emerged in Guayaquil in 2000 as essentially instrumental.

[27] Interview with an ex-President of INEC, June 10, 2008, Guayaquil (Interview E11).

made it harder, not easier, for provinces to secure formal autonomy by stipulating that two contiguous provinces must join together to petition for autonomy—no one province could become autonomous in its own right. Just as importantly, by formally relabeling all subnational governments as "autonomous decentralized governments," the 2008 constitution deflated the specificity and urgency of Guayaquil's specific push for autonomy.[28] Although autonomy was effectively blocked by the military in 2000, and by a new centralizing constitution in 2008, Nebot nevertheless used it successfully to boost participation in rallies and protests that have visibly demonstrated the breadth of his support base. Furthermore, his response to these setbacks was to promise that he would forge autonomy informally and from the bottom up—a process he referred to as "*autonomía al andar.*"

In addition to opting at times to play up the territorial rather than ideological nature of his conflict with Correa, Nebot has also sought to broaden his coalition by representing himself as a civic rather than a partisan figure. As Burbano de Lara (2014: 406) argues, "when Nebot replaced Febres Cordero as mayor, he initiated a gradual process of downplaying partisanship within the municipal government and embracing instead the cohesive discourse of 'civicness.'" Given Nebot's history as the standard-bearer of the Social Christian Party in the 1992 and 1996 presidential elections, this was a significant departure. After twice running for mayor as the *PSC* candidate in 2000 and 2004, Nebot abandoned the party and ran for re-election in 2009 as the candidate of a new civic movement that he created called *Madera de Guerrero* (*MG*) (Wood of the Warrior), which is the title of a popular 1943 song by Carlos Rubira glorifying the city of Guayaquil. Under the leadership of Nebot, the *MG* has emerged as the dominant political force in the city, even as it has continued to ally with the *PSC* to run candidates on a single list in national elections in 2009 and 2013. In addition to eschewing his former partisan identity, Nebot touted his civic credentials by allying closely with the Civic Board of Guayaquil (*Junta Cívica de Guayaquil* (*JCG*)), a non-partisan body that represents territorially specific civil society interests and that helped coordinate large pro-autonomy protests in 2000, 2005, 2008, and 2010. Increasingly, Nebot has sought to fashion himself a non-partisan civic leader in the tradition of War of Independence hero and poet José Joaquin de Olmedo, after whom Nebot renamed the Guayaquil airport when it was placed under private concession in 2006.

But, even as he used territorial autonomy and civic identities to broaden his appeal, Nebot also engaged in more tailored and concrete coalition-building activities to defend the local model from Correa. Here it is useful to distinguish

[28] Interview with a Subsecretary of Decentralization, SENPLADES, August 31, 2015, Quito (Interview E12).

between practices that have cemented the support of traditional elite groups and practices that have broadened the support coalition to include non-elite actors. While the former might appear to be far easier than the latter, in fact Nebot has had to work hard to maintain the loyalty of economic actors who have been frightened by Correa's willingness to use the powers of the state against ideological opponents, including libel laws and tax investigations (Conaghan 2015). In numerous interviews in Guayaquil, economic elites who support Nebot (and who insisted on anonymity) described a range of behaviors they have adopted to lessen their exposure to Correa, including placing businesses under their spouses' names, refraining from writing opinion columns, and investing in Panama and Perú rather than Ecuador. However, Correa's aggressiveness against elites has also created openings for Nebot. For example, when Correa sought to weaken business organizations like the Chamber of Industries by making membership voluntary rather than mandatory, the Chamber responded by ramping up its opposition and by allying with Nebot even more closely.[29] While Correa has used government-controlled media to attack Nebot, the mayor in turn has maintained tight relationships with local media elites, including a strong relationship with Carlos Pérez Palacios, the owner of a newspaper (*El Universo*) that has offered mostly celebratory coverage of the mayor's "urban regeneration" projects (Andrade 2004).[30]

As mayor, Nebot has also moved to integrate the city government more effectively with the local service institutions that were established and maintained by economic elites, but that experienced an antagonistic relationship with the municipality during Guayaquil's populist era before 1992, as described earlier in this chapter. Under Nebot, the city has generously donated both land and buildings to support these institutions, as well as sponsoring an annual telethon that helps finance the Coordinating Association of Voluntary Organizations of Guayas (*Asociación Coordinadora del Voluntariado del Guayas* (*ACORVOL*)). Several of *ACORVOL*'s top leaders previously worked in the municipality and served on the municipal council, reflecting a tight connection between Nebot and the elite "voluntariat."[31]

Nebot has also sought to widen his coalition significantly beyond the economic elites who have benefited from his foundations and the middle-class groups that have appreciated the urban renewal projects he has sponsored in

[29] Interview with a top official in the Chamber of Industries, January 9, 2014, Guayaquil (Interview E13).

[30] Before it was taken over by the national government, and especially when controlled by the Azpiazu group, *El Telégrafo* likewise provided consistent support for Guayaquil's neoliberal transformation (Silva 2013).

[31] Interview with two volunteer coordinators, *ACORVOL*, Guayaquil, January 15, 2014, Guayaquil (Interviews 14 and 15).

their neighborhoods. This has become more critical over time as memories have faded of the city's precarious existence before the liberals "took back" the municipal government in 1992. But reaching out to working-class and marginalized populations has been difficult for a number of reasons. First, Nebot's close identification with elite civil society organizations like the Chamber of Industry has generated strong opposition to the mayor among organizations that represent other economic interests. For example, according to José García, President of the Chamber of Microenterprises, Nebot has consistently favored large supermarkets such as SuperMaxi and Mi Comisariato over smaller food stores.[32] In response, García forged an alliance between his chamber and the Association of Informal Venders, long embattled with the mayor over his crackdown on the informal sector.[33] Second, through a number of counter-coalitional efforts, Correa has actively sought to prevent Nebot from widening his coalition to include popular sectors in Guayaquil. In 2009, for example, Correa established the Popular Civic Board of Guayaquil (*Junta Cívica Popular* (*JCP*)) as a popular-sector rival to the elite-dominated and pro-Nebot Civic Board (*Junta Cívica*). Correa used the *JCP* to organize pro-government rallies in Guayaquil, and subsequently appointed its president, Roberto Cuero, as Governor of Guayas so that he could coordinate civil society activities in favor of the national government and against the municipal government.[34] On February 11, 2010, Correa organized an anti-Nebot *minga* (an indigenous form of collective work) in marginalized neighborhoods in Guayaquil to compete with the massive rally convened by Nebot that same day to protest the decline in fiscal transfers (Isch 2011).

The response to these coalitional challenges by Nebot has largely been to skirt popular-sector organizations in favor of direct outreach to marginalized communities through new municipal policies and programs. According to one top official in the municipal Department of Social Action and Education (*Dirección de Acción Social y Educación* (*DASE*)), a chief difference between the Febres Cordero and Nebot administrations has been "the introduction of a social element that was missing under Febres Cordero."[35] Critics of Nebot refer to the *DASE* as the product of "a concerted effort to soften the model."[36] Most important have been the *Mi Lote* and *Mucho Lote* housing programs through which the city, in partnership with private organizations such

[32] Interview with a former President of the Chamber of Microenterprises, June 11, 2008, Guayaquil (Interview E16).

[33] Nebot's attempt in 2007 to restrict bus traffic on the Bridge of National Unity in order to reduce pollution also jeopardized his outreach to populations that are heavily dependent on bus transport.

[34] "Gobiernistas agitan las calles," *Hoy*, August 8, 2011.

[35] Interview with a high-level official in *DASE*, January 15, 2014, Guayaquil (Interview E17).

[36] Interview with a professor at the Universidad Católica Santiago de Guayaquil, January 15, 2014, Guayaquil (Interview E18).

as Rotary and *Hogar de Cristo*, build pre-fab houses with water, sewerage, phone, and electricity.[37] In addition to housing, Nebot also introduced a discount card called the "*Guayaquileña*" in 2009, which gives 900,000 low-income residents a discount (beginning at 5 percent) for purchases of clothes, food, and domestic appliances through an agreement with four large companies: Super Éxito (clothes, 10 percent), Tía (food, 5 percent), La Ganga (appliances, 5 percent), and Cruz Azul (pharmacy, 14–25 percent). More recently, Correa's violent response to squatters in the Monte Sinaí neighborhood on the outskirts of Guayaquil in the run-up to the 2014 elections gave an important opening to Nebot, who promised to support their legalization. Nebot's outreach to subaltern sectors has benefited from other unpopular moves by Correa in Guayaquil, including the forced displacement of poor residents to make way for a new nature reserve (*Guayaquil Ecológico*) and Correa's decision in 2010 to terminate a popular health program (*Plan de Aseguramiento Popular*) in the city.[38] Critics of Nebot within progressive NGOs in Guayaquil agree that attempts by Correa to penetrate local civil society—and thereby to contest Nebot's coalition-broadening strategy—have on the whole been sporadic and inconsistent.[39]

Similarly, though Correa's supporters have made inroads on the Guayaquil municipal council, Nebot has maintained a majority throughout his mayoralty, and this legislative coalition with *MG*, *PSC*, and independent councilors has played an important though underappreciated role in the defense of the local model. Under Nebot, the municipal council has not been a vibrant space for discussion or action, and the council has suffered from a lack of institutional capacity separate from the executive branch;[40] council meetings are brief and dominated by Nebot.[41] However, because the council retains the authority to remove the mayor, maintaining a majority coalition on the council has been a central objective in the attempt to preserve Guayaquil's model.[42] In the third Nebot administration between 2010 and 2014, Correa's party *Alianza Patria Altiva y Soberana* (*AP*) (Proud and Sovereign Fatherland party) party held five of seventeen seats on the council, and several interviews

[37] Interview with a member of the Chamber of Construction and former national Minister of Public Works, January 14, 2014, Guayaquil (Interview E19).

[38] "Se suspende Plan de Aseguramiento Popular para Guayaquil," *El Diario*, January 14, 2010.

[39] For example, despite a promising start, the *JCP* later fizzled out when Correa was forced to ask for Cuero's resignation over a police scandal. Interview with a member of the *Comité Permanente de Defensa de los Derechos Humanos*, January 10, 2014, Guayaquil (Interview E20).

[40] Interview with an opposition councilor in the Municipal Government of Guayaquil, June 11, 2008, Guayaquil (Interview E21).

[41] In the weekly council meeting that I attended on January 16, 2014, which lasted fifteen minutes, Nebot was the only participant to speak, one councilor ate a sandwich, and another took a phone call.

[42] Interview with a pro-Nebot councilor in the Municipal Government of Guayaquil, June 13, 2008, Guayaquil (Interview E22).

in the month before the 2014 elections pointed to widespread fears among Nebot supporters that the mayor would probably win a fourth term but lose his majority on the council, "which could prove just as fatal to the model."[43] In the end he retained his majority. While the legislative coalition in support of Guayaquil's policy regime thus remained in place, along with the societal coalition that Nebot has widened to defend it, the mayor's preponderant role in stitching together these coalitions does raise questions about the post-Nebot future of this policy regime.

The resilience of the Guayaquil model

Erected by two like-minded mayors over a period of more than two decades—but with roots that trace all the way back to the nineteenth century—Guayaquil's liberal subnational policy regime has proved to be quite resilient in the face of concerted and creative attempts to dismantle it by the national government. Since his first election in 2006, Correa has adopted a number of maneuvers toward the overarching goal of suppressing this local model. Some of these measures have been quite visible and blunt, while others are more subtle and indirect; likewise, some measures have been narrowly focused on Guayaquil while others are less obvious in that they focus on reversing earlier, generic decentralizing measures that disproportionately benefited or affected Guayaquil. Although they constitute a long list, Correa's efforts to defeat Nebot as his main ideological rival reached their zenith in 2014 when he took a temporary leave from the presidency in order to dedicate himself full time to the campaign to prevent Nebot's third re-election.[44] The memorable moments of this (unsuccessful) campaign against Nebot included derisive comments about the smell of (privatized) water and the quality of (privatized) bus service in Guayaquil, along with a press conference in which Correa—mimicking Nebot's own trademark gruff voice—ridiculed the mayor's constant references to the "successful model of Guayaquil."[45]

Interviews with a range of stakeholders in Guayaquil—including supporters of Nebot, supporters of Correa, and supporters of neither—revealed a range of views with respect to the success or failure of the president's assault on the Guayaquil model. For example, one interviewee de-emphasized the impact of Correa's measures, arguing that, while the price of oil has temporarily given the president more independence relative to Guayaquil, nothing could fundamentally alter the key geopolitical and spatial advantages upon which the

[43] Interview with a member of the *Nueva Junta Cívica de Guayaquil*, January 10, 2014, Guayaquil (Interview E23).

[44] "Rafael Correa pide dos días de licencia para campaña," *El Universo*, January 3, 2014.

[45] "45 días de campaña terminan hoy con recorridos y ofertas," *El Universo*, February 20, 2014.

liberal local model rests.[46] Another claimed that, after nearly a decade in which Correa has constantly chipped away at the model, Guayaquil's distinctive policy regime was virtually dead.[47] As demonstrated in the paragraphs below, I concur with one interviewee who concluded that the Guayaquil model is "alive but under attack and in dispute" (*vigente pero bajo ataque y en disputa*).[48] Even one of Ecuador's highest-level officials in charge of decentralization policy concurs with the view that Guayaquil's neoliberal model—"high on efficiency, low on solidarity"—remains intact.[49] While I agree that the core features of Guayaquil's neoliberal policy regime have survived, and see this outcome as essentially similar to the survival of the local Santa Cruz regime discussed in the next chapter, it is clearly the case that the former remains much more besieged than the latter, with its chief advocates operating in a much more defensive mode.[50]

Most important is the maintenance of the most distinctive part of the Guayaquil model, which is the use of private foundations to offer public services. In 2007, Correa pushed through congress a major tax reform that, among other things, revoked the right of taxpayers to "donate" a portion of their income-tax payment to these foundations (a right initially extended only to Guayaquil in 1997, but that was later generalized to all Ecuadorians). Subsequently, in 2008 pro-Correa legislators passed a new public contracting law (*Ley de Contratación Pública*), which reduced the flexibility of private foundations that receive public funds. While these changes have perhaps dissuaded Nebot from introducing additional foundations, the fact remains that critical public services are still provided by private foundations whose governing boards and employees receive far less monitoring and oversight than they would in the public sector. Unable to eliminate Nebot's foundations, Correa took up the battle against them by financing rival activities that would throw into relief their alleged middle- or upper-class biases. For instance, responding to the charge that the 21st Century and Malecón Foundations had privileged projects in wealthier neighborhoods, and hitting Nebot directly on his claims to have restored public space, Correa financed the creation of major new parks (*Parque Samanes* and *Guayaquil Ecológico*) in more marginalized parts of the city. With these micro-level interventions, "Correa has tried to show that he can be

[46] Interview with a former Governor of Guayas, January 14, 2014, Guayaquil (Interview E24).

[47] Interview E3.

[48] Interview with the director of a pro-Correa Ecuadorian daily, January 7, 2014, Quito (Interview E25).

[49] Interview E12.

[50] In the words of one supporter, "Nebot has successfully defended the Guayaquil model based on the foundations, but he is in a mostly defensive mode, having given up any hope of further advancing or deepening the model." Interview with the director of a prominent local philanthropic foundation, January 9, 2014, Guayaquil (Interview E26).

a better, more responsive mayor of Guayaquil than the actual mayor of Guayaquil."[51]

Nebot's preference for private solutions to public problems has also been challenged by the thrust of the 2008 Constitution, through which Correa sought to reverse the liberalizing and decentralizing effects of the prior Constitution. For instance, the new Constitution shortens the list of responsibilities that can be decentralized in Ecuador, including ports—the administration of which Nebot was forced to return to the center. Just as importantly, the constitution imposes new constraints on the use of concessions, including vis-à-vis water. For example, Article 12 of the new constitution identifies the right to water as fundamental, absolute, and inalienable, and outlaws any future privatization of water. While the constitution introduced a framework to review existing private water contracts, and while Nebot agreed to pro-poor amendments in 2010 to the city's contract with Interagua in response to the new constitution, the reality is that the provision of water remains privatized in Guayaquil.

As in the case of the foundations above, Correa has sought to challenge Nebot's preference for market solutions like the water concession by emphasizing state-centered solutions instead. One highly visible example to elevate the presence of the state in Guayaquil was the creation in 2007 of a special "Ministry of the Coast" (*Ministerio del Litoral*), a sort of "super ministry" that consolidated the activities in the city of all major national ministries (health, culture, education).[52] Located in the landmark ex-*Banco del Progreso* building opposite Guayaquil's city hall, and including an office on the third floor for Correa himself, the new ministry signaled the president's attempt to take his battle against neoliberalism and privatization to Nebot's own turf. Owing to pronounced bureaucratic inefficiencies, however, Correa was forced to dismantle this new ministry in 2009, and to subsume it within the National Planning Agency.[53]

In addition to the survival of his foundations and concessions, Nebot was also able to defend the use of city-chartered corporations, though here too he was put on the defensive. As described earlier, Nebot placed the city's civil registry office (responsible for issuing birth and death certificates, marriage licenses, and so on) under the control of a corporation in 2006, a privatizing move that was supported by Correa's predecessor as president. Unable to reverse privatization, Correa has sought to undermine the corporation (that

[51] Interview E10.

[52] "La nueva dependencia servirá para efectuar trámites de 15 subsecretarías," *Diariocrítico del Ecuador*, July 26, 2007.

[53] Interview with an advisor in the Subsecretaría General de Transformación del Estado, *SENPLADES*, August 31, 2015, Quito (Interview E27).

is, *Registro Civil de Guayaquil*) by instructing national government offices not to recognize the identification cards that it issues.[54] One parent, for example, complained that he can no longer use ID cards issued by the corporation to enroll his kids in school or take them to the hospital.[55] For activities that do not transcend the municipality, however, the privatized office remains in operation. A similar result can be seen with respect to the Citizen Security Corporation (*Corporación de Seguridad Ciudadana* (*CSC*)). Although Correa eliminated national funding for the corporation in 2007, and redirected those funds ($3 million) to the office of the (appointed) Governor of Guayas, the *CSC* continues to operate as an important player within Guayaquil (even if its surveillance cameras can no longer be linked to the national system).[56] For instance, the *CSC* has supported the long-standing efforts of the Metropolitan Police to crack down on informal vendors, a partnership that often pits the corporation against the officers of the National Police, with whom they have repeatedly clashed over the rights of informals.[57]

The resilience of the Guayaquil model can also be seen in the outcome of Correa's attacks against a broader set of local institutions identified with traditional economic elites. It is important to note that Correa did succeed in his crackdown on some of these institutions. For example, in 2008 he suppressed the independence of the historic *CTG* by forcing its incorporation into the national transit agency, and he subsumed Guayaquil's History Archive (*Archivo Histórico de Guayaquil* (*AHG*)) within the national Ministry of Culture. In response, the Director of the *AHG* argued that Correa was taking revenge on the archive for the prominent role it had played in the Guayaquil autonomy movement.[58] Other attacks were less successful, though no less sensational. In 2010, Correa's Interior Minister sought unsuccessfully to shut down the *JCG* over charges that its director had accused the president of authoritarianism and centralism, in violation of the board's own charter proscribing political activity.[59] More importantly, the *JBG* staved off an attempt by Correa to take its lottery away—a potentially devastating move that failed owing to the popularity and high quality

[54] "Cédula de identidad obtenida en Guayaquil no es válida en el resto del país," *El Universo*, January 31, 2008.

[55] Interview E23.

[56] Régimen retira fondos a Corporación para Seguridad Ciudadana de Guayaquil," *El Universo*, January 16, 2008.

[57] "El alcalde toma acciones tras los incidentes con los informales," *El Universo*, June 11, 2008.

[58] Interview E1. The publications of the *AHG* have consistently portrayed *guayaquileños* as a naturally liberal and commercial people.

[59] "Jaime Nebot ofreció defender a la Junta Cívica de Guayaquil," *El Comercio*, October 23, 2010. Correa also accused the JCG of meeting with CONAIE and forming an opposition alliance with the *Frente de Resistencia Nacional General Rumiñahui*.

of the free and subsidized services that it has provided for over a century.[60] According to the directors of *ACORVOL*, which provides technical assistance to hundreds of voluntary organizations in Guayaquil, Correa's animus toward Guayaquil elites and the voluntary organizations they have sponsored has led him to require that all volunteers register with the new Ministry of Economic and Social Inclusion (*Ministerio de Inclusión Económica y Social* (*MIES*)).[61] In the run-up to the 2014 elections, the president told *guayaquileños* that they need to choose between the city's "alms model" (*modelo de limosna*) and the national model of the citizen revolution.[62] Despite fears that Correa might terminate these organizations altogether with the authority he claimed in 2013 through Decree 16, which he used to shutter the environmental NGO Pachamama, in fact Guayaquil's "voluntariat" has survived the president's onslaught. In 2015, a major corruption scandal in the national government's largest hospital in Guayaquil (IESS) had the effect of further illuminating the professionalism and competence of the private hospitals run by the elite "voluntariat."[63]

Altogether, Correa's various acts of aggression against the "successful model of Guayaquil" have failed fundamentally to alter this model—to the obvious chagrin of the president, who has spent virtually every Tuesday of his presidency in the city. For example, in response to one of the larger anti-Correa protests that Nebot convened in Guayaquil in February 2010, Minister of Political Coordination Doris Solíz complained that "Nebot keeps claiming that his model is that of the market economy. He has not read the Constitution. This no longer exists in Ecuador."[64] Nebot, however, can indeed credibly claim that this model survives in Guayaquil. Not only did his campaign against the statist orientation of the new constitution lead a majority of voters in Guayaquil to reject it in the 2008 referendum—even as it passed with 64 percent of the vote nationwide. But Nebot can and does interpret his consistent electoral victories as evidence of the model's survival. As he announced on election night in 2014 in a reference back to Febres Cordero's first election as mayor in 1992, "for the sixth time in a row, the people of Guayaquil have now ratified our local model in the polls."[65]

[60] In response to the threat to its lottery, the JBG put up billboards around Guayaquil trumpeting the "400,000 Patients Served" by the hospitals that it manages. Interview E24.

[61] Interview E14.

[62] "Candidatos a la Alcaldía de Guayaquil y prefectura del Guayas participan en inauguración de obra," *El Universo*, November 19, 2013.

[63] "42 bodegas de medicamentos se descubrieron en el hospital del IESS de Guayaquil," *El Universo*, February 24, 2015.

[64] "Régimen muestra visión diferente de la concentración de GYE," *El Universo*, February 12, 2010.

[65] "Jaime Nebot: 'No interfiera en mis funciones,'" *El Universo*, February 24, 2014.

Guayaquil's Limited Leverage at the National Level

Guayaquil has remained a neoliberal space of exception relative to the statist transformation that Ecuador as a country has experienced since 2006. The architects and defenders of this subnational policy regime, however, have failed to exercise meaningful leverage at the national level, or to moderate in any significant way the ambitious state-centered model that Correa has built from Quito. Nebot has kept neoliberalism alive at the local level—against significant odds and tremendous pressure—but this success stands in sharp contrast to his growing irrelevance on the national stage, where he has been unable to promote more liberal approaches. Why did subnational neoliberals fail to mount this second type of subnational policy challenge when the first succeeded, especially given that Guayaquil remains a very important electoral, economic, and cultural space within Ecuador? To answer this question, I begin with structural challenges to Guayaquil's economic clout that are independent of the rise of Correa and that have weakened the policy influence it has traditionally wielded in Quito. Equally important are long-standing obstacles and tensions that also pre-date Correa and that impeded the formation of an anti-Correa coalition with Guayaquil at its center. Finally, if an inherited set of structural and coalitional challenges explains the inability of Nebot and his allies to reach beyond Guayaquil and influence the emerging national policy regime, Correa responded to this opportunity by adopting a broad and ultimately successful strategy of containment that explicitly exacerbated these same structural and coalitional challenges.

Structural challenges

The main source of Guayaquil's structural power within Ecuador could be found historically in the strength of its financial sector. Not only did bankers in the city take a leading role in building the local institutional model described earlier, but they also exercised considerable influence at the national level owing to pronounced weaknesses in the Ecuadorian state. Unable to extract revenues through direct taxes, the national government relied heavily on easy-to-collect trade taxes and loans from the Guayaquil banks that were established and capitalized by cacao exporters (Hurtado 1977; Rodríguez 1985; Conaghan and Malloy 1994: 27). Volatility in the price of commodity exports increased the reliance of the state on financing from Guayaquil; Ecuador's financial history is replete with episodes in which Guayaquil banks bailed out the national government in exchange for policy advantages. Even after the establishment of a central bank in 1927 and the implementation of modernizing reforms by the progressive military officers who took power in the July Revolution of 1925, public finance institutions remained susceptible to penetration by financial interests in Guayaquil (Quintero and Silva 1991; Pineo 1994).

Eventually, however, the absence of effective bank supervision by the central government proved to be devastating for Guayaquil's banks, whose "self-lending" to companies they owned rendered them vulnerable to the financial collapse that finally occurred in 1999 (North 2004; Martínez 2006). Two important banks owned by the Aspiazu group (Banco del Progreso) and Isaías group (Filanbanco) disappeared in 1999 and 2001, respectively, following the earlier bankruptcy of the Banco del Descuento in the 1980s. The only important remaining bank is the Banco de Guayaquil, whose owner Guillermo Lasso represents a clear example of a Guayaquil liberal who has indeed sought to influence the national policy regime, but who can no longer count on any important sectoral allies. The Banco de Guayaquil is also much weaker than other Quito-based banks, including ProduBanco and the Banco de Pinchincha, which now owns the large stadium in which Guayaquil's popular Barcelona soccer club plays—a powerful symbol of the financial decline of Guayaquil relative to Quito.[66]

The structural deterioration of Guayaquil's financial sector had the effect of significantly expanding the range of options available to Correa as he sought to assert the state's regulatory authority over the banking industry. Blaming bankers for a crisis that caused the economy to contract by 7.5 percent in 1999 and an estimated 10 percent of the population to leave the country in search of jobs in Europe and the USA, Correa took direct control over numerous businesses owned by the bankers, including the expropriation of 195 businesses in the Isaías group. Just as noteworthy, Correa put together a cabinet in 2007 that included no representatives of the Guayaquil financial sector (Ramírez Gallegos 2012: 121). Having removed Guayaquil bankers from their previous positions of influence within national institutions, Correa then worked consistently to enhance the state's ability to intervene in privately owned banks, a project that culminated in 2014 with the passage of the *Código Orgánico Monetario y Financiero* (*COMF*) (Organic Monetary and Financial Code). According to Conaghan (2015: 7–8), bankers view the *COMF* as a "quasi-statization"; among other prerogatives, it enables the government to "require banks to direct their reserve funds to loans on projects that the government identifies as developmental priorities."

Guayaquil's structural decline is a function not only of the decreasing vitality of its banking sector but of the state's increasing access to fiscal revenues—the absence of which was precisely what enabled Guayaquil banks to leverage their considerable influence in the past. According to one

[66] Interview with a high-level official in the Barcelona Sporting Club, June 13, 2008, Guayaquil (Interview E28).

local historian who descends from the founders of both the *JBG* and *CTG*, "the discovery of oil in the Amazon in the 1970s may have allowed the modernization of Ecuador, but it constituted a historic blow to the fortunes of Guayaquil and the coast."[67] Although the decline in the price of oil in the 1980s and 1990s arrested this trend—a period that corresponds with the aggressive pursuit by Guayaquil banks of liberalizing reforms at the national level—the return of high prices after 2003 has once again bolstered the fiscal autonomy of the Ecuadorian state. Revenues from oil exports nearly quadrupled under Correa, increasing from US$3.2 billion in 2006 to US$13 billion in 2011 and US$11 billion in 2012, 2013, and 2014 (Burbano de Lara 2015: 21). Oil, however, is only half the story. Correa may be the passive beneficiary of a sustained, exogenous spike in the price of oil, but he has simultaneously pushed through a series of reforms in tax policy and tax administration that have contributed just as much to boost the state's fiscal resources. As Burbano de Lara (2015: 22) notes, what is especially striking is improved performance vis-à-vis the collection of direct taxes, which constituted 40.5 percent of total taxation in 2014 as opposed to only 28.5 percent in 2004. Equally important, according to Bowen, is the introduction of a series of other taxes, including a capital export tax, a windfall profits tax, and a tax on rural properties of more than 25 hectares, all of which significantly increased Ecuador's tax to GDP ratio—even at a time when Correa insisted on lowering the rate of value added tax (Bowen 2015: 98).[68] By 2012, taxation displaced oil as the largest source of fiscal revenues in Ecuador (Weisbrot, Johnston, and Lefebvre 2013).

Increases in the price of oil and in the extractive capacity of the state have also lessened Guayaquil's structural power as the port through which 93 percent of Ecuador's outgoing and incoming container traffic passes.[69] With respect to exports, Correa has displayed a striking indifference to the concerns of agro-exporters, to whom he can pay less attention given the lesser role they are playing as generators of government revenue. In 2008, Correa removed representatives of business chambers from the Council of Foreign Trade and Investment (*Consejo de Comercio Exterior e Inversiones* (*COMEXI*)), and then replaced the council with a purely public body, Pro Ecuador (Wolff 2016). Correa also unilaterally renounced US trade preferences through the Andean Trade Promotion and Drug Eradication Act, and has remained hostile to the negotiation of free trade agreements demanded by Guayaquil exporters. Particularly notable is the president's failure forcefully to promote banana exports and his expropriation of one of the largest and most productive

[67] Interview E3.

[68] See Bowen (2014) for the argument that oil resources, in combination with the incomplete nature of neoliberal reforms, have kept Ecuadorian elites dependent on the state and therefore less willing to invest in party-building activities than their peers in Bolivia.

[69] "More than Just a Port of Call, a Destination," *New York Times Magazine*, July 1, 2007, p. 72.

banana producers in the country. Because of his failure to pay an overdue tax bill in the amount of US$800 million, Alvaro Noboa's *La Clementina* is now a worker collective.[70] Correa has likewise disregarded the concerns of importers, who complain that the president's imposition of unreasonable quality standards will devastate the importing business.[71] Correa's obvious disinterest in the Guayaquil agro export model can be understood as the flipside of his deep interest in the return to an oil-financed model of import-substituting industrialization.

Coalitional impediments

Not only has the structural decline of Guayaquil *decreased* the national leverage previously enjoyed by the city's neoliberal protagonists, but these same protagonists have also failed to *increase* their leverage through the formation beyond Guayaquil of a broader anti-Correa coalition. Forming a territorial alliance against the president proved to be a tall order considering the many impediments to coalition-building that are discussed in this section, which include the lack of shared interests with other subnational units on Ecuador's coast, the history of animosity toward Guayaquil on the part of many other municipalities, and the scarcity of possible partisan allies owing to the decline and fragmentation of the *PSC*. Simply put, as mayor of Guayaquil it proved easier for Nebot to construct an internal coalition to defend neoliberalism within the city than an external coalition on behalf of neoliberalism nationally.

In contrast to the Bolivian case, where the president's statist orientation led neoliberals in Santa Cruz to form an effective coalition with neighboring departments in the east, advocates of neoliberalism within Guayaquil formed no equivalent coalition among neighboring provinces on the coast. At first blush, the absence of a coalition between the five coastal provinces (El Oro, Esmeraldas, Guayas, Los Ríos, and Manabí) is surprising given the presence in Ecuador of a prominent cleavage between the coast and the sierra. Along the lines of this territorial cleavage, inefficient producers in the highlands who traditionally benefited from statist approaches clashed with more competitive producers on the coast who stood to benefit from liberal trading policies (Hurtado 1977). A deeper look at the historiography, however, paints a much more complicated picture. Unlike in Bolivia, where the national government in La Paz neglected the eastern lowland departments until the 1950s and 1960s, across Ecuador's history as an independent republic much more extensive and variegated ties have been established between the

[70] Interview E26. [71] Interview E13.

national government and the five coastal provinces. Deep conflicts between coastal provinces have frequently emerged, as in the 1950s textile crisis when Guayaquil free traders criticized Sierra-based industries for constructing a colonial relationship with cotton producers in neighboring, coastal Manabí province (Quintero and Silva 1991: 55).[72] From the colonial period onward, the northern coastal province of Esmeraldas—home to the country's largest Afro-Ecuadorian population—has been tightly integrated into and dominated by highland economies. These historical struggles and structural differences between coastal provinces help explain why the nearly simultaneous holding of pro-autonomy votes in 2000 in four of them (El Oro, Guayas, Los Ríos, and Manabí, but not Esmeraldas) failed subsequently to generate a shared movement—in stark contrast to the 2008 autonomy referenda in Bolivia's four eastern departments.

The prospects for a more encompassing coalition of opposition forces under the leadership of Nebot were also diminished by decades of grievance on the part of other municipalities toward Guayaquil. Even as Guayaquil has long nursed grievances against Quito, which proved handy for Nebot as he set out to widen the coalition to defend his neoliberal local model, smaller subnational jurisdictions across Ecuador have articulated a critique of "bicentralism," which argues that Quito and Guayaquil have in fact together monopolized power since independence, to the detriment of all other cities and provinces (Muñoz 1999; Verdesoto 2001). Resentment against Guayaquil intensified in the 1990s over the design of decentralizing legislation. In 1994, subnational officials opposed a decentralization law proposed by Febres Cordero (1992–2000) that would have used an origin-based formula to share revenue from the value added tax and that would have disproportionately benefited Guayaquil relative to other jurisdictions. Two years later, Febres Cordero used his considerable political clout to veto a more redistributive bill that emerged from a nationwide consultation process and that would have benefited most subnational districts (Frank 2004: 219). At the same time, resentment about the small size of its contribution to the Ecuadorian Association of Municipalities led Guayaquil to withdraw from the association, further alienating other, poorer municipalities.[73] In the complaint of one subnational official, "What Guayaquileños want is to make Guayaquil into Singapore and let the rest of the country fend for itself" (Noboa 2004: 202).

Partisanship might also have served, but did not, as a glue for the formation of a more robust opposition coalition across territorial boundaries. After all,

[72] Guayaquil elites dismissed the prospects of an alliance with other coastal provinces such as Manabí or Esmeraldas. Interview with the president of the board of directors of one of Ecuador's largest sugar producers, June 6, 2008, Marcelino Maridueña (Interview E29).

[73] "AME se aleja de Nebot y logra acuerdo con régimen," *El Universo*, January 7, 2010.

although the right-of-center *PSC* declined as a national party, it persisted as an important local party in multiple subnational jurisdictions, able to run successful mayoral candidates if no longer viable presidential candidates (Freidenberg and Alcantara 2001). In Bolivia, a shared history of membership in traditional parties (e.g. *ADN* and *MNR*) facilitated the anti-Morales coalition that emerged among opposition governors in the east. In Ecuador, membership in the *PSC* did indeed generate the basis for a strong coalition between the mayors of Guayaquil (Febres Cordero and Nebot) and Nicolás Lapentti, who served as the elected *PSC* Prefect of Guayas province for an uninterrupted sixteen years (1992–2008). The *PSC* maintained its stranglehold not just on the office of the elected prefect, who represents the province vis-à-vis its appointed governor, but on the provincial council of Guayas as well, where the party maintained an overwhelming majority throughout this period.[74] With an office down the block from city hall, Lapentti operated as a predictable ally for the mayors of Guayaquil in their many conflicts with the center (even as the lesser importance of the office of the prefect and the lesser political stature of Lapentti meant that the two mayors were undisputedly the dominant figures in this Guayaquil–Guayas coalition).

Elsewhere, however, the *PSC* failed to serve as a binding force, and not just because the collapse of the party system led elected officials at the subnational level to de-emphasize all traditional partisan labels. Part of the challenge facing the *PSC* was the spatial pattern of its victories, which were not all clustered in the coast—even as this region has become the most important electoral redoubt for the party. In the 2005–9 electoral period, for instance, when the *PSC* held the prefecture (alone or in alliances) in four of the twenty-four provinces, two of these provinces were on the coast (Guayas and Manabí) but the other two were located in the distant and far less developed Amazon region (Napo and Zamora-Chinchipe). In this same period, the victory in two other coastal provinces (El Oro and Los Ríos) of the populist *Partido Roldosista Ecuatoriano* (*PRE*) (Ecuadorian Roldosist Party)—long considered the ideological rival of the *PSC* on the coast—imposed clear limits on the possibility of a neoliberal *PSC*-led alliance on the coast. This contrasts with the territorial alignment (in contiguous eastern departments) of victories by conservative opposition parties in Bolivia. Another challenge for the *PSC* was the significant ideological distance among elected officials who belong to the party. For example, while some *PSC* subnational leaders, like Prefect Mariano Zambrano of Manabí Province and Mayor Carlos Falquez in the city of Machala, advocated pro-foreign investment positions and sought to emulate Nebot's "urban regeneration" projects, others were far less market identified.

[74] Interview with a top official in the Prefectural Government of Guayas, June 12, 2008, Guayaquil (Interview E30).

The containment of Guayaquil

As a consequence of these structural and coalitional weaknesses, all of which were present before his rise to power, Correa has been relatively free to build his preferred national policy regime—without having to confront or negotiate with a powerful neoliberal opposition. The president, however, has not taken this favorable scenario for granted. In a series of bold and aggressive maneuvers that reflect his acumen as a politician, Correa has also sought actively to worsen the structural and coalitional challenges facing his ideological opponents in Guayaquil, and to reinforce still further their isolation. The result is that Correa has successfully contained neoliberalism within Guayaquil, even if he has failed to asphyxiate and replace its local model with the more state-centered vision he favors for the city.

One of the boldest measures has been the further shrinking of the province of Guayas by dividing it into two separate provinces: Santa Elena and the rump Guayas. Shortly after taking power, and having promised to do so on the campaign trail, Correa pushed his *AP* party to pass legislation giving the Santa Elena peninsula within Guayas its own provincial status. With its direct access to the Pacific Ocean, the Santa Elena peninsula contributed significantly to the economy of Guayas, and the city of Salinas on the coast served as an important vacation destination for generations of Guayaquil elites. Because communities in Santa Elena's lesser-developed municipalities had long complained that Guayas' provincial government always favored Guayaquil, the president could use the administrative elevation of Santa Elena as a high-profile way once again to excoriate the "oligarchs" of Guayaquil. Patricio Cisneros won the 2009 election as the new province's prefect, subsequently converted to Correa's party, and then won reelection in 2014 with nearly 80 percent of the vote.[75]

In addition to carving up Guayas, Correa pursued two other territorial measures that deserve mention here. First is an institutional re-engineering plan borrowed from the military-era *Junta de Planificación* in the 1970s that would transform regionalism by replacing the three essentially vertical traditional regions in Ecuador (that is, the coast, the highlands, and the Amazon) with eight new regional governments in the form of horizontal bands that cross these traditional regional lines. For example, each coastal province would be inserted into a bigger region with other provinces from the highlands and/or Amazon, and Guayaquil would be refashioned as a stand-alone "Metropolitan District." In other words, having separated Santa Elena from

[75] Having created Santa Elena and brought it under his political control, Correa subsequently invested heavily in the province, most importantly in the new gas terminal at Monteverde. "La Revolución Ciudadana construye megaobras como el terminal de GLP El Chorrillo," *El Ciudadano*, November 11, 2013.

Guayas, this plan would then remove Guayaquil from Guayas. Pitched as a project that could better integrate the nation, the new regionalism would have the effect of further fragmenting the coast. Approved as part of the new Constitution in 2008, the regions have yet to be formally created, although they are already in use by the state planning agency *Secretaría Nacional de Planificación y Desarrollo (SENPLADES)* (National Secretariat for Planning and Development).[76] Second is the adoption in 2013 of a new law (*Ley de fijación de limites*) that seeks to impose clear borders between subnational districts, but that has led to divisive fights between the governments of these districts. For example, by giving municipalities in Guayas the right to decide whether they want to continue to belong to Guayas or switch to El Oro, Manabí, or Santa Elena, the law has generated protracted conflicts among these coastal provinces.[77]

But by far the most threatening maneuver, from the perspective of liberals in Guayaquil, are the president's proposals vis-à-vis its port. Before the rise of Correa, and in addition to putting the port's bulk and container terminals under private control in 1999 and 2006, respectively, Nebot successfully lobbied the national government to support his idea of building a new deep-water port through a new concession with a Spanish company. Nebot chose Posorja, a location still within the city limits of Guayaquil and still on the Gulf of Guayaquil, but that sits far closer to the Pacific and that can handle the heavy vessels that are able to access the current port only at high tide. In 2013, however, Correa announced a new Strategic Mobility Plan (*Plan Estratégico de Movilidad*) that (1) downgrades the current maritime port in Guayaquil into a port that would merely service tourist vessels and traffic to the Galapagos islands (roughly 2 percent of the ships it currently receives), (2) suspends the construction of the deep-water port at Posorja, and (3) proposes building this new deep-water port further up the coast beyond the city limits of Guayaquil, either at Chanduy (in Santa Elena province) or at Manta (in Manabí province).[78] Critics of the plan argue that neither Chanduy nor Manta offers the protection from ocean waves that Posorja does.[79] In addition to disputes over the location of the new deep-water port, Correa and Nebot have fought over the mayor's plan to defend the viability of the current port by paying to dredge the Guayas river, which the president has indicated would require a special permit from the Ministry of the Environment. Considering the

[76] Interview with a former Subsecretary of Deconcentration, *SENPLADES*, August 26, 2015, Quito (Interview E31).

[77] "Asamblea aprueba proyecto de Ley para fijación de limites territoriales," *La República*, February 26, 2013.

[78] "Nebot asegura que el Puerto de Posorja es vital para el desarrollo del Ecuador," *El Universo*, July 23, 2013; and "Nebot asegura que se quiere despojar a Guayaquil de su naturaleza portuaria," *El Universo*, August 11, 2013.

[79] Interview E24.

significance of the port as the anchor of Guayaquil's liberal model, the prospect of losing it poses an existential sort of threat to the very identity of this port-city, one that would significantly worsen the structural decline already discussed.

In addition to proposing to wrest the port away from Guayaquil, Correa has also embarked on a number of other state-led infrastructure projects that have accentuated its relative structural decline, and that thereby put into question its traditional role as the most important subnational region on the coast. Many of these projects have sought to strengthen the position of neighboring Manabí province to the north of Guayaquil, site of the Manta Air Base whose contract with the US Air Force was terminated by Correa in 2008 in a rebuke to the US-led war on drugs. In 2007, Correa instructed the Army Corps of Engineers (*Cuerpo de Ingenieros del Ejército*) to begin work on a 2,000-meter bridge between the cities of Bahía and San Vicente in Manabí province, which cost US$100 million and was inaugurated as the country's longest bridge in 2010.[80] The president also identified Manabí as the site of a much larger project, the US$11 billion Refinery of the Pacific (*Refinería del Pacífico*). The refinery would give Ecuador the ability to refine gasoline, which it has never been able to do, and represents an important part of Correa's broader critique of neoliberal trading policies (though he has yet fully to secure the requisite Chinese financing to finish the project, estimated for completion in 2018 or 2019). Beyond Manabí, and in addition to the proposal to remove the main maritime port from Guayaquil, Correa has also proposed introducing specialized new ports in other locations on the coast, including one for fruits in Puerto Bolívar (in El Oro province) and one for auto imports in the province of Esmeraldas.

Finally, turning from structural to coalitional challenges, Correa has been able to further what Burbano de Lara (2009a: 25) described as the "disappearance of the Social Christian Party [*PSC*] as a regional network for the construction of alliances." On the coast, Correa has engaged in a successful process of either eliminating subnational officials who belong to the *PSC* or recruiting them into vertical alliances with the governing *AP* party. One important example is Mariano Zambrano, who governed as Prefect of Manabí as a member of the *PSC* in 2005–9, but then left the party to run for re-election with Correa's support as part of a new entity called *Manabí Primero* (First Manabí). Having secured significant investment projects in his province on the part of the central government, Zambrano was re-elected in 2014, again in alliance with the president. In the 2014 local elections, Correa also successfully prevented popular *PSC* Mayor (and Nebot ally) Carlos Falquez of the city

[80] "El puente más largo del país está listo," *La Hora*, Nov. 3, 2010.

of Machala (capital of El Oro province) from running for re-election on charges that the mayor's radio license represented a conflict of interest. But most important for the *PSC* is the loss of the prefecture of Guayas itself. When Nicolás Lapentti decided not to run for a fifth term as *PSC* Prefect of Guayas, Nebot supported as his replacement Jimmy Jairala, a former newscaster who defeated the president's own sister Pierina Correa in the 2009 elections. Subsequently, however, in a major betrayal of Nebot, Jairala forged an alliance with the president's party and won re-election with the support of Correa in 2014. By reducing the possibility of ideological alliances with other opponents of the president in other subnational jurisdictions, these adroit partisan moves by Correa have had the effect of further fencing in the mayor of Guayaquil.

Conclusion

According to the central argument of this chapter, the two types of subnational policy challenges that are examined in this book resulted in hybrid outcomes in the Ecuadorian case: subnational officials succeeded in implementing and defending a unique and coherent neoliberal policy regime in Guayaquil, even as they failed to check the statist orientation of the new national policy regime that has taken shape under the Correa presidency. These mixed results can be distinguished from the Peruvian case, where, in addition to failing to shape the national policy regime, subnational officials were also unable to create any policy regime at the subnational level that deviated from the (neoliberal) preferences of the national government. As will be seen in the following chapter, the outcome in Ecuador also differs from that in Bolivia, where the president shared Correa's state-centered vision but was forced to moderate that vision in response to a much more powerful subnational policy challenge.

In addition to these mixed results, Ecuador stands out for the intensely personalized nature of the territorial and ideological conflicts that it has experienced since 2006. To a large extent, these conflicts have unfolded in the form of a political rivalry between just two individuals: Rafael Correa and Jaime Nebot. In contrast to Peru, where a series of neoliberal presidents have done battle with a number of regional presidents, and Bolivia, where Santa Cruz Governor Rubén Costas built a coalition with other opposition governors against the president, in Ecuador Correa and Nebot have personified the two disparate models in dispute. In some respects, this has led to a simpler dynamic in Ecuador, one of raw political combat between a charismatic right-wing mayor committed to defending his neoliberal experiment and an equally charismatic left-wing president devoted to ending that experiment and the neoliberal "nightmare" that it spawned. Despite the greater personification of

Ecuador's ideological and territorial struggles, this chapter has demonstrated that the same institutional, structural, and coalitional variables highlighted in my theoretical framework do a better job explaining the outcome of these struggles than any individual-level attributes. First, the resilience of Guayaquil's distinctive local model lies fundamentally in the city's robust and lengthy history of liberal institutionalism. Second, the structural decline of Guayaquil must be considered the critical factor that explains the stunning loss of national leverage on the part of liberals in the city who have historically enjoyed such outsized influence. Third, coalitions matter at both levels; Nebot's success in building a vibrant internal coalition to defend Guayaquil's liberal model from a decade of assaults by Correa contrasts sharply with his failure to build a wider coalition in defense of neoliberalism beyond the city.

5

Territorial Conflict and Reconciliation in Bolivia

If the connection between ideological and territorial conflict has been tightening across Latin America, nowhere is it tighter than in Bolivia. In contrast to both Peru and Ecuador, I argue that each of the two types of subnational policy challenges that are examined in this book has succeeded in Bolivia: subnational neoliberals in Santa Cruz successfully defended their local model *and* forced liberal changes upon the national government. As a result, Bolivia can be considered the country that is characterized by the most effective territorial resistance of my three cases. In the first decade of the twenty-first century and in response to the rise to national power of a popular-indigenous movement that sought to end neoliberalism, leaders in the important department of Santa Cruz mobilized to preserve a neoliberal subnational policy regime whose precepts clashed with the state-centered logic of the new national policy regime then emerging in La Paz. Many of the dynamics associated with this first type of subnational policy challenge echo the Guayaquil experience discussed in Chapter 4; in both cases right-of-center subnational officials were able to defend more market-oriented policy regimes in each country's most economically vibrant subnational unit.

In contrast to Ecuador, however, the second type of subnational policy challenge also succeeded in Bolivia. Advocates and defenders of the more market-centered approach that took shape in Santa Cruz beginning in the 1950s were not only able to defend this distinctive local model, but also succeeded in their attempts to challenge the national policy regime, culminating in a significant degree of ideological reconciliation and policy moderation. On the verge of civil war in 2008 over two very distinct ideological agendas, Bolivia subsequently experienced rapid depolarization in the wake of a territorial pact that was negotiated between the national government—now firmly under the control of the *MAS*—and its former subnational challengers and neoliberal opponents in Santa Cruz. In other words, while

Bolivia appeared poised to enter into a potentially prolonged period of policy regime juxtaposition, marked by the simultaneous election in 2005 of the indigenous President Evo Morales and the landowning Governor Rubén Costas, in practice the significant policy concessions offered by Morales have served to align the national and subnational policy regimes to a considerable degree, and in a mostly liberal direction.[1]

Drawing on the theoretical arguments developed in Chapter 2 about capacity, structure, and coalitions, this chapter seeks to describe and explain the success of both types of subnational policy challenges in Bolivia. In the first half of the chapter I trace the strength of Santa Cruz's neoliberal policy regime—along with its resilience in the face of the national left turn—to the private-sector economic elites who invested heavily and consistently in the development of local institutional capacity. Not unlike their counterparts in Guayaquil, *cruceño* economic elites responded to what they perceived to be an absent central state by creating and controlling a set of local quasi-public institutions that over time proved to be critical for the development of markets and for the region's economic success. As in Guayaquil, the local institutional capacity accumulated through this essentially private initiative was eventually and partially incorporated into subnational government, especially after appointed prefects gave way to elected governors in Bolivia in 2005. Here too we see the same apparent paradox as in Guayaquil: significant levels of subnational state capacity whose origins can be traced back in large part to the private sector. This is a surprising outcome given the historically hostile stance of many economic elites toward formal state-building activities in Latin America.

If anything, this trajectory is even more surprising in Santa Cruz than in Guayaquil given the relative economic obscurity and structural insignificance of Santa Cruz as recently as 1950, when it was a marginal town of 43,000 residents largely unconnected to national and international markets (Molina 2013; Burbano de Lara 2014). Whereas economic elites in Guayaquil had the country's main port around which to build the liberal local model, their counterparts in Santa Cruz faced greater challenges and would depend even more heavily on the institutions they designed to promote and sustain economic activity. Two key clarifications are in order. First, while I emphasize in this chapter the leading role played by local economic elites in devising the institutions at the center of Santa Cruz's subnational policy regime, it would be a mistake to overlook the various forms of investment by the central state that also facilitated the transformation of Santa Cruz after 1950. Second, it is

[1] For more on the moderation of Evo Morales, see also Dunkerley (2007), Petras and Veltmeyer (2009), Kaup (2010), Postero (2010), and Webber (2011).

also important to question how well these local institutions served non-elite interests in Santa Cruz. Nevertheless, the development of local institutional capacity—which is directly reflected in the comparatively high quality of the water, electricity, and telecommunication services provided by these institutions in Santa Cruz—helps explain the success of later efforts to defend the *cruceño* model when it came under assault in the early years of Evo Morales's rise to power.

In addition to the accumulation of high levels of institutional capacity in Santa Cruz, I argue that the construction of a broad coalition within Santa Cruz was also critical in the struggle to defend the department's policy regime in the face of opposition from the national government. In effect, the same concentrated set of economic elite interests that built and operated the model began after 2000 to assemble a much broader local coalition in the ultimately successful attempt to preserve this model. Particularly instrumental in the construction of this coalition was the Pro-Santa Cruz Committee (*Comité Pro-Santa Cruz* (*CPSC*)), a civic institution formed in the 1950s with extensive ties to a number of functional and professional organizations in the department. Beginning with the fall of the neoliberal Sánchez de Losada government in 2003 and culminating in the violent polarization of 2008, the *CPSC* knit together a strong territorial coalition composed of disparate local organizations that together leveraged significant mobilizational strength in defense of the Santa Cruz model.

In the second half of the chapter, I turn from the successful defense of Santa Cruz's subnational policy regime to the effective challenge it posed to the preferred national policy regime of the *MAS*. Here I emphasize the importance of structural leverage and the construction of a powerful coalition that transcended the borders of the city and department of Santa Cruz. The absence of similar structural and coalitional strengths in Ecuador is what explains why and how the case of Guayaquil differs from Santa Cruz in its inability to exert national-level policy influence. In terms of structural power, the preponderant role of Santa Cruz as the supplier of critical and price sensitive agricultural goods generated a great deal of bargaining leverage for Morales's ideological opponents in the department. When important agricultural producers responded to export and price controls in 2008 and 2009 by cutting production and threatening not to supply the domestic market, Morales responded with a series of policy compromises that undermined some of the most sacrosanct elements of the *MAS*'s critique of neoliberalism. Most critically the president, along with his vice president Alvaro García Linera, offered initially vague but increasingly explicit guarantees not to threaten existing land tenure patterns in the department. Fearing invasions by landless workers who would be encouraged by a government that had promised to redistribute land and end land inequality, in the end the *MAS* government has reconciled with rather than threatened the interests of these agricultural elites. Ironically, then, by transforming Santa Cruz into an agricultural powerhouse with real veto power, it was the revolution in the 1950s led by the Nationalist Revolutionary Movement (*Movimiento Nacionalista Revolucionario* (*MNR*) that seriously limited the scope of the *MAS*-led revolution in the 2000s. This dynamic differs not only from Ecuador, where Guayaquil's national-level influence has been undercut by its long structural decline, but Peru as well, where the structure of natural resource extraction and ownership has made it difficult for subnational officials to effect meaningful changes in the national (neoliberal) policy regime.

If structure made a difference in the outcome of this second type of subnational policy challenge, so did coalitions. While the construction of a department-wide coalition under the auspices of the *CPSC* sufficed in the defense of Santa Cruz's local model, the emergence of a still broader pan-departmental coalition proved to be critical in forcing Morales to conciliate at the national level. Rather than do battle with Morales on a bilateral basis, Santa Cruz and its governor Rubén Costas were able to build a coalition with opposition governors in other departments in the eastern lowlands of Bolivia whose economic elites were far less powerful than their *cruceño* counterparts, but who were likewise threatened by the economic policy proposals of Morales and the *MAS*. Grouped together in the National Council for Democracy (*Consejo Nacional Democrático* (*CONALDE*)) that they formed to contest Morales, and representing two-thirds of Bolivia's national territory, the opposition governors of the eastern *media luna* were able to coordinate amongst themselves, as well as with civic committees in each department. This coordination, as I describe in greater detail in this chapter, heightened the effectiveness of a series of measures, including wildcat referenda on departmental autonomy in May and June of 2008, which ultimately forced compromise upon the national government. Although it subsequently fizzled out once these compromises had been won, the success of this Bolivian coalition of opposition governors stands in sharp contrast both to the isolation of Jaime Nebot in Ecuador and to the atomized landscape that faces regional presidents in Peru.[2]

[2] While I emphasize structural and coalitional strengths in explaining why subnational officials were able successfully to challenge the national policy regime in Bolivia but not in Peru or Ecuador, it is also important to note another difference that may have contributed to this outcome. Only in Bolivia was the national government under the control of an organization (the *MAS*) with a serious party-building project across the national territory. The *MAS*'s attempt to build electoral support in Santa Cruz may also help account for its greater willingness to adopt serious policy compromises. For this comparative insight, I am grateful to Carla Alberti.

The Construction and Defense of Santa Cruz's Subnational Policy Regime

According to the argument developed in this first half of the chapter, landowning elites in Santa Cruz built a distinctly liberal policy regime over the course of the second half of the twentieth century, and then assembled a broad (but local) coalition to defend this regime when it came under attack by the national government at the start of the twenty-first century. I present this argument in three parts. First, I describe the gradual accumulation of capacity in the subnational institutions that were established and controlled by the private sector, and that cohered in support of the department's distinctly liberal policy regime. The central claim here is that economic elites responded to the absence of the central state by investing in the construction of local quasi-public institutions whose administrative capacity would ultimately redound to the benefit of the subnational state. Second, I analyze the logic of the coalition-building efforts that local elites subsequently championed in the attempt to preserve these local institutions by broadening their support base. Outreach to workers, migrants, and indigenous groups was especially concerted, in addition to new discursive strategies that elites adopted to reframe their policy disagreements with the center as a fundamentally territorial struggle that threatened all who lived in Santa Cruz. Third, I examine a number of indicators to demonstrate that, notwithstanding sharp conflicts with the *MAS*, the core elements of Santa Cruz's subnational policy regime remain intact today—an otherwise surprising outcome that can be explained only with reference to the successful institution- and coalition-building efforts of local elites.

Although my focus in this section is on Santa Cruz, it is impossible to understand what happened within that department without reference to national-level politics. As we will see, the relationship between Santa Cruz's liberal policy regime and that of the national government has been quite volatile over time, shifting from a period of considerable hostility in the aftermath of the national Revolution in the 1950s and 1960s, to a period of alignment after the national government had embraced neoliberalism in the 1980s and 1990s, and back to the episodes of conflict that were produced by the national turn to the left in the 2000s and that are showcased in the discussion here.

Institution-building and the emergence of Santa Cruz's policy regime

What Bolivia's 1952 Revolution did—and did not do—in Santa Cruz offers a useful starting point for the analysis of the distinctive institutions that developed in this department over the next five decades. In the western highland departments of Bolivia, which were dominated by private mining interests and semi-feudal haciendas, the Revolution had an enormous impact by nationalizing the mining industry and by eliminating the traditional landowning class through the redistribution of lands to peasants on a collective basis. Peasant unions (*sindicatos*) were simultaneously incorporated into the political system via a new set of corporatist institutions (Malloy 1970; Klein 2003; Yashar 2005). The radical changes in land tenure instituted by the *MNR* make this one of Latin America's most significant social revolutions ever.

In hindsight, the Revolution was equally consequential for the sparsely populated departments of the eastern lowlands (these are the departments of Beni, Pando, Santa Cruz, and Tarija in Map 5.1), which did not play a significant role in the events of the Revolution itself. Drawing directly on the Plan Bohan, a study mission to Bolivia financed by the US State Department during the Second World War, the victorious *MNR* identified Santa Cruz as the region best suited for modern agricultural production—both to supply the domestic market and to diversify Bolivia's export profile away from its dependence on minerals (Soruco 2008). Critically, the *MNR* decided not to engage in land redistribution in the lowlands and to encourage instead the formation of large agribusinesses owned by individual families. In the words of historian José Luis Roca (2001: 578), "what was called 'land reform' in the east was nothing other than an extensive program of land titling in favor of those who wanted to dedicate themselves to agriculture and/or cattle ranching." By the end of the 1970s, 96 percent of the new titles extended in Santa Cruz went to individual rather than collective landowners, and 72 percent of the land under production belonged to large farms of more than 1,000 hectares (Sandoval 2003: 46, 47). The Revolution dramatically expanded the agricultural frontier and, surprisingly, given what it did in the highlands, put those new lands under the control of a concentrated new class of landowning elites (Prado 2007). Also in sharp contrast to the western highlands, the type of peasant union organizations that could coordinate land invasions was altogether missing in the east (Waldmann 2008).

In addition to the fateful decision not to apply agrarian reform in the east, the Revolution was momentous for Santa Cruz because, after four centuries of isolation, it finally connected the department to the rest of the country through the completion of long-promised but never-delivered infrastructure projects (Roca 1980). For example, the *MNR* government used national revenues to complete a newly asphalted highway linking Santa Cruz to Cochabamba that was inaugurated in 1954 and fully operational in 1957. Even more symbolically important, the national government completed the railway connection to Santa Cruz in 1960, more than fifty years after the articulation of this and other regionalist demands in the famous 1904 Memorandum of the Santa Cruz Society of Geographers. Although *cruceño*

Map 5.1. Bolivia: Administrative Divisions
Source: Perry-Castañeda Library Map Collection at the University of Texas.

elites emphasized that the railway was built not with Bolivian but with Brazilian funds, which were paid to La Paz for the eastern territories in Acre that Bolivia had ceded to Brazil in 1938, these new transport connections gave eastern landowners access to new markets at a time when Bolivia's population was overwhelmingly concentrated in the west. Infrastructural investments in transport proved to be just as consequential for the success of these emerging economic elites as the absence of land reform (Bozo 2013: 178).

Although the Revolution did much not just to advance the interests of Santa Cruz's landowning class but to create that very class, *cruceño* elites nevertheless opposed the *MNR* party that led the Revolution, largely because of its centralizing logic and political ideology (Whitehead 1972). As Dunia Sandoval (2003: 42) writes, "while economic elites in Santa Cruz preferred a liberal approach to modernization, the *MNR*'s national economic project promoted a much more centralist vision of development in the east." Elite opposition to and fear of territorial penetration by the *MNR* fueled the formation and strengthening in the 1950s of the *CPSC*, an officially non-governmental and non-partisan body that for a variety of reasons has operated as a quasi-public institution. Founded in 1950 by a group of university students who were affiliated with a right-wing party (*Falange Socialista Boliviana*) opposed to the *MNR*, the *CPSC* identified the lack of public services in Santa Cruz as the region's chief problem and the decentralization of oil royalties as its chief solution. Financed and led by men from socially prominent families, including most importantly a doctor named Melchor Pinto, the *CPSC* responded to the *MNR*'s Revolution by focusing its demands on the transfer of 11 percent of all oil revenues to producer departments—the most significant of which was then Santa Cruz (Barragán 2008). When the *MNR* responded by accusing the *CPSC* of separatism, dispatching militias to Santa Cruz, and sending Pinto into exile, conservative *cruceño* youths formed the *Unión Juvenil Crucenista* (*UJC*) (Crucenista Youth Union), a body that would function in later disputes as the "shock troops" of the *CPSC* (Iskenderian Aguilera 2010; Marca 2012). After a prolonged period of violence, including a coup attempt by *cruceño* leaders and a massacre in Santa Cruz at the hands of *MNR* militias, *MNR* President Hernán Siles agreed to negotiate directly with the *CPSC* and ultimately acquiesced to its 11 percent demand in 1959.

The successful struggle for oil royalties generated a tremendous amount of legitimacy for the *CPSC*, bolstering not just its claim to represent regional rather than elite interests, but also the view that it functioned as "the moral government of the *cruceños*" (Peña 2003).[3] The quasi-public status of the *CPSC* was further reinforced by the decision of the *MNR* after the Revolution to cancel local elections in all nine departmental capitals, which were not held again in Bolivia until 1985. In the absence of either an elected mayor or prefect, the President of the *CPSC*, who is elected for a two-year period by the committee's members, emerged overtime as Santa Cruz's most influential leader. In the words of one *CPSC* President, "the most important role of my predecessors was to monitor the prefects appointed from La Paz."[4] The suppression of local elections elevated the importance of the *CPSC* as a political space, even as it continued to be dominated by a small number of

[3] Interview with a former director of the Bolivian Chamber of Hydrocarbons, October 26, 2005, Santa Cruz (Interview B1).

[4] Interview with a former President of the *CPSC*, September 7, 2012, Santa Cruz (Interview B2).

interconnected elite families. When the military overthrew the *MNR* in 1964, initiating nearly two decades of direct military rule, the shift to authoritarianism further strengthened the quasi-public nature of the *CPSC*. Searching for channels of communication and engagement with local societal actors, but preferring not to engage with political parties or to reinstate local elections, military presidents opted to privilege Santa Cruz's civic committee as their main interlocutor, in addition to similar civic committees in other departments (Roca 1980; Sandoval 2003). Through time, even in moments of intense ideological conflict with the national governing party in the 1950s, early 1960s, early 1980s, and 2000s, the *CPSC* leadership has assiduously defended the body's non-partisan and civic status, which has had the effect of further bolstering its claim to a semi-public status.

Even as the *CPSC* emerged as Santa Cruz's most important institution, the elite interests who dominate it have spun off a number of other key institutions that are critical in understanding the region's liberal, outward-oriented, and market-centered policy regime. As described here, these include the Regional Development Corporation of Santa Cruz (*Corporación Regional de Desarrollo de Santa Cruz* (*CORDECRUZ*)), three service cooperatives (*Cooperativa de Telecomunicaciones Santa Cruz* (*COTAS*) (Telecommuncations Cooperative of Santa Cruz); *Cooperativa Rural de Electrificación* (*CRE*) (Rural Electrification Cooperative); *Servicio de Agua Potable* (*SAGUAPAC*) (Potable Water Service)), and a number of business chambers (*Cámara de Industria y Comercio* (*CAINCO*) (Chamber of Industry and Commerce); *Cámara Agropecuaria del Oriente* (*CAO*) (Eastern Agricultural Chamber); *Federación de Empresarios Privados de Bolivia–Santa Cruz* (*FEPB–SC*) (Federation of Private Entrepreneurs of Bolivia–Santa Cruz)). Each of the pieces of what are together referred to as "*la institucionalidad cruceña*" (Ferreira 2010: 163) has played a special role in supporting the region's neoliberal policy regime: *CORDECRUZ* enabled private sector elites to determine where and how public revenues would be invested in infrastructure and services, cooperatives generated a preponderant role for non-governmental social provision, and business chambers offered strong and consistent support for private property and an outward-looking economic orientation. Given the coordinating role that it has played as the central node in this network of proliferating institutions, the *CPSC* can indeed be seen as the "institution of institutions" in Santa Cruz (Roca 2001: 604). The number and strength of these elite-dominated, but quasi-public, institutions are particularly striking considering the persistent problems of weak capacity in the official institutions of the state that continued to plague Bolivia across this period.

One of the most legendary local institutions in Santa Cruz is *CORDECRUZ*, established in 1970 and widely credited with making possible Santa Cruz's transformation into Bolivia's largest and most dynamic city and department

(Pinto 2009: 235). If the *CPSC* operated as a sort of de facto local government in Santa Cruz, *CORDECRUZ* assumed the role of identifying, financing, and delivering the range of public services that were never provided by the national government, and whose absence had fueled a deep sense of grievance and neglect in Santa Cruz vis-à-vis La Paz. Financed by the transfer to Santa Cruz of a portion of "its" oil royalties, *CORDECRUZ* sowed these revenues into infrastructure projects in the areas of sewerage, water, electricity, and roads, but also engaged heavily in planning and promoted the city's distinctive growth pattern in the form of an expanding set of concentric circles. Moving beyond basic service delivery and urban planning, and as greater revenues became available in the commodity boom of the 1970s, *CORDECRUZ* increasingly focused on higher order challenges, including financing for the construction of an industrial park (directed by the *Financiera de Desarrollo de Santa Cruz* (*FINDESA*) (Development Finance Company of Santa Cruz)) and international airport (Viru Viru). According to one prominent Santa Cruz businessman who served as its President in the mid-1980s, the success of *CORDECRUZ* can be attributed to the strong *esprit de corps* that developed among administrative staff. *CORDECRUZ* employees developed lengthy time horizons and saw their mission as building directly upon the earlier work of the Public Works Committee (*Comité de Obras Públicas* (*COP*)), which had been established in 1945. "From 1945 to 1995, *CORDECRUZ* and the *COP* before it gave several generations of professional *cruceños* the opportunity to acquire high-level technical and managerial expertise."[5]

Although *CORDECRUZ* was created by the military government and representatives of national ministries sat on its board of directors, by all accounts it was another board member—the *CPSC*—that dominated and controlled the corporation, which was officially independent of the state. According to José Luis Roca (2001: 613), "because of the role it had played in the 1950s in securing funding for *CORDECRUZ*, the *CPSC* possessed virtual veto authority over all of the corporation's decisions." One former President of *CORDECRUZ* confirmed this view: "Although I was appointed by the President of the Republic, *CORDECRUZ* functioned with a great deal of autonomy from La Paz, and in close coordination with the *CPSC*, in which I was an active member." In essence, although *CORDECRUZ* as an institution was financed by public revenues, it operated largely under the control of the private-sector interests that were grouped together in the *CPSC*. Just as importantly, one can observe an uninterrupted process of capacity-building over many decades as the *COP* was subsumed by *CORDECRUZ* in 1970, which was then put under

[5] Interview with a former President of *CORDECRUZ*, February 24, 2014, Santa Cruz (Interview B3).

the direct control of the departmental prefect in 1995 and of the departmental governor in 2005 after the introduction of direct elections.

Perhaps the most emblematic feature of the liberal policy regime that developed in Santa Cruz can be seen in the three important non-governmental cooperatives that were established beginning in the 1960s in electricity, telecommunications, and water. In contrast to other departments in Bolivia, citizens in Santa Cruz receive these crucial services not from state-owned enterprises but rather from cooperatives to which they belong as quota-paying members. Drawing on the mutual aid societies (*sociedades mutuales*) that proliferated in Santa Cruz in the 1920s, the cooperatives are officially governed by their membership, with each member receiving one vote in electing its leadership. Any surpluses generated are supposed to be invested in improving service provision (rather than paid out as dividends). The first modern cooperative, which emerged in 1962, was *CRE*, an entity that has offered key support for private agriculture in Santa Cruz by distributing electricity to over 112,000 members and 1,300 farms. Although the *MNR* government in the 1950s sought to suppress *CRE* in favor of the state-owned electricity company, the cooperative survived and prospered under military rule after 1964 (Roca 2001: 630–5). The second to emerge was the telephone cooperative, *COTAS*, in 1963, which grew to 123,000 members by the 2000s, when it successfully made the transition to the internet and fought off an acquisition attempt by Italian and Spanish investors (Roca 2001: 621–9). More recently, the water cooperative *SAGUAPAC* was spun off from *CORDECRUZ* in 1979 and provides water to a third of the city with 31 wells and 1,700 kilometers of pipe (Roca 2001: 634). Thanks to their broad membership base and the widespread perception that they provided better (though not necessarily cheaper) service than public-sector agencies elsewhere in Bolivia, the cooperatives helped broaden support for the Santa Cruz model when it came under fire from Evo Morales, who claimed that elites and not rank-and-file members controlled the cooperatives.

In addition to *CORDECRUZ* and the cooperatives, a number of business chambers were also critical as institutional supports in the development and subsequent defense of Santa Cruz's liberal development model. Most important is the Chamber of Industry and Commerce (*CAINCO*), which unusually brought together economic sectors that were organized separately elsewhere in Bolivia, and which served as a critical forum for the identification of problems hindering the region's progress. In addition to *CAINCO*, the *CAO* provided a vigorous defense of the interests of large agribusinesses and cattle ranchers, while *CADEX* lobbied for infrastructural investments that would facilitate foreign trade. No other department in Bolivia witnessed the development of similar private-sector institutions. Although these sectoral business chambers participated as a federation in the national umbrella structure of the

Confederation of Private Entrepreneurs of Bolivia (*Confederación de Empresarios Privados de Bolivia (CEPB)*), the *FEPB-SC* formally withdrew from the *CEPB* in 2004 over fears that national business leaders had failed to mount a vigorous defense of private property rights vis-à-vis Evo Morales and the *MAS* (Eaton 2007).[6]

Finally, in addition to the coordinating role played by the *CPSC* at the center of all these *cruceño* institutions (for example, *CORDECRUZ, COTAS, CRE, SAGUAPAC*, and *CAINCO*), another critical feature that united them was the importance in each of membership in one of Santa Cruz's two elite fraternities or lodges (*logias*). Defined by Reymi Ferreira (2010: 97–8) as "closed power groups" that are distinct from Masonic lodges because of their pursuit of economic benefits and their Catholic identity, the lodges became increasingly important in the late 1970s, when the country's imminent return to democracy provoked fears among Santa Cruz elites of a "highland invasion" (*invasión de collas*) and "communist agitation" (Ferreira 2010: 97–8, 164). Despite their secretive nature, it is clear that affiliation with one of these lodges (either *Caballeros del Oriente* or *Toborochi*) has been essential in order to rise to positions of influence within any of Santa Cruz's important institutions. Whereas the *Caballeros del Oriente* are understood to control *COTAS* and *CAINCO*, for example, *Toborochi* (which split from the *Caballeros* in the early 1980s) has remained dominant within *CRE* and *SAGUAPAC* (Ferreira 2010: 168). Although there have been attempts to dispute the power of the lodges within the cooperatives, including a challenge to the candidate endorsed by *Toborochi* in *CRE* elections in 1992, Ferreira (2010: 185) argues that these have been defeated because of threats of reprisals and the incidence of electoral fraud in cooperative elections. The two lodges have alternated in their control of the *CPSC*; every president was affiliated with one or the other lodge until the election of Herland Vaca Diez in 2011.[7] Growing media attention to and public awareness of the behavior of the two lodges over the course of the 1990s increased the importance of coalition-building efforts in the following decade, which were designed to expand support for the Santa Cruz model beyond the economic elites who took the lead in its construction.[8]

Coalition-building to defend the policy regime

Despite tension between the *MNR* and the *CPSC* in the 1950s and 1960s, and the contrast that emerged in those years between Santa Cruz's liberal

[6] Interview with a former President of *CAINCO*, October 26, 2005, Santa Cruz (Interview B4).
[7] Interview B2.
[8] Interview with the ex-Rector of the Universidad Autónoma René Gabriel Moreno, August 31, 2012, Santa Cruz (Interview B5).

approach and the statist preferences of the national government, military rule in the 1970s and economic liberalization in the 1980s produced a considerable degree of policy alignment between Santa Cruz and La Paz. Santa Cruz elites played a leading role in the internal military coup against left-leaning military president Juan José Torres in 1971, and benefited directly when he was replaced as dictator by Santa Cruz native Hugo Banzer (1971–8). Santa Cruz agribusinesses, for example, received 66 percent of the agricultural credit extended under Banzer by Bolivia's Agricultural Bank (Conaghan and Malloy 1994: 57). While Santa Cruz elites feared redemocratization and opposed the statist policies of President Hernán Siles (1982–5)—the same president whom they had forced to share 11 percent of oil royalties back in 1959—Bolivia's transition to democracy was followed in short order by one of the most ambitious and radical programs of economic liberalization anywhere in Latin America. The adoption of market-friendly and pro-export economic policies in La Paz, along with the encouragement of direct foreign investment, had a strongly positive impact in the east, where the bulk of the country's agricultural exports are generated, and a negative impact on the western highlands, where the producers of non-tradable goods dominated. One especially important indicator of the policy alignment that took place between Santa Cruz and La Paz after 1985 was the consistent representation of leading *cruceño* agribusiness owners in important cabinet positions, including the critical Ministry of Agriculture.

In 1997, the return of Santa Cruz's own Hugo Banzer to the presidency—this time as the result of democratic elections—seemed to give elites in the department reason to celebrate. Banzer, however, failed to provide an effective response to the major social upheavals that defined his second presidency (1997–2000), and this weakness was cause for growing alarm among Santa Cruz elites—despite the favoritism Banzer had shown them in the past. Most important are the two widespread social protests that took place in 2000: the so-called *guerra del agua* (water war) in April and the events of *septiembre negro* (Black September) five months later. In the water war, indigenous groups, anti-market activists, and environmentalists coordinated a successful mobilization against a subsidiary of the Bechtel Corporation, which then decided to abandon its bid to supply water to Cochabamba (Laserna 2004: 51–7; Simmons 2016). Santa Cruz elites were disturbed by the forced eviction of a major international investor as well as by the renewal of violence in September that saw a coordinated set of blockades by Morales's *MAS* in protest against Banzer's US–backed coca eradication efforts.[9]

[9] Interviews in Santa Cruz with a prominent participant in Nación Camba, October 25, 2005 (Interview B6); with a former Prefect of Santa Cruz, October 28, 2005 (Interview B7); and with a local business leader, October 28, 2005 (Interview B8).

In this generalized environment of growing political and social turbulence, the June 2002 elections generated additional cause for concern among elites in Santa Cruz.[10] First, although by law Congress should have used the results of the 2000 census to grant additional legislative seats to Santa Cruz, whose population had surged because of migration from the west with the closing of mines in the highlands, legislators from western departments vetoed any such changes.[11] This fight over seats (*escaños*), which returned in a more virulent form in the run-up to the 2005 elections, exacerbated fears among *cruceño* elites that they could no longer count on adequate representation in the national government.[12] The second and more important factor in the 2002 elections was the inferior performance of Bolivia's traditional parties, including the *MNR* (by now a neoliberal party), and *Acción Democrática Nacionalista* (*ADN*) (Nationalist Democratic Action), which virtually disappeared in the wake of Banzer's death in May (Cyr 2017). The combined vote for the three traditional parties (*ADN, MIR, MNR*) declined from 57 percent in 1997 to 42 percent in 2002 (Mayorga 2005: 156). Because of the fragmentation of the vote, Sánchez de Losada's *MNR* was still able to secure the presidency in 2002 but without the support of an effective inter-party pact of the sort that had sustained past democratic governments.

In the end, Sánchez de Losada was able to complete only fifteen months of his second term, which did much to convince elites that Bolivia's political system was experiencing profound change and that the high levels of governability achieved in the post-1985 period were at an end (Mansilla 2007; Molina 2013). Perhaps worse, it was opposition to the neoliberal economic policies so faithfully implemented in Bolivia for the previous decade and a half that fueled the devastating protests against Sánchez de Losada. In February 2003, thirty-three people died in protests and lootings in La Paz and El Alto over tax reform proposals that were designed to close the budget deficit. Eight months later, in the so-called *guerra del gas* (gas war), nearly sixty people died when Sánchez de Losada called in the military to control protests over his proposal to build a new pipeline for the export of natural gas (Mayorga 2007). Amid invitations from Santa Cruz business elites that he transfer the national capital to Santa Cruz, Sánchez de Losada resigned the presidency on October 17, 2003, triggering a statement by the *CPSC* that "it now doubted whether Santa Cruz would stay within Bolivia" (Barragán 2004: 36).

With the overthrow of Sánchez de Losada, for the first time since the transition to democracy more than two decades earlier the Bolivian presidency

[10] On electoral reform as a cause of regional polarization, see Centellas (2009).

[11] Interview with Senator from the department of Oruro, October 18, 2005, La Paz (Interview B9).

[12] Interview with a staffer in the *Comisión de Descentralización y Participación Popular*, October 19, 2005, La Paz (Interview B10).

was no longer occupied by one of the country's three established parties (*ADN*, *MIR*, and *MNR*). While it was Congress that chose Carlos Mesa to finish out Sánchez de Losada's term, Mesa ascended to the presidency in October 2003 without any partisan support in the legislature. In response, the new president sought to bolster his authority by constructing an extra-congressional alliance with the *MAS* and by engaging in direct negotiations with Morales. From the standpoint of Santa Cruz's business leaders, Morales was not yet president, but he was now exerting substantial influence on the chief executive (Rada 2004: 157). Mesa's dialogue with Morales was particularly threatening because no representatives of Santa Cruz's powerful agricultural sector were invited into the presidential cabinet—for the first time since the transition to democracy in 1982.[13]

The cumulative effect of these changes was to displace economic elites in Santa Cruz from the advantageous position they had enjoyed in the national political system throughout the neoliberal period (1985–2003).[14] Worse, from the standpoint of these elites, was the reality that these changes would not easily be reversed; rather, they appeared to constrict for the foreseeable future the channels of influence on which elites had long depended. Particularly at the national level, the meteoric rise of the *MAS*—in a party system in which no single party in the post-1982 period was ever able to win a majority—signified a deep challenge to elite interests in Santa Cruz. Whereas the fragmentation of Bolivia's party system forced all presidents since the transition in 1982 to negotiate inter-party pacts in order to govern (Gamarra 1997), the emergence of the *MAS* as a majority party after 2002 meant that Morales would not need to negotiate with any traditional parties. This dynamic was rendered more threatening still by the reality that the *MAS* is a movement-based party with deep and extensive connections to grassroots social movements (Anria 2016). As a result, economic elites in Santa Cruz did not perceive their loss of voice in the national government to be a temporary matter, and believed instead that the defense of their economic model would now require departmental autonomy from that government (Plata 2008; Urenda 2009).[15]

But building the case for autonomy required building a broader coalition in Santa Cruz—one that would go substantially beyond the economic and social

[13] The significance of this change was underscored in interviews with a former President of the Cattle Ranchers Federation, October 25, 2005, Santa Cruz (Interview B11); and a top-level official in the Agricultural Chamber of the East, October 24, 2005, Santa Cruz (Interview B12).

[14] Businessmen in the highlands, meanwhile, saw this as a necessary corrective that would reverse the marginalization of private-sector actors outside Santa Cruz. Interviews in La Paz with the former Manager of the National Chamber of Industries, October 18, 2005 (Interview B13); with the ex-Director of Social Relations of the Confederation of Private Businessmen of Bolivia, October 19, 2005 (Interview B14); and with the former President of the Chamber of Industries of the Department of La Paz, October 18, 2005 (Interview B15).

[15] Interview with a Senator from the department of Santa Cruz, October 27, 2005, Santa Cruz (Interview B16).

elites that had dominated the *CPSC* for nearly fifty years. Three non-elite actors loomed large in this coalition-building exercise: workers, indigenous groups, and migrants. With respect to workers, the *CPSC* took advantage of divisions within the Departmental Labor Federation (*Central Obrera Departamental* (*COD*)), an affiliate of the corporatist Bolivian Labor Confederation (*Central Obrera Boliviana* (*COB*)). While labor leaders such as Lucio Vedia supported Evo Morales and the *MAS*, others including Elio Pedraza, Gabriel Helbing, and Edwin Fernández argued that Santa Cruz's workers had more in common with the *CPSC* than the *COB*.[16] For example, Elio Pedraza, who led the *COD* delegation to the *CPSC*, maintained that the *COB*'s traditional focus on public-sector employees squared poorly with the reality of Santa Cruz's small public sector. Pedraza argued for the *COD* to leave the *COB*, just as the *FEPB-SC* had withdrawn from the national *CEPB*.[17] In 2006, the *CPSC* supported attempts by Edwin Fernández forcibly to take control of the *COD* office in Santa Cruz from the more left-leaning Lucio Vedia.[18] The *CPSC* also supported the election campaign of *COD* operative Gabriel Helbin, who successfully ran as the candidate of a center-right party in the December 2005 legislative elections.[19]

Divisions within Santa Cruz's indigenous population likewise created coalition-building opportunities for the *CPSC*, many of whose leaders insist on the myth of "happy miscegenation" (*feliz mestizaje*) in the lowlands, and ascribe to the view that, "while the Incan empire in the west was highly statist, eastern indigenous groups prevented the Inca from descending into the lowlands [*el inca no pudo bajar*] and have always rejected statist initiatives."[20] Many indigenous political leaders criticized the *CPSC* for supporting autonomy for the department when it simultaneously resisted the autonomy claims of indigenous communities *within* the department.[21] One such politician is José Bailaba, who parlayed his experience as a leader of the anti-*CPSC* indigenous group *Coordinadora de Pueblos Étnicos de Santa Cruz* (*CPESC*) (Coordination of Ethnic Peoples of Santa Cruz) into a successful campaign for Congress representing Evo Morales's *MAS* party.[22] Bailaba's *CPESC* was sharply critical of the *CPSC* for promising food and other benefits to members of indigenous communities who agreed to travel to the city of Santa Cruz to participate in a Special Assembly of the *CPSC* for the department's indigenous inhabitants.

16 "La COD sin solución y los militares custodian locales," *El Deber*, July 6, 2006.

17 Interview with a high-level labor leader in the department of Santa Cruz, October 25, 2005, Santa Cruz (Interview B17).

18 "La COD sin solución y los militares custodian locales," *El Deber*, July 6, 2006.

19 "Helbing será el primer plurinominal de Tuto," *El Nuevo Día*, September 4, 2005.

20 Interview B2.

21 "En Santa Cruz no todos están de acuerdo con la autonomía," *El Diario*, May 25, 2005.

22 Interview with a national deputy representing Santa Cruz for the *MAS* party, October 28, 2005, Santa Cruz (Interview B18).

At the end of this assembly on February 12, 2004, Bonifacio Barrientos, a Guaraní leader from the province of Cordillera, was named "Representative of the Indigenous Peoples of the Department to the *CPSC*."[23] Although Barrientos's participation split the Guaraní population and led to charges that he had betrayed his community, he and other indigenous leaders have been attracted to the *CPSC* by the perks that it can offer and by the support it can deliver in political campaigns.[24] After his elevation to the *CPSC* as its top indigenous representative, for example, Barrientos used the committee's support to run for Congress in December 2005 as the candidate of three right-of-center parties.[25]

Strongly objecting to the argument that they have been co-opted, other indigenous members of the *CPSC* insist that they support the committee out of a shared set of beliefs. In the words of one Mojeño indigenous leader within the *CPSC*, "I don't buy the 'happy miscegenation' argument—the conquest was as brutal here as in the highlands. But, unlike the indigenous groups in the *MAS*, I don't want to just 'live well' [*vivir bien*]. We want improvements and progress and a share of the profits that are generated by agriculture in this department."[26] As a reflection of their wooing of lowland indigenous groups, in 2007 *CPSC* leaders agreed to introduce additional articles in their draft autonomy statute that had been demanded by indigenous leaders.[27] More recently, in opposition to Evo Morales's controversial attempt to construct a highway through the lowland *TIPNIS* forest in 2011, four of the five legislators who occupy reserved indigenous seats in the departmental assembly joined the coalition in support of former *CPSC* President and current Santa Cruz Governor Rubén Costas. Ironically, these four indigenous legislators would provide the critical votes that protected Costas from a *MAS*-led attempt in the Santa Cruz department assembly to suspend him from office in 2012.[28] After *TIPNIS* had led the lowland indigenous organization *Confederación de Pueblos Indígenas de Bolivia* (CIDOB) (Confederation of Indigenous Peoples of Bolivia) to withdraw its support for the Morales government, Costas was also able to form an alliance with *CIDOB* leader Adolfo Chávez.

In a more diffuse but also demonstrable fashion, the *CPSC* as the ultimate arbiter of *cruceñidad* (that is, what it means to be *cruceño*) also reached out to

[23] See "Alertan sobre la manipulación de organizaciones indígenas en Santa Cruz," <http://www.derechos.org/nizkor/bolivia/doc/cpesc9.html> (accessed November 1, 2015).

[24] "Pueblo Guaraní se decepciona con Barrientos," *El Mundo*, October 11, 2005, p. 126.

[25] "Dirigente indígena está inscrito como candidato en tres listas," *El Deber*, September 9, 2005.

[26] Interview with a high-level indigenous representative to the *CPSC*, September 6, 2012, Santa Cruz (Interview B19).

[27] Interview with a former Vice President of the *CPSC*, September 6, 2012, Santa Cruz (Interview B20).

[28] Interview with a top official in the Departmental Government of Santa Cruz, September 3, 2012, Santa Cruz (Interview B21).

migrants. Given the considerable flows of migration from the highlands to Santa Cruz, a major challenge for the *CPSC* has been to cultivate the support of migrants who make up ever-larger shares of the department's population (Kirshner 2010; Fabricant and Postero 2013). By 2001, 25 percent of Santa Cruz's population had been born in another department.[29] According to the *CPSC*'s media coordinator, Daniel Castro, the committee made a conscious choice to strike a more inclusive tone by defining *cruceños* as "*vivientes en Santa Cruz*" (those who live in Santa Cruz) rather than "*nacidos en Santa Cruz*" (e.g., those who were born in Santa Cruz). "We support the idea that anybody who lives here now is a *cruceño*. You don't have to be born here to consider yourself *cruceño*."[30] The *CPSC* also liberalized its internal rules; whereas in the past one had to be born in Santa Cruz to serve as the President of the Committee, now it is enough if either parent was born there. More recently, Herland Vaca Diez, the first *CPSC* President who was not a member of an elite lodge and who publicly criticized the lodges, reorganized the committee to include representation of migrants who live in the city's poorest neighborhoods, including Plan 3000.[31]

Two caveats about the *CPSC*'s coalition-building efforts are in order. First, while the *CPSC* engaged in extensive outreach to include previously marginalized actors, it also responded harshly and often violently to discordant voices in the form of organizations and groups who questioned the model that autonomy was meant to protect (Gustafson 2006; Argirakis and Parejas 2009; Pedraza 2011; Peña 2011). One example is the Cáritas Social Pastorate (*Pastoral Social Cáritas* (*PASOC*)), a progressive Catholic organization under the leadership of Father Mauricio Bacardit, who questioned the inequality associated with the Santa Cruz model and organized workshops critical of autonomy in the absence of structural reforms.[32] Conservative Cardinal Julio Terrazas, widely seen as an opponent of Evo Morales and ally of Rubén Costas, banished Bacardit from Santa Cruz in 2008, after which *PASOC* largely disappeared as a political actor.[33] More generally, many individuals who were critical of the *CPSC* experienced what became called "civic death," harassed or shunned on the streets of Santa Cruz and pulled out of cafés and restaurants. In the violence of September and October 2008, much of which was directed by *CPSC* President Branko Marinkovic, it was not just state institutions that

[29] Pastoral Social Cáritas, "La migración interna y externa en Bolivia," documento no. 18, 2005.

[30] Interview with the former Media Coordinator of the *CPSC*, October 27, 2005, Santa Cruz (Interview B22).

[31] Interview B2.

[32] Interview with a high-level official within *PASOC*, October 24, 2005, Santa Cruz (Interview B23).

[33] Interview with a former analyst at the *Centro de Investigación y Promoción del Campesinado* (*CIPCA*) (Center for Research and Promotion of the Peasantry), February 26, 2014, Santa Cruz (Interview B24).

were sacked and burned but progressive organizations such as *CPESC* and *CEJIS* (*Centro de Estudios Jurídicos e Investigación Social*) (Center for Juridical Study and Social Investigation). Second, it is important to note that the decision to broaden its coalition in order to secure autonomy and defend the Santa Cruz model *did* produce backlash within the *CPSC*. Shifting the *CPSC* in a more inclusive direction alienated some of the committee's traditional elite families and financiers, and the *CPSC* snapped back under the control of the lodges in 2013.[34]

Notwithstanding these caveats, the success of the *CPSC* in broadening its coalition can be clearly seen in the consistently massive pro-autonomy activities that it organized between 2004 and 2008, activities that were bankrolled by *CPSC*-affiliated businesses. Of great importance are the two days in June 2004 and January 2005 when hundreds of thousands of *cruceños* answered the call issued by the *CPSC* to demonstrate on behalf of autonomy for Santa Cruz. More than 350,000 people participated in the second of these events, the so-called Second Great Open Town Hall (*Segundo Gran Cabildo Abierto*), which made it Bolivia's largest-ever public demonstration.[35] Subsequent to this second and larger rally in January 2005, the "Agenda of January" came into use as shorthand in Bolivia to describe Santa Cruz's autonomy movement, in contrast to the "Agenda of October" (2003), which refers to the leftist movement that ousted Sánchez de Losada from the presidency in October of 2003 (Chávez 2009). In the period between these two demonstrations, the *CPSC* collected approximately 500,000 signatures in support of a referendum on autonomy and led a civic strike in November 2004 in the attempt to force the national government to hold this referendum, which it agreed to do in July 2006.[36] In addition to protests and strikes, the *CPSC* also unilaterally moved to create a departmental assembly, which was not allowed within Bolivia's constitution, and symbolically declared its own president as governor of Santa Cruz in January 2005.[37] Just as important are the events (including work stoppages, hunger strikes, and demonstrations) that led up to the approval of an illegal referendum on autonomy in Santa Cruz on May 4, 2008, which passed with 86 percent of the vote.

[34] Interview with a consultant in the Secretary of Economic Development in the Departmental Government of Santa Cruz, September 3, 2012, Santa Cruz (Interview B25).

[35] Interview with the former Rector of the Universidad de Aquino, October 27, 2005, Santa Cruz (Interview B26). According to one analyst at *CEJIS*, businesses affiliated with the *CPSC* spent approximately US$400,000 on the production of the Second Great Open Town Hall meeting, including the transport of individuals from the provinces to the city of Santa Cruz. Interview with a research analyst at *CEJIS*, October 27, 2005, Santa Cruz (Interview B27).

[36] Interview with one of the main intellectual architects of the autonomy movement, October 25, 2005, Santa Cruz (Interview B28).

[37] Interview with a high-level official in the Museum and Archives of Santa Cruz, February 24, 2014, Santa Cruz (Interview B29).

Evidence of policy regime juxtaposition

The demand in Santa Cruz for autonomy from the national government was nothing less than a demand to opt out of the historic "process of change" (*proceso de cambio*) that Evo Morales was leading from La Paz, and through which he hoped to "refound" the republic. Considering how important Santa Cruz had become to the national economy by the year 2000, departmental autonomy for Santa Cruz would directly threaten the new president's efforts to replace Bolivia's neoliberal model (which was developed over the course of two decades by five presidents from the three traditional parties) with a different model centered on much more robust action by the state—including vis-à-vis land tenure patterns in the east (Valdivia 2010). In his first years as president, Morales adopted a number of bold, aggressive, and harsh measures against Santa Cruz that speak to the profound nature of this threat posed by the autonomy movement. For instance, in October 2007, Morales imposed a 70 percent cut in the size of revenue-sharing with departments from the new direct tax on hydrocarbons, a measure that produced widespread protests in Santa Cruz coordinated by the *CPSC*. In the wake of his nationalization of hydrocarbons in 2006, which Santa Cruz business chambers interpreted as a major attack on private property and the sanctity of contracts, Morales threatened to nationalize the three Santa Cruz cooperatives (*COTAS*, *CRE*, and *SAGUAPAC*) and complained of the high rates they charge for services. Most sensationally, the national government arrested or drove into exile some thirty civic and business leaders in Santa Cruz charged with financing and directing a plot to overthrow Morales that was led by Eduardo Rozsa, a mercenary who was killed by police operatives in a Santa Cruz hotel in April 2009. Leaders of the autonomy movement saw in these arrests a policy of political persecution against Santa Cruz (Valverde 2012).[38]

But these highly visible critiques and sensational attacks against some of the opposition should not obscure a more fundamental dynamic, which is a series of measures that together ensured the continuity of the Santa Cruz model. First is the introduction of direct elections for departmental prefects (henceforth called governors) in December 2005, a key concession granted by President Carlos Mesa just weeks before he fell from power and in response to the strength of the demands articulated by the *CPSC*. The introduction and subsequent institutionalization of gubernatorial elections meant both that Morales could no longer appoint a prefect who shared his ideological vision, and that the main defender of Santa Cruz's liberal policy regime would now have direct democratic legitimacy. The election of important landowner and

[38] Interview with a Senator from the Department of Santa Cruz, February 28, 2014, Santa Cruz (Interview B30).

former *CPSC* President Rubén Costas as governor in 2005, along with his easy re-election in 2010 and 2015, have made it harder for detractors to dismiss the Santa Cruz model merely as an elitist manipulation. In his decade as governor, Costas has built new partnerships with the cooperatives and focused on infrastructural improvements to facilitate exports by large privately held farms. He also articulated a critique of *asistencialismo*, a word he used to stigmatize the new income transfer programs or *bonos* that were introduced by the Morales government, and claimed that instead his government would offer "seeds not bonds."[39] Though Costas in 2005 sat atop a brand new government, unlike his counterparts in other departments he could draw upon deeper reserves of administrative capacity thanks to Santa Cruz's unique process of institution-building, as already described.

The Bolivian experience suggests that policy regime juxtaposition is indeed furthered by the introduction of subnational elections, particularly after the Constitutional Tribunal ruled in 2013 against the constitutionality of an article in the 2010 Autonomy Law that enabled Morales to suspend governors merely when a prosecutor files charges against them (and before any sentence is emitted). Morales used this article to suspend opposition governors in two eastern departments (Beni and Tarija) and began movements against Costas, in addition to a number of mayors from Costas's party in municipalities across Santa Cruz. That the national government can no longer suspend subnational elected officials so easily is a key development that reinforces the possibility of deviant subnational models.

While the 2005 introduction of elections for governor pre-dated the constitutional revision process (and was ratified by it), the other critical measures that have served to accommodate the Santa Cruz model were introduced in the course of this process, which stretched from the election of constitutional assembly members in July 2006 to the final approval of the constitution in January 2009 (Bohrt 2012). The number of constitutions that Bolivia has written since independence suggests that it is important not to put too much stock into the constitutional protections that were inserted to defend the Santa Cruz model, and yet these victories in the constitutional revision process are nevertheless consequential. After months debating decision rules and a symbolic attempt to move the Bolivian capital to Sucre from La Paz, the *MAS* delegation pushed through a draft of the constitution in December 2007 that denied substantive input from the Santa Cruz opposition, including the possibility of departmental autonomy, which had been approved in the July 2006 referendum in the four lowland departments but not nationwide. When

[39] Interviews in Santa Cruz with a high-level public finance expert in the Department of Santa Cruz, September 5, 2012 (Interview B31); and with a former Secretary of Finance in the Department of Santa Cruz, February 24, 2014 (Interview B32).

the adoption of this December 2007 draft triggered widespread and violent resistance in Santa Cruz, Morales and the *MAS* offered two important institutional concessions as the result of negotiations mediated by Cardinal Julio Terrazas. First the government agreed to the establishment of full-fledged departmental legislatures with lawmaking powers, rather than weaker departmental councils.[40] Henceforth, voters would elect not just departmental chief executives but a departmental legislative branch as well. Looking to the future, several of the top leaders of the autonomy movement emphasized this critical extension of lawmaking authority to the departments.[41] Second, Morales agreed to reinsert bicameralism back into the draft of the constitution that was approved in December 2007. When the *MAS* failed to win a majority in the Senate in 2005, the upper chamber emerged as an important space for the opposition, and its restoration represented an important concession given its ability to block legislation.

But the most important and explicit concessions for the Santa Cruz policy regime were extended only after the violence had worsened in September and October 2008, culminating in a blockade of Santa Cruz by the highland peasant federation (Unified Syndical Confederation of Rural Workers of Bolivia (*Confederación Sindical Única de Trabajdores del Campesinado de Bolivia* (*CSUTCB*))), and *CPSC*-led attacks on a number of state institutions, including police stations and the land reform agency.[42] In the attempt to de-escalate the violence and move beyond the impasse, over 100 changes in the draft constitution were agreed to in a 72-hour period negotiated by a three-person team composed of *MAS* representative Carlos Romero, Senator Carlos Bohrt from Oruro, and Deputy Alejandro Colanzi from Santa Cruz.[43] According to Colanzi's detailed account of the negotiations, three changes were especially critical in protecting Santa Cruz's policy regime.[44] First, the national government agreed to remove language that would have altered Santa Cruz's cooperatives by placing them under "social control" (*control social*), which is a practice through which the *MAS* has sought to democratize a range of political, economic, and social institutions throughout Bolivia (Farthing and Kohl 2010). Arguing that the service cooperativess already have internal oversight mechanisms, Colanzi successfully proposed removing language from Article 54 that would have challenged the cooperative status quo. One high-level *CPSC* official credits Colanzi with thereby "saving Santa

[40] Interviews in La Paz with a former Planning Director (Interview B33), and high-level official in the Indigenous Autonomies Unit (Interview B34) of the Ministry of Autonomies, August 29, 2012, La Paz.

[41] Interviews B4, B16, and B28.

[42] For more on the violence of this period, see Barndt (2012).

[43] For more on these negotiations, see Zegada (2010) and Centellas (2013).

[44] Interviews with a former national deputy representing the department of Santa Cruz, September 1, 2012 and February 7, 2014, Santa Cruz (Interviews B35 and B36).

Cruz's coops."[45] In the words of one Santa Cruz-based journalist, "no coop can survive without the protection of the state because they are monopolies, and as long as elites still control the coops, they will still have the material conditions necessary to maintain their model and their ideology."[46] Although several elite figures in *COTAS* and *CRE* were later arrested in the investigations into the Rozsa plot in 2009, the cooperatives at the heart of the Santa Cruz model have been substantively unaffected by these individual prosecutions.[47] Indeed, Costas as governor has worked closely with *CRE* to expand access to electricity, and *CPSC* President Fernando Castedo has proposed paying for a new private security corporation in Santa Cruz through an additional fee that would be levied on *SAGUAPAC* water bills.[48]

The second important concession granted in October 2008 related to the fundamental question of departmental autonomy, which had been suppressed in the December 2007 draft in favor of indigenous autonomy. Frustration with this draft led Santa Cruz Governor Costas to organize a referendum in May 2008 through which the department's residents expressed their overwhelming support for an autonomy statute that had been drafted by leaders of the autonomy movement, including Juan Carlos Urenda in the lead role.[49] Although Morales criticized the referendum as illegal, and affirmed that he would not recognize the statute when he authorized Cardinal Terrazas to negotiate with Santa Cruz over the summer of 2008, in the end he agreed to recognize the statute so long as it would be adjusted to the new constitution through a process of *adecuación*. One top official in the Autonomy Ministry considers this to be the most significant of the October 2008 concessions,[50] and it was an especially meaningful concession given Carlos Romero's view that "the liberal vision espoused in the autonomy statute was incompatible with the *MAS*'s goal of building a pluri-national state."[51] In the words of a former Minister of Sustainable Development, this compromise "recognized the legitimacy if not the legality of the May 2008 autonomy statute."[52] In

[45] Interview with a former Vice President of the *CPSC*, February 7, 2014, Santa Cruz (Interview B37).

[46] Interview with a journalist and editor of a Santa Cruz-based political magazine, March 5, 2014, Santa Cruz (Interview B38).

[47] Interview B29 and interview with a Santa Cruz investigative journalist and TV personality, January 25, 2014, Santa Cruz (Interview B39). For instance, the prosecutor who accused *COTAS* President Juan Carlos Velarde of letting Rozsa use the *COTAS* booth at the *FEXPOCRUZ* fair clarified that "we're not investigating *COTAS* because those who committed these crimes were individuals; we are not looking into the coops themselves." "Soza cita a tres funcionarios de COTAS," *El Deber*, May 25, 2010.

[48] Interview with a former President of *CPSC*, February 27, 2014, Santa Cruz (Interview B40).

[49] For Urenda's position on autonomy, see Urenda (2003, 2005, 2009).

[50] Interview with a top official in the Ministry of Autonomies, August 28, 2012, La Paz (Interview B41).

[51] "Desafío: Estatutos autonómicos con pactos sociales," *Cambio*, January 16, 2011, p. 11.

[52] Interview with a former Minister of Sustainable Development, August 30, 2012, Santa Cruz (Interview B42).

addition to the recognition of departmental autonomy, Colanzi was able to eliminate language from the December 2007 draft that would have enabled the formation of subdepartmental regional governments, which provoked fears among elites in Santa Cruz that lowland indigenous communities could form their own regional governments within the department, effectively undermining it "from within" (Ayo 2010: 171). Romero conceded that regional bodies could be administrative but not governmental units.[53]

Finally, the third major concession achieved in October 2008 relates back to the central issue described at the beginning of this chapter: agrarian reform and the concentrated landholdings that define Santa Cruz as a department. For many years, the *MAS* had articulated a sharp critique of land tenure patterns in Santa Cruz, including the charge that many large landowners failed to make productive use of their extensive lands (Valdivia 2010). Likewise, it was fear of *MAS*-endorsed land invasions that animated agribusinesses in their aggressive support for autonomy as a means to defend the Santa Cruz model. This background renders all the more remarkable the deal worked out by the three-person negotiating team, which focused on both the size and the applicability of the new constitutional limits on landownership that were endorsed in Oruro in December 2007. According to Colanzi, while Romero maintained that he could not agree to raise the limit from 5,000 to 10,000 hectares, he offered to submit this question to a separate and specific vote in the referendum and, much more importantly, acquiesced to language that would impose these limits only on future land transfers.[54] By agreeing not to apply the new limits retroactively, the structure of landownership in Santa Cruz was effectively preserved (Chumacero 2009: 28). While 85 percent of voters favored the lower limit of 5,000 hectares in the January 2009 referendum that approved the new constitution, non-retroactivity means that agrarian reform in the eastern lowlands, in the words of Gustavo Pedraza, would continue to be "a policy fiction" (*una política ficticia*).[55]

Reconciliation and the Moderation of Bolivia's National Policy Regime

The concessions extracted from the Morales government in the 2005–8 period that have been analyzed in the preceding section served to preserve and defend the core features of Santa Cruz's liberal policy regime, including the non-governmental provision of services, concentrated landholdings under

[53] Interviews with a former Director of Autonomous Development in the Department of Santa Cruz, September 5, 2012 and February 24, 2014, Santa Cruz (Interviews B43 and B44).
[54] Interview B35. [55] Interview B42.

the control of agrarian and agribusiness elites, and an export-driven economic orientation. While the victory of this first type of subnational policy challenge was noteworthy considering Santa Cruz's weight in the national economy, more striking still is the outcome of the challenge posed by Santa Cruz to Bolivia's *national* policy regime as it evolved under *MAS* rule. In contrast to Vice President Alvaro García Linera's claim in 2010 that the national government had defeated the oppositional autonomy movement "electorally, militarily, and politically" in 2008 and 2009, I argue that the reverse is true when it comes to economic models, and that the opposition largely succeeded in moderating the government's preferred, more statist policy stance.[56] While the arrest or exile of leading members of the Santa Cruz opposition made headlines, a deeper policy-based process of territorial reconciliation—initially subtle and hesitant but increasingly explicit and public—unfolded over the course of Morales's second term as president (2009–14). In effect, Santa Cruz compelled Morales to end the historic "*proceso de cambio*" through which he had proposed to transform Bolivia, dramatically shifting his government in a liberal direction. In the discussion in this section, I examine the structural and coalitional factors that forced moderation upon the president, followed by a review of the most significant evidence of this moderation.

Structural leverage in the east

The source of Santa Cruz's structural power lies in the preponderant role it plays as the provider of foodstuffs in Bolivia, a role that was envisioned and promoted during the *MNR* revolution in the 1950s and that would serve to constrain the revolutionary potential of the *MAS* five decades later. By 2006, agricultural and livestock production in Santa Cruz amounted to 45 percent of the national total, followed by just 13 percent for Cochabamba and 12 percent for La Paz (del Río 2012: 127). Edilberto Osinaga, General Manager of the Eastern Agricultural Chamber (*Cámara Agropecuaria del Oriente* or *CAO*), estimated in 2014 that Santa Cruz controlled 53 percent of the country's beef production, 72 percent of wheat, 80 percent of sugar, and 99 percent of soy beans and sunflower seeds, which are used to produce domestic cooking oil.[57]

In its first years in power, the *MAS* government faced the troubling reality that much of this production took place under the control of a small group of large-scale producers who had united behind the *CPSC* against Morales, and who had bankrolled the autonomy movement. In the words of one former

[56] "García: La clave del porvenir son los lazos pueblo-gobierno," *Cambio*, October 7, 2010.

[57] Interview with the former General Manager of the Agricultural Chamber of the East (CAO), February 25, 2014 (Interview B45).

head of the Santa Cruz-based human rights organization *CEJIS*, "Branko Marinkovic (President of the *CPSC*), alone controlled three or four of the items in the basic food basket" (*canasta familiar*, which is used to calculate the cost of living in Bolivia).[58] Although Morales eventually did expropriate Marinkovic's landholdings and drove him into exile for his role in the Rozsa affair, he was unable to alter the underlying, concentrated structure of production in the east.[59] Unlike the regional presidents in Peru discussed in Chapter 3, the source of Santa Cruz's structural power lay not in its ability to disrupt exports, the most important of which are publicly owned in Bolivia and produced in the gas fields of Tarija, not Santa Cruz. Rather, Santa Cruz's oppositional leverage was a function of the supply role it plays internally, which proved to be a much more significant form of leverage.

Bolivia's so-called food emergency between 2008 and 2010 is an important case in point. One of the many ways that Morales hoped to transform Bolivia was through the promotion of food security and sovereignty, not simply through the insertion of these goals into the new constitution, but through the creation of new state-owned enterprises like *Empresa de Apoyo a la Producción de Alimentos* (*EMAPA*) (Company to Support the Production of Foodstuffs), whose twin goals were to stabilize prices and boost agricultural production by small and medium-sized enterprises. Beginning in the aftermath of Morales's tense stand-off with Santa Cruz in 2008, the national government began to impose price controls on goods such as sugar, rice, bread, and cooking oil, in addition to the direct marketing of soybean oil to urban markets through *EMAPA*. Arguing that the supply of the domestic market was his first priority, and that Santa Cruz business-owners were withholding products from the domestic market, Morales in 2009 then imposed a series of restrictions on exports of non-traditional agricultural goods (all such exports except for oil are considered non-traditional in Bolivia). These included quotas on some goods and outright bans on others, in addition to specific permits to export certain items only at the discretion of the national government. According to the Santa Cruz Chamber of Exporters (*Cámara de Exportadores de Santa Cruz* (*CADEX*)), quotas were often perceived to be just as negative as all-out prohibitions, since exporters typically lose their markets abroad if they cannot meet a minimum level of supply in a given year.[60]

Export restrictions and price controls were especially resonant in 2009 because they exacerbated persistent anxiety among the landed elite about the prospects of their continued control of the countryside, notwithstanding the concessions about limits on the size of landholdings that were won in the

[58] Interview with a former head of *CEJIS*, Santa Cruz, February 26, 2014 (Interview B46).
[59] "Branko fuge del país, fiscal pide declararlo en rebeldía," *Cambio*, January 19, 2010.
[60] Interview with a strategic analyst in *CADEX*, February 25, 2014 (Interview B47).

October 2008 constitutional deal. For instance, landowners still worried about constitutional language requiring them to demonstrate the productive use of their land as measured by its social and economic function (*función económica y social* (*FES*)) every three years. Large agribusinesses claimed the *FES* raised questions about their ownership status, and would make it harder to raise commercial bank loans and expand production at a time when the government was using *EMAPA* to promote its rivals (that is, small and medium-sized enterprises). They also worried about a number of land invasions that took place in 2009 amid allegations that workers were placing metal debris on fields to damage tractors, even on productive farms. That same year the liberal Bolivian Institute for Foreign Trade (*Instituto Boliviano de Comercio Exterior*) organized visits by journalists to farms that had been affected in this way, hoping to tap into widespread public opposition to land invasions of productive farms.[61]

In the end, Morales's attempt to promote food security through price controls and export restrictions resulted in food shortages across the country. According to his chief representative in Santa Cruz, Santa Cruz producers who withheld rice, oil, sugar, and meat from the domestic market in 2009 were engaged in a concerted campaign of economic destabilization designed to bring down the government. "When their attempt to overthrow the president through a political coup failed in 2008, the Santa Cruz elite tried to do the same thing in 2009 but through an economic coup."[62] Morales's representative in Santa Cruz claimed that elite control of the media in general, and of two media conglomerates controlled by ranching interests in particular (Red Uno and Unitel, owned by the Monasterio family), was especially critical in creating a sense of panic about food shortages. The shortages were real, however, and they clearly translated into inflation in the price of foodstuffs, despite the efforts of *EMAPA*, which faced a number of logistical and capacity challenges.[63] Confronted with the failure of his attempt to generate food security through statist policies, Morales was forced in 2010 to lift both the price controls and the export restrictions. In hindsight, this was just the first sign of a broader and more proactive process of reconciliation with Santa Cruz, which is discussed in greater detail later in this chapter.

What is striking is the degree to which analysts across the political spectrum, including the private sector, the departmental government, and the NGO community, agree that Santa Cruz producers were able to force Morales to stand down and alter his policy course. According to one business

[61] Interview B45.
[62] Interview with the former Coordinator for the Ministry of Autonomies in Santa Cruz, September 5, 2012, Santa Cruz (Interview B48).
[63] Interview B37.

association leader, "so much of the country depends on Santa Cruz for food that Evo discovered he could not just do whatever he wants here."[64] Likewise, in the words of a public finance expert who analyzes fiscal issues for the departmental government of Santa Cruz, "all of the value added occurs here in Santa Cruz, with the exception of beer and cement in La Paz, and this creates real limits on how far Morales can push us."[65] Finally, as summarized by an analyst in the progressive research institute *Centro de Investigación y Promoción del Campesinado* (*CIPCA*) (Center for Research and Promotion of the Peasantry): "If the price of food increases or there are shortages in Bolivia, El Alto will rise up against Evo, so he's got to keep Santa Cruz happy..."[66]

Building the media luna *coalition*

In addition to Santa Cruz's structural power, another sobering geopolitical reality obliged Morales to step back from the national policy regime he had hoped to build. This constraint took the form of a coalition among opposition governors who were elected in 2005 in Bolivia's four lowland departments: Beni, Pando, Santa Cruz, and Tarija. None of these three other departments can rival Santa Cruz's economic heft, as already described, and combined they represent only approximately one-third of Santa Cruz's population (which is roughly three million). And yet, for a number of reasons, the ability to forge a coalition with opposition governors in these other departments generated an important political advantage in the policy stand-off with the president. Together, the four departments contribute nearly half of the country's GDP and represent nearly two-thirds of its national territory, identified as a *media luna* or half-moon shape that wraps around the highlands to the west. Three of the four (Beni, Pando, and Santa Cruz) are contiguous, with Tarija separated from the others by a narrow band of territory belonging to the (mostly highland) department of Chuquisaca. These factors bolstered the perception that Bolivia between 2005 and 2008 was indeed at a potentially "catastrophic impasse" (*empate catastrófico*), if not on the verge of outright civil war. The strength of the opposition coalition constructed by subnational officials in Bolivia, along with its ability to derail Morales's national project, contrasts sharply with the Ecuadorian case, where Jaime Nebot has stood more or less alone in his struggles with Correa.

A number of factors—structural, political, cultural—facilitated the emergence of a conservative coalition among opposition governors in the lowlands, who essentially wanted to preserve the pro-market status quo against the statist proposals emanating from La Paz. First is the same concentration of

[64] Interview B47. [65] Interview B31. [66] Interview B24.

productive assets in the hands of a small class of landowners who were similarly spared from the redistributive effects of agrarian reform in the 1950s, and who were similarly motivated to defend existing land tenure patterns. Second is the pronounced ethnic diversity, physical isolation, and small population size of lowland indigenous communities in the *media luna* departments, which reduced these groups' electoral voice even as they achieved important organizational successes in the 1990s and 2000s (Albó 2004; Yashar 2005). When gubernatorial elections were introduced in 2005, prominent representatives of the traditional landowning class won these elections in Beni (Ernesto Suárez), Pando (Leopoldo Fernández), and Santa Cruz (Rubén Costas). In addition to their shared class position, all three governors developed strong personal and familial ties with one another.[67] A further similarity that brought the governors together was their common origin in Bolivia's traditional parties, which continued to be able to win offices in the east even as they disappeared in the west. For example, Fernández began his career in Banzer's *ADN*, and Cossio and Suárez belonged to the *MNR*.

Just as important in the construction of this oppositional coalition were the cultural practices and territorial identities shared by those who live in these four departments. Common identities as *cambas* (lowlanders) among the residents of Beni, Pando, and Santa Cruz were especially important; investors from the latter department essentially colonized the two former departments during the rubber room of the nineteenth century, thereby establishing important cultural similarities. In the past, *camba* was used pejoratively by white and mestizo elites as an ethnic term to describe *guaraní*-speaking rural laborers (Gustafson 2006). Over time, however, these elites began to appropriate *camba* cultural forms and to embrace the label *camba* as part of a regionalist discourse that would distinguish the lowlands from the highlands (Plata 2008). *Camba* now signifies a lowlander, in contrast to the *colla* or highland inhabitants of the western departments (Waldmann 2008). This transformation of *camba* from an ethnic to a territorial identifier was fortuitous for the governors, because it meant that residents with distinct ethnic identities and class positions could come together as lowlanders. It also emboldened residents in different jurisdictions to feel that they were part of a larger and shared struggle, one that transcended their specific departmental identities (as *cruceños*, *benianos*, or *pandinos*). It is important to note that residents of non-contiguous Tarija are referred to as *chapacos* and not *cambas*, and that Tarija was not included in the demands for separate statehood for the *camba* nation (*Nación Camba*), which marked the more extreme fringes of the eastern autonomy movement.[68] Nevertheless, in all four lowland

[67] Interview B46. [68] Interview B6.

departments opposition governors were able to play up common fears of domination and invasion by highlanders in the west, now led by the *MAS*.

The notion that lowlanders were under attack helps explain why so many residents of eastern departments—not all of them elites—participated in the various protest activities coordinated by the governors against Morales. These included signature-gathering campaigns on behalf of autonomy, work stoppages and hunger strikes, and demonstrations attended by hundreds of thousands of protesters who together generated an overwhelming sense of polarization in Bolivia. But it is also important to underscore the coordinated nature of these activities, which heightened their political impact. One critical development was the formation by opposition governors of the National Council for Democracy (*Consejo Nacional Democrático* (*CONALDE*)), which enabled them jointly to plan and schedule oppositional activities, including the four autonomy referenda held in May and June 2008, and to negotiate with Morales on a collective rather than a bilateral basis. The rise of *CONALDE* as a coalitional pivot was facilitated by the decline of traditional parties, and by the general weakness of opposition parties that might otherwise have played a more important role piecing this coalition together.

The governors grouped in *CONALDE*, however, could not have implemented their decisions without the help of each department's civic committees. While the civic committees in Beni, Pando, and Tarija were not as powerful as the *CPSC* in Santa Cruz, they too served as central nodes through which functionally and territorially organized groups in each department could be quickly mobilized and coordinated against the national government. Ultimately, the behavior of this oppositional coalition triggered the expulsion of the US ambassador, as well as external intervention in the form of a high-level visit to defuse Bolivia's crisis from the Union of South American Nations (*Unión de Naciones Suramericanas* (*UNASUR*)). In neither Ecuador nor Peru did subnational policy challenges provoke such direct incursion by international actors, a key difference that is largely due to the strength of the coalition constructed among the Bolivian government's subnational challengers.

In arguing for the importance of the *media luna* coalition as a factor that explains policy reconciliation in Bolivia, I do not mean to overstate its coherence or durability. *CONALDE*, for instance, was characterized by internal tension over which governor would lead the organization, with Costas and Cossio jockeying for advantage. More importantly, before it was found to be unconstitutional by the Constitutional Tribunal, Morales used Article 144 of the new constitution to suspend from office both Ernesto Suárez of Beni and Mario Cossio of Tarija, each of whom was replaced by pro-Morales governors (though the opposition later reclaimed the governorship of Beni in fresh elections in 2013). Even more dramatically, the national government arrested Pando Governor Leopoldo Fernández for his role in the massacre of indigenous *MAS* supporters at Porvenir in September 2008. However, just as the arrest of individual civic and business leaders in Santa Cruz in 2009 because of their support for the Rozsa plot failed to shake Santa Cruz's local model, I argue that the coalition formed by opposition governors was critical in forcing moderation upon the national government, even if Morales was subsequently able to remove several of these individuals from office. According to the logic of the dynamic that is explored further in the following section, Morales has pursued a successful divide and conquer strategy, attacking eastern political elites while simultaneously adopting economic policies to satisfy eastern economic elites.

From the "catastrophic impasse" to territorial and ideological reconciliation

From a variety of angles, this section portrays the territorial and ideological reconciliation—between east and west and between advocates of liberal and statist approaches—that took place in Bolivia over the course of the second Morales administration (2009–14). Building on the argument developed in the first half of this chapter, the argument here is that not only did Morales let Santa Cruz's local model stand in 2008, but that he subsequently made a pact with the advocates of this model in ways that shaped the national policy regime. In the words of a former Minister of Sustainable Development, "the *MAS* has signed onto the Santa Cruz model and not the reverse; the result is a liberal economy with an indigenous face [*una economía liberal con rostro indígena*]."[69] Compromise pleased the eastern economic elites who were brought into the pact with Morales, but alienated both the left flank of the *MAS* and the president's hardcore political opponents in Santa Cruz (who continued in their oppositional stance vis-à-vis the president despite his policy moderation). Polarization along a central east–west cleavage in the first decade of the twenty-first century gave way as each of the two sides in the "catastrophic impasse" fractured, and as a new cross-regional alliance emerged to maintain a national policy regime that resembled the neoliberalism of Gonzalo Sánchez de Losada in several key respects. In the words of one eastern politician, "Evo has stolen the liberals' banner."[70]

Policy moderation unfolded along a number of dimensions, not all of which was due to the subnational policy challenge examined here. For example, largely in response to resistance by small-scale mining groups in the highlands, Morales was unable to replace the neoliberal mining law of the 1990s. After the "nationalization" of the oil industry in 2006, which actually preserved an

[69] Interview B42. [70] Interview B35.

important role for the private sector, Morales refrained from other major nationalizations and pledged no new nationalizations at the start of his third term in 2014 (several electricity firms were nationalized in 2010 and 2012). The president stuck to consistently prudent macroeconomic policies and adopted a weak new financial regulation law that angered his progressive base.[71] But it is Morales's policies in the agrarian sector, which caused so much of the earlier anxiety and tension between east and west, where policy moderation can most clearly be attributed to Santa Cruz's subnational policy challenge.

Four agrarian measures adopted since 2009 have been especially important in signaling the fundamental reality of continuity in the countryside. First, in a pointed 2012 speech in Santa Cruz to the *CAO*, Vice President García Linera promised that the government would use force (*la fuerza pública*) to evict invaders, followed by the adoption in 2013 of a harsh anti-invasion law (*Ley contra el avasallamiento*) that established prison sentences of three to five years for land invasions.[72] Second, the government substantially relaxed the rules requiring farms to prove their productivity, shifting the cycle for *FES* reviews from every three to every five years in a concession that was particularly important for cattle ranchers given their extensive use of land. At the time of writing (2016), no landowners have suffered land redistribution for failure to prove *FES*.[73] Third, in a subversion of the 2009 referendum setting the upper limit of landownership at 5,000 hectares, the government unilaterally raised this limit to 8,000 hectares.[74] Finally, Morales decided not to tighten the state's control over the illegal clearing of forests (*desmontes*) in the lowlands, a widespread practice that has contributed to the concentration of landownership. Instead, through the 2013 *Ley de desmonte*, he offered an amnesty to farmers (*perdonazo agropecuario*) in the hopes of further extending the agricultural frontier.[75] While interviews in 2012 and 2014 with an array of business leaders uncovered a number of complaints about red tape and the difficulty of getting credit, the harsh policy critiques of earlier years were far less common. Instead, often using the same language, most of them admitted that Santa Cruz's agribusinesses are making "more money under Evo than they ever did under Goni [Sánchez de Losada]."[76]

In addition to critical policy adjustments, infrastructure projects or the lack thereof also point to victory for economic elites in Santa Cruz. Most importantly, the government agreed to meet the historic demand by Santa Cruz agribusinesses for investments to improve two external river ports (Puerto Suárez and Puerto Busch) through which agricultural exports pass to Brazil.

[71] Interview with a former Director of *CEJIS*, February 6, 2014, Santa Cruz (Interview B49).
[72] "Según el Vice, avanzan leyes de producción," *El Deber*, September 1, 2012.
[73] Interviews B46 and B49. [74] Interview B36.
[75] "Ley de desmonte busca la expansión del área agrícola," *El Día*, May 8, 2013.
[76] Interviews B45 and B47.

Existing agribusinesses will benefit disproportionately from these investments. In the area of infrastructure, it is also important to note that economic interests in Santa Cruz have benefited from the collapse of another major infrastructure project, which was the government's intended highway through the *TIPNIS* reserve in Beni. Morales did not abandon this project to please Santa Cruz agribusinesses, and it is not therefore an example of reconciliation; instead advocates of the highway in the national government alleged that Santa Cruz businesses were financing the protests by lowland indigenous groups that led to the suspension of the project. Without the highway, agricultural products from Beni must pass through Santa Cruz in transit to the highlands; the highway would have threatened Santa Cruz by providing a direct route from Beni to Cochabamba, bypassing Santa Cruz.

Beyond the significance of the policy adjustments and infrastructure projects that Morales offered to his former ideological enemies in Santa Cruz is the significance of the venues in which these changes were negotiated. In the aftermath of the violence in Santa Cruz in late 2008 and early 2009, and as one of the first steps toward reconciliation, Morales's vice president used a press conference to issue what sounded like an admonition at the time, but which in hindsight could also be taken as an invitation. Here García Linera explicitly told *cruceño* economic elites to "get out of politics and just focus on their businesses."[77] After individual appearances in 2010 and 2011 by García Linera and other high-level government officials in Santa Cruz, eastern business chambers decided to participate in formal conversations with the national government in January 2012 in Cochabamba in an event designed to negotiate a "Great National Accord" (*Gran Acuerdo Nacional*). One noteworthy aspect of this event, according to Gisela López, is that *cruceño* business chambers actively participated in the thematic workshops while Santa Cruz Governor Costas boycotted the event.[78] The next sign of this increasingly public rapprochement was the "summit" (*cumbre*) on July 11, 2013 that took place between representatives of national ministries and *CAINCO*, *CAO*, and *CADEX*. But by far the most symbolically important development involved Santa Cruz's most important annual event every September, the *Feria Exposición de Santa Cruz* (*FEXPOCRUZ*), a hybrid trade fair and civic festival that showcases the department's economic strengths. After years of either being uninvited or failing to attend, García Linera attended in 2012, and Morales himself attended in 2013.[79] More recently, Morales presided over a meeting of

[77] "Alvaro García Linera advierte a medios y empresarios que no hagan política," *El Diario*, November 30, 2009.

[78] Interview B48.

[79] "Discurso del Presidente Morales en la inauguración de la Feria Internacional de Santa Cruz," September 20, 2013, Ministerio de Comunicación.

the international G77 conference in Santa Cruz in 2014, a crowning moment in his reconciliation with the east.

Evidence of reconciliation can also be seen in the evolution of the views of one particularly influential *cruceño* businessman, Gabriel Dabdoub, who has served in a variety of high-level positions in the "*institucionalidad cruceña*" (including President of *CAINCO* and President of *FEPB-SC*). Dabdoub was one of the most important business leaders advocating for autonomy from the national government after the fall of Sánchez de Losada in 2003. At that time, Dabdoub expressed fears about the restrictions on private property that would probably come out of *MAS* demands for a new constitution, worried about the underrepresentation of Santa Cruz in a constituent assembly, and explained that Santa Cruz would need substantial fiscal and policymaking autonomy from La Paz in order to continue to prosper under a Morales government.[80] Under Dabdoub's leadership, *CAINCO* provided critical support for the opposition rallies against Morales between 2005 and 2008, and in 2010 its then President (Eduardo Paz) was detained for his alleged involvement in the Rozsa affair.[81] By 2014, however, the year following his historic invitation to Morales to speak at the *FEXPOCRUZ*, Dabdoub's views of the national government were much more benign than his views of the departmental government under Costas, which he criticized for accomplishing little in office, and of the *CPSC*, which he criticized for imposing rather than negotiating the content of the autonomy statute approved back in 2008.[82]

Dabdoub's distancing from the *CPSC* is part of a much larger pattern according to which the pursuit of an economic partnership with Morales under the aegis of an essentially liberal model has led many *cruceño* business leaders to abandon the *CPSC*. Under the leadership of Branko Marinkovic, the *CPSC* played a key role in coordinating the violence of September and October 2008; although many moderate voices within the committee disagreed with Marinkovic's more radical, separatist stance, its association with violence has discredited the *CPSC* to a significant degree and many *CPSC* members face legal problems over their involvement in the Rozsa plot (Peña 2011). Interviews with high-level officials in the *CPSC* in 2012 and 2014 revealed a deep sense of abandonment by the department's business interests, both in the sense that they no longer attend *CPSC* events and that they no longer fund the committee's operations. One official complained that the younger generation of economic elites in Santa Cruz "are neoliberals interested merely in making

[80] Interviews in *CAINCO* with an economic advisor (Interview B50) and legal analyst (Interview B51), October 26, 2005, Santa Cruz.

[81] "Retienen sin arraigo al presidente de CAINCO," *El Deber*, March 11, 2010.

[82] Interview with a high-level official in the Federation of Private Businessmen of Santa Cruz, February 26, 2014, Santa Cruz (Interview B52).

money and are not motivated to defend their identities as *cruceños*."[83] Another complained that businesses, seeking to partner with and not alienate the national government, refused to support *CPSC* plans for a major protest in 2013 over the claim that national census procedures had damaged Santa Cruz's interests. "We simply couldn't pull it off without business support."[84]

The key point is that reconciliation between the national government and Santa Cruz business elites, who care more about economic policy than politics, has driven a wedge between these elites and the more purely political or civic leaders with whom they used to share control over the autonomy movement. Morales' continued antagonism toward civic leaders in the *CPSC*—even as he has reconciled with economic leaders in Santa Cruz—points to a fundamental irony: the very body that built the Santa Cruz model now feels cast aside by the operators of that model.[85]

Finally, perhaps one of the most telling signs of policy moderation can be seen in the results of a set of elections that took place in Bolivia in 2014 and 2015. In the 2005 and 2009 presidential elections, Evo Morales won landslide victories at the national level, but was defeated in Santa Cruz by more conservative candidates: Jorge Quiroga in 2005 and Manfred Reyes Villa in 2009. But when Morales decided, at the end of the process of reconciliation with Santa Cruz that is described above, to run for a third term in 2014, he finally emerged victorious, winning 49 percent of the vote in the department and defeating the conservative Samuel Doria Medina by more than 10 percentage points.[86] Six months later, Rubén Costas also coasted to his third term by receiving more than double the vote received by the *MAS* candidate, his closest competitor for governor of Santa Cruz (60 percent to 31 percent).[87] In December 2005, the simultaneous election of Morales and Costas pointed toward the coming battle that would take place between advocates of two very different economic agendas and ideologies. Nearly a decade later, Costas's re-election in the wake of Morales's historic victory in Santa Cruz pointed toward something very different—namely, the end of Bolivia's cycle of polarization and the consolidation of a new period of territorial and ideological reconciliation.

[83] Interview B2. [84] Interview B40.

[85] Another major exception to reconciliation, in addition to the *CPSC*, is the Catholic Church, whose Cardinal Julio Terrazas has continued to confront Morales. Interview with the former Assistant Director of *PASOC*, September 4, 2012, Santa Cruz (Interview B53).

[86] For more on the *MAS*'s growing strength in Santa Cruz, see Vergara 2011.

[87] In the 2015 subnational elections, Santa Cruz Mayor Percy Fernández also won re-election. Though once Costas's ally in the autonomy movement, Fernández subsequently forged an alliance with *MAS* deputies on the Santa Cruz city council in order to secure a two-thirds majority to protect himself from corruption charges. Morales called him the "best mayor in Bolivia" on the campaign trail in 2014. Interviews in Santa Cruz with a former President of the Municipal Council in the City of Santa Cruz, February 27, 2104 (Interview B54); and with a *MAS*-affiliated municipal councilor, February 6, 2014, Santa Cruz (Interview B55).

Conclusion

Bolivia in recent years has undeniably experienced a historic set of transformations. These include the collapse of the traditional party system and the emergence of the *MAS*, a hegemonic governing party, three landslide electoral victories for the country's first indigenous president, and a new constitution that among other departures makes it possible for indigenous communities to petition for autonomy and self-governance. In the field of political economy, however, one can see important examples of continuity rather than change. Although Evo Morales's *MAS* was forged in the struggle against neoliberalism, and, although its rise to power led most observers to predict a pronounced shift from market-centered to statist economic policies, the reality is that no wholesale substitution of one national policy regime with another actually occurred.

In this chapter, I have argued that this important outcome cannot be understood without reference to two distinct subnational policy challenges posed by Bolivia's most economically dynamic department. Prompted in part by the 1952 Revolution and in part by centuries of isolation and underdevelopment, economic elites in Santa Cruz designed and invested in quasi-public local institutions that over time incubated a distinctly liberal policy regime. When this regime seemed threatened by the rise to power of the *MAS*, those elites then engaged in a bold and successful process of defensive coalition-building. Rather than initiate a new era of policy regime juxtaposition, in which liberalism would be confined to Santa Cruz while the national government embarked on a heavily statist project, in fact the erstwhile Santa Cruz opposition pulled the *MAS* strongly toward its preferred policies. Neoliberalism may have been the spark that ignited Morales's movement, but Santa Cruz's structural power in the national economy combined with the breadth of the coalition formed by opposition governors were ultimately enough to prevent its replacement.

6

Conclusion

This book began with the observation that the relationship between ideology and territory has become increasingly complicated and contentious. Over the past several decades, subnational territories have been emboldened by the cumulative effects of globalization, democratization, and decentralization. As the nation state has become a less dominant unit in the international state system, some of the authority shed by national governments has been taken up by subnational governments. The pressures created by these large macro-processes have encouraged leaders at the subnational level to strike much more aggressive postures vis-à-vis the ideological struggles over the market that are taking place within their countries. In this way, conflicts over economic development models that are not at all new have become progressively more territorialized. Rather than being mere observers of, or pawns in, these struggles, subnational leaders such as mayors and governors are now much more appropriately conceptualized as active participants. Transformed into principals in their own right rather than mere agents of the center, elected subnational officials now have direct sources of democratic legitimacy and forms of authority that are often sufficient to galvanize and sustain policy challenges from below.

Subnational officials may succeed or fail in these challenges—which is the central outcome this book has sought to explain—but there are good reasons to anticipate that their challenges will only become more frequent in the years to come. This is especially important because there are also good reasons to debate whether the greater territorial friction and dissonance that result from these challenges are positive or negative for a host of outcomes that matter dearly to citizens and social scientists alike. On the one hand, growing territorial heterogeneity in the pursuit of economic development models might dampen destabilizing policy swings, promote pragmatic convergence between models, and expand the range of meaningful policy choices for voters. On the other hand, territorial heterogeneity probably raises transaction costs for economic actors, creates a much less harmonized policy environment, and can generate nearly constant—rather than mostly episodic—conflict over economic development models between ideological combatants.

The book has sought to demonstrate that conceptualizing and theorizing this phenomenon requires more fully integrating the literature on multilevel governance with the literature on economic development. For example, scholars working in the literature on multilevel governance will need to go substantially beyond the study of decentralization and federalism to ask whether and why subnational officials are able to use their newfound powers in ways that reflect ideological commitments vis-à-vis the market. As the focus shifts from the study of the causes of decentralization to its consequences, one of the most transformative consequences is the tendency of decentralization to draw mayors and governors into ongoing debates over the appropriate roles for state and market. For the literature on economic development, successfully grappling with this phenomenon means abandoning views that have privileged the national arena and overlooked subnational governments as relevant sites for ideological struggles and policy conflicts. It also means taking seriously the specifically subnational expression of economic models such as statism and neoliberalism, and doing the work of documenting the opportunities and challenges associated with these models when they are deployed at subnational rather than national levels.

In addition to examining how territorial actors such as mayors and governors are shaping ideological conflicts, which is the direction of the causal relationship explored in this book, it is also becoming more important to examine causal patterns in the opposite direction by asking how ideological conflict can in turn shape territorial outcomes—including, most importantly, the territorial distribution of power within countries. In recognition of the multidirectional nature of the relationship between ideology and territory, this final chapter concludes the book with two related exercises. In the first half of the chapter, I review my argument that structural, institutional, and coalitional variables can help explain whether subnational officials are able to advance successful subnational policy challenges, and I assess the more general theoretical implications of my findings about each of these three variables. In the second half of the chapter, I reverse the focus by exploring how ideological conflict over the market also shapes territorial outcomes; most significantly, it has produced identifiable shifts in the distribution of authority and resources between levels of government. As national governments recognize the growing import of the type of policy challenges that are examined in this book, one increasingly prominent response is to adopt and implement a range of recentralizing measures in the attempt to undercut those challengers. In other words, just as decentralization set the stage for subnational policy challenges, the strength of those challenges has in turn set in motion various forms of recentralization. We may still live in an "age of decentralization"

(Snyder 2001), but the serious policy challenges that resulted logically from decentralization have nevertheless encouraged new and important attempts by the center to reassert itself.

Key Implications about Structure, Capacity, and Coalitions

My core argument is that subnational officials need structural leverage, institutional capacity, and broad coalitions if they are to wage successful policy challenges vis-à-vis the center. At the same time, the relative importance of these three ingredients is not constant across the two main types of subnational policy challenges that I conceptualize and study in this book. In order to create viable and coherent subnational policy regimes (challenge no. 1), elected officials must be able to draw upon significant levels of administrative capacity, and they must be able subsequently to broaden coalitions within their districts in order to sustain these regimes when confronted with aggression from the center. In contrast, when subnational elected officials seek to transform the national policy regime (challenge no. 2), what matters more is the structural significance of the subnational regions they govern, along with their ability to extend support coalitions beyond their home regions to include sympathetic peers who preside over other subnational jurisdictions.

Guided by this theoretical framework, the empirical chapters have remained tightly focused on the structural, institutional, and coalitional resources that are available (or not) to subnational officials in their conflicts with the center. While I have consciously privileged the subnational over the national, the empirical chapters are also loaded with evidence that presidents themselves believe these three types of subnational resources to be of paramount importance. This is why they have actively sought to weaken the structural significance of key subnational regions, to sabotage subnational capacity-building efforts, and to contest and disrupt the strategies subnational officials have used to widen both internal and external coalitions. Chapters 3–5 show that this three-part theoretical framework helps explain critical outcomes in each of my three cases: the remarkable persistence of neoliberalism in Peru despite widespread and often violent subnational opposition, the equally momentous moderation of Evo Morales's initially radical vision for the transformation of Bolivia, and the dramatic policy regime juxtaposition that has developed and persisted for the decade beginning in 2006 in Ecuador.

Starting with structure, one of the main implications of my argument about a region's structural significance is that some countries in the years to come are likely to experience much more powerful subnational policy challenges than others—at least with respect to challenges against the national policy regime where structure matters most. This is because the distribution of structural power across subnational regions varies considerably from one country to the next, even among countries that are otherwise similar in terms of territorial extension, demographic size, or levels of economic development. In some countries, economic activity is highly concentrated in and around national capital regions, often as the result of earlier policies of state-led industrialization but also because of exogenous factors like topography, while other countries are characterized by bipolarity or multipolarity in terms of the number and type of economically significant subnational regions (World Bank 2009; Soifer 2015). As a region, Latin America contains both types of countries; Argentina, Chile, Peru, and Uruguay are classic examples of the former type, while Bolivia, Brazil, Colombia, and Ecuador are salient examples of the latter type. My claim is that this latter type is more likely to enable effective challenges by subnational officials who govern regions that cannot easily be ignored by the center. Simply put, the territorial concentration or dispersion of economic activity sets the parameters within which subnational policy challenges unfold.

A subnational region's structural power emerges from multiple sources—in contrast to the structural power of business, which can typically be attributed to its underlying and fundamental control over capital (Lindblom 1977; Vogel 1987). One important distinction can be seen in the difference between threats of disinvestment and threats of disruption as two key sources of the leverage that subnational officials can wield as a result of their structural positions. According to the former, subnational officials can ally and coordinate with regional economic elites to threaten to withhold investment in the attempt to force the center to cooperate and/or compromise. According to the latter, subnational officials can use the powers of their offices in the attempt to block investment by others, including investments by both private-sector actors outside the region and public-sector investments by the center. While subnational officials can pose both types of threats, my research suggests that it is the threat of disinvestment rather than disruption that generates greater structural power for a subnational region. This is because threats of disruption are often quite time-bound and impermanent, working temporarily to halt investment projects without necessarily forcing change in underlying policies. In Peru, regional presidents have used their structural positions to lead, finance, and coordinate protests against private mining projects. While they have often been able to suspend major projects for varying lengths of time, in no case have they managed to extract substantive changes in the policies that promoted these projects. In Bolivia, in contrast, the disinvestment threat from Santa Cruz, and the fears of inflation in critical foodstuffs that it provoked in the national government, led the president to offer substantively and symbolically important policy concessions.

On the one hand, it may be safe to assume that the structural significance of a subnational region is best understood as a mostly exogenous factor, unlikely to change rapidly and thus typically beyond the control of elected incumbents at the national and subnational level who are chiefly focused on winning the next election. On the other hand, where elected officials are able to win re-election and thereby extend their time horizons, structural variables might not entirely escape the control of incumbent politicians and instead become endogenous to the behavior of these politicians. Agency can be said to shape structure. The Ecuadorian case here is especially instructive, where President Rafael Correa could and did respond to the aggressive opposition he encountered in the city of Guayaquil and in the province of Guayas by systematically favoring other coastal provinces and cities over the course of his decade in power. As a measure of how badly he wanted to defeat the neoliberal opposition in Guayaquil, Correa promoted a number of expensive (and in some cases technically questionable) infrastructure projects in politically compliant regions in order to limit the disruptive power enjoyed by Guayaquil—even at the cost of dramatically deepening the country's dependence on investment flows from China. In contrast to Ecuador, presidents in Bolivia and Peru were more highly circumscribed and less able to manipulate structural realities. The national government in Bolivia could not quickly sponsor agricultural production in compliant regions to respond to the supply threat from the eastern lowland departments, whose lands are by far the most apt for large-scale agribusiness production. In Peru, the overwhelming importance of mineral wealth and the desire to advance specific high-value mining projects in specific subnational regions has likewise forced the center to deal with the specific regional presidents who govern these regions (though, unlike Bolivia, they have been able to do so through a mixture of repression and co-optation rather than policy accommodation).

To turn from structure to capacity, the case studies generate three main insights for the growing literature on state-building, particularly as it finally begins to pay more attention to why and how state capacity varies within countries and not just across countries (Ziblatt 2008; Harbers 2015; Pribble 2015). At first blush, the country cases appear to generate contradictory findings with respect to the role of the private sector as a force that can either promote or hinder capacity-building and state formation. For Bolivia and Ecuador, I have argued that private-sector elites took the lead in designing and running local institutions and in contributing to the accrual of local institutional capacity over time—capacity that was ultimately subsumed in part into the subnational state, and that eventually helps explain how subnational governments were able to defend discordant subnational models. The argument is not that private-sector elites intentionally contributed to state capacity, but rather that their initial control over these originally quasi-public institutions encouraged them to invest heavily in administrative capacity that would later redound to the benefit of subnational state administrations. In contrast, for Peru I have emphasized the overwhelmingly negative role played by the private sector in the form of transnational mining companies that have undermined state capacity by taking on roles in service provision that directly and indirectly displace subnational governments. Together, the three cases point to the importance not only of distinguishing between domestic and foreign owners of capital, but further of disaggregating the former category to appreciate the particular preferences of private-sector elites who have regional (subnational) identities, locations, and commitments. Foreign and domestic capital-owners alike often face weak incentives to invest in state capacity because they fear states that are strong enough to tax, regulate, and/or expropriate them, and therefore generally resist state-building efforts. Regionalized economic elites, however, may have greater cause to invest in institutional capacity, particularly if it can be limited to those subnational regions in which they have great influence.

Second, if the book points to the private sector as a possible source of state-building, and to economic elites as the unlikely and unsung heroes of state formation in certain contexts, it also points, equally ironically, to the negative role that the state itself can play vis-à-vis state formation. Considering the more important roles subnational governments are now called on to play, the literature on decentralization has highlighted the deficient capacity of these governments as one of the greatest governance challenges of the century (Oxhorn, Tulchin, and Selee 2004; Eaton, Kaiser and Smoke 2010). To date, this literature has focused on two core problems: how to create capacity where none exists, and how to transfer it from one level of government to another. The problem, unfortunately, is even worse when we consider the lessons of the Peruvian case, where the national government has adopted a series of behaviors that have derailed and circumvented capacity-building efforts at the local level. Whether under the aegis of the "Voluntary Contributions" program of President García, or the "Works for Taxes" approach of President Humala, the national government has empowered corporate actors to play the kinds of governance roles that are typically assigned to subnational governments in representative democracies. Under the former, mining companies were allowed unilaterally to decide what kinds of goods and services they wanted to provide with little or no consultation with local governments. The latter program formalized and extended this dynamic by letting companies deduct the costs of these goods and services from their tax bill, further harming subnational governments. Going forward, efforts by practitioners and donors to deepen local capacity should refrain from assuming either the goodwill or the neutrality of the center, recognizing instead that the problem is not simply that the national government is indifferent to subnational capacity-building, or that it is technically and/or politically difficult to transfer extant capacity, but that the center may face incentives actively to undermine capacity in order to forestall subnational policy challenges.

Third, the analysis points to important asymmetries between subnational statism and subnational neoliberalism when it comes to capacity. If insufficient subnational state capacity deserves to be considered a key constraint on those mayors and governors who are seeking to challenge the center, this is probably a bigger problem for subnational officials who favor state-centered rather than market-centered approaches. Subnational statism requires higher levels of state capacity, and, if capacity is in short supply generally, this may mean that the deck is stacked against this type of subnational policy regime and in favor of more neoliberal approaches (Geddes and Sullivan 2012; Leopold and McDonald 2012). Consider the following thought exercise. While the institutions built up over time by economic elites in Guayaquil and Santa Cruz were effective at sustaining and supporting the liberal policy regime that emerged in both spaces, it is not necessarily the case that these institutions would suffice if a different, more state-centered model were now to emerge in these two subnational regions. What is clear is that, when liberal economic elites take the lead in building subnational state capacity, they contribute to the construction of a subnational state that does certain things better than others. As the literature on state capacity shifts from explaining national-level variation to within-country variation in the capacity of the subnational state, we need to learn much more about how different levels and types of subnational capacity open up or foreclose state-centered approaches. Using the language of Corrales (2003), what does the relationship between stateness and statism look like at the subnational level?

The final component of the theoretical framework—coalitional dynamics—is the most important in the sense that coalitions are critical for both types of subnational policy challenges. What I call the coalitional imperative reflects the profound disadvantages that face subnational chief executives when they dare to challenge the president, whose position at the pinnacle of the state and at the center of power gives him or her tremendous leverage. Even in structurally significant subnational territories, whose policy challenges the center cannot easily ignore, these are often struggles of David versus Goliath. Extending the metaphor, Goliath can indeed lose, but only if David has lots of local followers and is able to join forces with other Davids. The scope of the requisite coalition, along with how subnational officials can build these coalitions, depends on the type of challenge in play. Defending a deviant model in a given subnational district requires the construction of a defensive coalition internal to that district, and my research shows that officials can use both material and discursive strategies to broaden these coalitions. In contrast, external coalitions that transcend any one subnational district are necessary in order successfully to challenge the national model—coalitions that are exceedingly difficult to construct and maintain, but that can be easier for subnational chief executives to build when they, as in the Bolivian case, govern in territorially contiguous regions.

I argue that one of the most effective ways that subnational officials can broaden their internal coalitions, and therefore make it costlier for the center to respond with aggression, is to deploy rhetorical and discursive strategies that portray their ideological conflicts with the national government as fundamentally territorial conflicts. My research in Bolivia and Ecuador suggests that these strategies are particularly appealing to subnational officials on the right of the political spectrum as they seek to defend market-oriented models, whose content typically finds more support among local elites and less support among local residents who are not elites. If non-elite residents in subnational districts decide that they actually have more to gain from the state-centered approaches articulated by the center, then the mayors and governors who are seeking to defend neoliberal approaches face real trouble. Seeking to shift the terms of the debate from the class-centric frame preferred by the center, subnational neoliberals can try to embrace instead a territorial frame in the attempt to draw many more local residents—independent of their class positions—into their struggle against the center. While playing the territorial card in this fashion may thus be especially appealing for subnational officials with neoliberal as opposed to statist preferences, the strategy may not be widely available. In Guayaquil and Santa Cruz, Jaime Nebot and Rubén Costas were indeed able to widen their coalitions by tapping into long-standing grievances about the perceived neglect of the center, but their counterparts in other countries may not have similar historical legacies to activate and manipulate. Though potentially quite effective, these territorial strategies can also be dangerous considering the violence that resulted in the Bolivian case from high levels of territorial polarization.

By emphasizing the importance of coalitions, I face the same thorny questions that bedevil all coalitional analysts: how do coalitions come together, what is the exact role of leadership in the construction of coalitional arrangements, and how much does the maintenance of these coalitions depend on the continued presence of the actors who initially stitched them together? On the one hand, coalition-builders cannot construct coalitions out of thin air, and I have emphasized here the importance of the presence or absence of societal beneficiaries such as business groups and labor unions as key constraints on coalition-building (Gourevitch 1986; Schamis 1999). On this score, subnational officials on the left in Peru were seriously disadvantaged relative to their counterparts in Bolivia and Ecuador on the right, who had much more to work with in terms of the constituent elements available for the type of coalitions they needed to build. On the other hand, subnational leaders and the particular leadership talents they can bring to bear do loom large in the successful coalition-building that took place in Bolivia and Ecuador. The neoliberal models that Mayor Jaime Nebot and Governor Rubén Costas sought to defend pre-dated the rise of these two politicians by many decades—by over a century in the case of Guayaquil—and the viability of the models can by no means be reduced to these two individuals. And yet it would be a mistake to understate the critical roles played by each individual leader, whose multiple re-elections have been positive for the persistence of their preferred models, even as they have been subjected to widespread charges of personalism and *caudillismo*.

The Impact of Ideological Conflict on the Territorial Distribution of Power

This book has focused on how territorial actors such as mayors and governors are increasingly shaping the outcomes of ideological conflict over the market. Though derived from the close study of three countries in the central Andes over the past decade, the theoretical argument developed here should help illuminate the prospects for subnational policy challenges in other parts of the world and in other time periods. If my argument is valid beyond these three cases, the general claims I have made about structure, capacity, and coalitions should find empirical support in these other contexts. Empirical research on policy challenges by subnational governments in other parts of Latin America—as well as in other world regions—would help further to refine the core hypotheses I have derived from my Andean cases, and would probably lead to the formulation of additional hypotheses about this important phenomenon. What we need is a more robust theoretical debate about the territorialization of ideological conflict; there is a lot to learn about why, how, and to what effect subnational governments are challenging the policy preferences of national governments.

But perhaps the best way to conclude the book is to point toward a different and equally important research agenda going forward, which is to ask the opposite question: not how territory shapes ideology, but rather how ideological conflicts over the market are in turn shaping territorial outcomes. More specifically, how are struggles between advocates of different economic ideologies affecting the distribution of power between levels of government? Whereas the theoretical framework developed and assessed in this book privileged subnational chief executives, in this closing section I shift the focus back toward national chief executives. Whether the president is seeking to defend a neoliberal or a statist model from subnational challengers, one of the best strategies at his or her disposal is to pursue recentralizing changes that undercut these challengers. Furthermore, although I have argued throughout this book that decentralization cannot be assumed automatically to translate into successful subnational policy challenges (and that this outcome is better explained as the result of structural, institutional, and coalitional factors), it does make sense to argue that recentralization—should it succeed—would probably impose real limits on these challenges in the future.

In this closing section, I briefly review the multifaceted nature of current strategies by national governments to recentralize in response to the policy threats that they are now facing more frequently from below. I then give representative examples of these strategies from each of my three cases in order to illustrate how ideological conflict in Peru, Ecuador, and Bolivia has in fact culminated in significant efforts by national governments to recentralize authority and resources. The goal is to show that ideological conflict shapes territorial outcomes just as certainly as territorial conflict shapes ideological outcomes; the relationship between ideology and territory is indeed an increasingly complex one. According to the core dilemma identified in this section, national governments can deploy a surprisingly wide range of territorial options as they seek to undercut policy challenges; across the ideological spectrum presidents in post-decentralization Latin America have tried to defend their policy preferences through a dizzying array of recentralizing measures. But they cannot do so without running the risk of alienating citizens in subnational territories, and thereby strengthening the two kinds of coalitions that subnational politicians try to build in order to defend their own preferred approaches. In other words, the center can deploy numerous methods in the attempt to recenter politics, but my theory anticipates that these methods can also backfire and play into the hands of subnational challengers.

As national governments in the wake of decentralization have encountered increasingly powerful challenges from subnational officials, they have become more proactive, bold, and creative in designing and pursuing a host of strategies to recentralize power. Some of these strategies are symmetrical in the sense that they treat all subnational governments alike irrespective of who governs them or how much of a challenge they pose; others are focused asymmetrically on challengers alone. Likewise, it is important to note that not all these strategies have been adopted with the sole purpose of undercutting ideological challenges; instead, national leaders may try to recentralize for a variety of reasons. However, recentralization in a number of areas can certainly boost the position of the national government as it seeks to fend off policy challenges from below. In addition to seeking formally to reverse earlier policies of decentralization, national leaders can pursue many other (often less visible and controversial) strategies that have the effect of shifting power back to the center and undercutting subnational challengers.

Consider the following four types of strategies to recenter power (policy -based, bureaucratic, institutional, and societal) that have become increasingly common in post-decentralization Latin America (Dickovick 2011; Dickovick and Eaton 2013; Eaton 2013). First, national governments can experiment with new policy innovations like conditional cash transfer programs that have the effect of dramatically increasing the prominence and protagonism of the center in policy fields (like social policy) that have been officially decentralized. Second, presidents can use their tremendous power over the bureaucracy to challenge the independent behavior of subnational officials. Most importantly, they can suppress or sideline bureaucratic organizations that give voice to subnational governments, and they can prioritize deconcentration over devolution; whereas the latter transfers control to subnational governments, the former shifts authority to bureaucrats who may be located in subnational territories but who remain under the control of the center. The third type of strategy is institutional, including the use of national institutions like electoral courts to influence the outcome of subnational elections and even suspend subnational candidates and incumbents. Fourth, presidents can adopt societal strategies, allying with and promoting the work of subnational civil society actors whose ideological preferences align with the national government rather than with the government of the subnational district where they are located. Despite their subnational identities, these societal allies under certain conditions may favor recentralization as the best way to secure their policy preferences.

Since the start of the new century, evidence of the pursuit of these different strategies can be seen across the central Andes, beginning in Peru, where a series of presidents have pursued territorial strategies that undermine neoliberalism's subnational opponents. For example, in 2007 President García eliminated the only organization (the National Council of Decentralization (*Consejo Nacional de Descentralización* (*CND*)) that formally represented the interests of subnational governments in Lima; its disappearance has reduced the leverage of oppositional regional presidents and impeded their coalition-building efforts. García's successor as president, Ollanta Humala, introduced rule changes that divert revenues from subnational governments, reducing the fiscal resources that could otherwise be used to subsidize local challenges. From Fujimori on, presidents have appointed finance ministers whose liberal commitment to limited government has taken the form of a full-throated defense of Peru's national accounting system (National System of Public Investment or *Sistema Nacional de Inversión Pública* (*SNIP*)), which sharply limits the ability of subnational officials to use public monies from the canon system that are legally theirs to invest. More recently, the national government launched investigations into allegations of corruption against nineteen of twenty-five regional presidents in 2014; while corruption is a real problem at subnational and national levels alike, Lima has clearly put the regions on notice that there are limits to how much they can challenge the center. That corruption charges are in many cases well founded has hindered the emergence of local societal coalitions to defend impugned subnational officials, and yet taken together these various recentralizing measures are likely further to fan the flames of deep-seated and explosive anti-Lima sentiment across Peru's interior regions.

In Ecuador, President Correa has been especially active in the pursuit of territorial measures designed to undercut subnational policy challenges in general, as well as the especially galling challenge that is posed by his home town of Guayaquil in particular. Most obvious are the new institutional rules established in the 2008 Constitution that shrank the list of services eligible for decentralization under the prior 1998 Constitution, and that eliminated the possibility of offering concessions to the private sector as a means of delivering these services. But Correa has not stopped there. Bureaucratically, he has embraced deconcentration as a means of strengthening the presence of the central state across subnational territories, and of directly and aggressively rebutting the privatizing logic that continues to dominate within Guayaquil's city hall. Institutionally, Correa has directed officials in politically compliant electoral institutions to bar popular opposition candidates from running for local office. With respect to policy, he introduced technical changes that reduced municipal participation in oil export revenues and thereby increased resources under the control of the national government, which it has used to expand popular new entitlements like Ecuador's cash transfer program (the human development bond). At the societal level, Correa has sponsored sympathetic local groups like the Popular Civic Board (*Junta Cívica Popular*) of Guayaquil, organizations that can be mobilized by the center to trumpet the superiority of its preferred (and more generous) approach to social policy than that endorsed by the neoliberal mayor. More generally, Correa's powerful new central planning body (*SENPLADES*) has officially repudiated the approach to decentralization that was introduced during Ecuador's "long dark night of neoliberalism" in the 1990s.

Recentralization in the service of ideological commitments has also occurred in Bolivia—even though President Morales has indeed been forced to moderate his policy agenda in response to the structural and coalitional realities that I have emphasized in Chapter 5. Morales has compromised on his party's preferred economic policy orientation, but this has not prevented him from proposing and implementing a number of recentralizing changes that constrain subnational governments. At the level of policy, Morales in 2007 introduced deep cuts in revenue transfers to departmental governments from the lucrative tax on hydrocarbons, a revision of revenue-sharing rules that galvanized widespread protests in opposition-governed eastern departments, but that has stuck. Morales explicitly justified this fiscal recentralization as necessary to fund the new safety net that he introduced for Bolivians over sixty years of age now eligible for the so-called Dignity Pension (*Renta Dignidad*). As in Ecuador, recentralization to fund cash transfer programs was doubly appealing to Morales in that it simultaneously increased funds necessary for a more statist approach to social policy and reduced funds under the control of subnational opponents. Early on, Morales also pursued a number of centralizing institutional strategies to undercut his ideological opponents at the subnational level. Most controversially, the president used ambiguous language in the new constitution to suspend a number of opposition mayors and governors—until this was determined to be unconstitutional by Bolivia's Constitutional Tribunal in 2013. Like his presidential counterparts in Peru (but in the pursuit of a different set of ideological preferences), Morales sought aggressively to use national institutions to discipline subnational challengers. Finally, subnational bureaucrats in Santa Cruz complain about a whole host of onerous new requirements in the 2010 framework Law for Autonomy and Decentralization that have had a strongly recentralizing effect.

In all three of my cases, then, ideological combat with subnational officials has led to a quite heterogeneous mix of recentralizing changes through which presidents have tried to defend their preferred policy approaches, whether these are market centered or state centered. This willingness to introduce potentially long-lasting changes in intergovernmental relations in order to defend the center's preferred policy orientation is a phenomenon that cuts across ideological lines. The aggressive nature of these changes in the territorial division of power speaks to the radical nature of the challenges that subnational governments are posing, as well as to the lengths to which the center will go to defend its prerogatives. These recentering changes amount to changes in the scope of authority for subnational governments, and certainly alter the parameters within which future subnational policy challenges will unfold. They should probably be seen as making it harder for mayors and governors to advance challenges in the future.

At the same time, there are good reasons to anticipate that these recentering changes will not eclipse subnational policy challenges, and may in fact encourage them still further. First, despite the varied and aggressive nature of recentralization in recent years, it has rarely taken the form of the cancellation of direct subnational elections. Much as the presidents in my cases deeply resent subnational policy challengers, and much as they have been willing to engage in heavily repressive political actions against them (including jailing subnational officials, suspending them, or barring them from running for office), they have mostly refrained from annulling elections for subnational governments. One exception here is the baldly authoritarian experience of Alberto Fujimori in Peru, who cancelled regional elections in

1992 at the same time that he closed congress as part of his "self-coup" (*autogolpe*). But the idea of returning to a world in which presidents appoint mayors and governors seems to be off the table in Latin America, and presidents in response have focused on a range of other measures to constrain the threats posed by the individuals who come to power through subnational elections. This is a crucial exception to the trend of recentralization; as long as mayors and governors continue to be directly elected, and as long as they seek to win election and re-election on the basis of their proposals and performance, the possibility of subnational policy challenges will remain very much alive.

Second, although many recentralizing measures have been nearly invisible and stealth-like—so much so that they might not even register as having a recentralizing effect—others are highly visible and more likely to be controversial and contested. For example, while very few people may know or care about technical changes in organic laws that limit the autonomy of subnational governments, more of the local population will know and care when the center freezes revenue transfers to their province, or bars popular local candidates from running for re-election. Recentralizing measures that threaten territorial prerogatives and identities run the risk of antagonizing subnational populations, and thereby make it easier—not harder—for opposition mayors and governors to broaden subnational coalitions against the center. This is true for both of the types of coalitions whose importance I have highlighted in this book. Internally, local residents who might not feel particularly invested in the defense of the policy views of their mayor or governor may turn out to support him or her if they think that their city or department is under attack, as we saw in Bolivia and Ecuador. Externally, recentralizing measures that undermine the power, resources, and authority of subnational officials as a class of actor may help these officials to overcome the differences that otherwise make it quite difficult for them to construct durable coalitions. In this sense, recentralization as a means to defend and reinforce the center's preferred ideological model may ultimately prove to be self-defeating, setting the stage for further and more robust subnational policy challenges in the future.

References

Abers, Rebecca, and Margaret Keck (2009). "Mobilizing the State: The Erratic Partner in Brazil's Participatory Water Policy," *Politics & Society*, 37(2): 289–314.

Abers, Rebecca, and Margaret Keck (2013). *Practical Authority: Agency and Institutional Change in Brazilian Water Politics*. Oxford: Oxford University Press.

Aguirre, Xavier Flores (2007). "Criminalización de la libertad de expresión: Protesta social y administración local en Guayaquil," *Iconos*, 27: 65–75.

Albó, Xavier (2004). "Bolivia: From Indios and Campesino Leaders to Councilors and Parliamentary Deputies," in Rachel Seider (ed.), *Multiculturalism in Latin America. Indigeneous Rights, Diversity and Democracy*. London: Palgrave.

Andrade, Pablo (2009). *La era neoliberal y el proyecto republicano*. Quito: Corporación Editora Nacional.

Andrade, X. (2004). "Burocracia: Museos, políticas culturales y flexibilización laboral en Guayaquil," *Iconos*, 20: 64–72.

Anria, Santiago (2016). "Democratizing Democracy? Civil Society and Party Organization in Bolivia," *Comparative Politics*, 48(4): 459–77.

Arce, Moises (2005). *Market Reform in Society: Post-Crisis Politics and Economic Change in Authoritarian Peru*. University Park, PA: Penn State University Press.

Arce, Moises (2008). "The Repoliticization of Collective Action after Neoliberalism in Peru," *Latin American Politics and Society*, 50(3): 37–62.

Arce, Moises (2014). *Resource Extraction and Protest in Peru*. Pittsburgh: University of Pittsburgh Press.

Arellano-Yanguas, Javier (2011). *Minería sin fronteras? Conflicto y desarrollo en regiones mineras del Perú*. Lima: Instituto de Estudios Peruanos.

Argirakis, Helena, and Jaime Parejas (2009). "Identidad, política y poder en Santa Cruz," in Alejandra Boschetti and Claudia Peña (eds), *Los cruceños según sus intelectuales*. Santa Cruz: El País.

Avellaneda, Claudia (2009). "Municipal Performance: Does Mayoral Quality Matter?," *Journal of Public Administration Research and Theory*, 19(2): 285–312.

Ayo, Diego (2010). "Las autonomías entre 'hegemonistas' y 'consociativos'," in *Miradas: Un Nuevo texto constitucional*. La Paz: IDEA Internacional.

Azpur, Javier (2012). "Analísis de la legislación sobre planificación territorial en el Perú," *Cuadernos Descentralistas*, 7: 9–68.

Bache, Ian, and Matthew Flinders (2004) (eds). *Multi-Level Governance*. Oxford: Oxford University Press.

Baiocchi, Gianpaolo (2003). *Radicals in Power: The Workers' Party and Experiments in Urban Democracy in Brazil.* London: ZED.

Ballon, Eduardo (2011). "Decentralization," in John Crabtree (ed.), *Fractured Politics: Peruvian Democracy Past and Present.* London: University of London Press.

Barber, Benjamin (2013). *If Mayors Ruled the World: Dysfunctional Nations, Rising Cities.* New Haven: Yale University Press.

Bardhan, Pranab (2002). "Decentralization of Governance and Development," *Journal of Economic Perspectives*, 16(4): 185–205.

Barndt, William (2012). "Destroying the Opposition's Livelihood: Pathways to Violence in Bolivia since 2000," *Journal of Politics in Latin America*, 4(3): 3–37.

Barragán, Rossana (2004). "'La media luna': Autonomías regionales y comités cívicos," *T'inkasos*, 7/16: 9–45.

Barragán, Rossana (2008). "Oppressed or Privileged Regions?: Some Historical Reflections on the Use of State Resources," in John Crabtree and Laurence Whitehead (eds), *Unresolved Tensions of Bolivia.* Pittsburgh: University of Pittsburgh Press.

Battle, Margarita (2012). "Sistema de Partidos Multinivel en Contextos Unitarios en América Latina," Ph.D. Dissertation, University of Salamanca.

Bebbington, Anthony (2007) (ed.). *Minería, movimientos sociales y respuestas campesinas.* Lima: Instituto de Estudios Peruanos.

Bebbington, Anthony (2011). *Los movimientos sociales y la política de la pobreza en el Perú.* Lima: Instituto de Estudios Peruanos.

Bebbington, Anthony, and Jeff Bury (2013) (eds). *Subterranean Struggles.* Austin: University of Texas Press.

Bebbington, Anthony, and Martin Scurrah (2013). "Hydrocarbon Conflicts and Indigenous Peoples in the Peruvian Amazon," in Anthony Bebbington and Jeff Bury (eds), *Subterranean Struggles.* Austin: University of Texas Press.

Bethell, Leslie (1985). *The Cambridge History of Latin America*, iii. *From Independence to 1870.* Cambridge: Cambridge University Press.

Bland, Gary, and Luis Chirinos (2014). "Democratization through Contention?: Regional and Local Governance Conflict in Peru," *Latin American Politics and Society*, 56(1): 73–97.

Blecher, Marc (1991). "Development State, Entrepreneurial State: The Political Economy of Socialist Reform in Xinji Municipality and Guanghan County," in Gordon White (ed.), *The Chinese State in the Era of Economic Reforms: The Road to Crisis.* Basingstoke: Macmillan.

Bohrt, Carlos (2012). *El andar de la autonomía departamental en Bolivia: Caminantes y senderos.* La Paz: UNDP.

Boone, Catherine (2003a). *The Political Topographies of the African State.* New York: Cambridge University Press.

Boone, Catherine (2003b). "Decentralization as Political Strategy in West Africa," *Comparative Political Studies* 36(4): 355–80.

Bowen, James (2014). "The Right and Non-Party Forms of Representation and Participation: Bolivia and Ecuador Compared," in Juan Pablo Luna and Cristóbal Rovira Kaltwasser (eds), *The Resilience of the Right in Latin America.* Baltimore: Johns Hopkins University Press.

Bowen, James (2015). "Rethinking Democratic Governance: State Building, Autonomy and Accountability in Correa's Ecuador," *Journal of Politics in Latin America*, 7(1): 83–110.

Bozo, Angel Castro (2013). *Santa Cruz: La mayor inversión boliviana (1825–2000)*. La Paz: Centro de Estudios para la América Andina y Amazónica.

Brenner, Neil (2004). *New State Spaces: Urban Governance and the Rescaling of Statehood*. Oxford: Oxford University Press.

Brenner, Neil, Jamie Peck, and Nik Theodore (2010). "Variegated Neoliberalization: Geographies, Modalities, Pathways," *Global Networks*, 10: 182–222.

Brenner, Neil, and Nik Theodore (2002) (eds). *Spaces of Neoliberalism*. Oxford: Blackwell.

Burbano de Lara, Felipe (2009a). "La lucha por Guayaquil," *Iconos*, 33: 21–6.

Burbano de Lara, Felipe (2009b). "Las luchas autonómicas de Guayaquil y Santa Cruz," in Enrique Arceo and Eduardo Basualdo (eds), *Los condicionantes de la crisis en América Latina*. Buenos Aires: CLACSO.

Burbano de Lara, Felipe (2014). *La revuelta de las periferias: Movimientos regionales y autonomías políticas en Bolivia y Ecuador*. Quito: FLACSO Ecuador.

Burbano de Lara, Felipe (2015). "El complejo ensamblaje estatal en el Ecuador posneoliberal: Retorno del Estado, recentralización y dominio territorial," paper presented at the 2015 Congreso Latinoamericano y Caribeño de Ciencias Sociales, FLACSO.

Burt, Jo-Marie (2010). *Political Violence and the Authoritarian State in Peru: Silencing Civil Society*. New York: Palgrave.

Bury, Jeff (2007). "Neoliberalismo, minería y cambios rurales en Cajarmarca," in Anthony Bebbington (ed.), *Minería, movimientos sociales y respuestas campesinas*. Lima: Instituto de Estudios Peruanos.

Cáceres, Eduardo, and Jaime Rojas Huerta (2013). *Minería, desarrollo y gestión municipal en Espinar*. Lima: Asociación SER.

Cameron, John (2009). *Struggles for Local Democracy in the Andes*. Boulder, CO: Lynne Rienner Press.

Cameron, Maxwell (1994). *Democracy and Authoritarianism in Peru: Political Coalitions and Social Change*. New York: Palgrave.

Cameron, Maxwell (2011). "Peru: The Turn Left that Wasn't," in Steve Levitsky and Kenneth Roberts (eds), *Resurgence of the Latin American Left*. Baltimore: Johns Hopkins University Press, 375–98.

Campbell, Timothy (2009). *The Quiet Revolution: Decentralization and the Rise of Political Participation in Latin American Cities*. Pittsburgh: University of Pittsburgh Press.

Campodónico, Humberto (2011). "García, óbolo, y impuesto a las sobreganancias mineras," *La República*, April 1.

Cardoso, Fernando, and Enzo Faletto (1979). *Dependency and Development in Latin America*. Berkeley and Los Angeles: University of California Press.

Carey, John, and Matthew Shugart (1992). *Presidents and Assemblies: Constitutional Design and Electoral Dynamics*. New York: Cambridge University Press.

Carothers, Thomas, and Saskia Brechenmacher (2014). *Closing Space: Democracy and Human Rights Support under Fire*. Washington: Carnegie Endowment for International Peace.

Carrión, Fernando (2003). "La descentralización en América Latina: Una perspectiva comparada" in Fernando Carrión (ed.), *Procesos de descentralización en la comunidad andina*. Quito: FLACSO.

Carrión, Fernando (2015). "El giro a la izquierda en los gobiernos locales de América Latina," in Fernando Carrión and Paúl Ponce (eds), *El giro a la izquierda: Los gobiernos locales en América Latina*. Quito: FLACSO.

Carrión, Fernando, and Paúl Ponce (2015) (eds). *El giro a la izquierda: Los gobiernos locales en América Latina*. Quito: FLACSO.

Castells, Manuel, and Jordi Borja (2004). *Local y global: La gestión de las ciudades en la era informática*. Barcelona: Taurus.

Centellas, Miguel (2009). "Electoral Reform, Regional Cleavages and Party System Stability in Bolivia," *Journal of Politics in Latin America*, 1(2): 115–31.

Centellas, Miguel (2013). "Bolivia's New Multicultural Constitution: The 2009 Constitution in Historical and Comparative Perspective," in Todd Eisenstadt, Michael Danielson, Moisés Bailón, and Carlos Sorroza (eds), *Latin America's Multicultural Movements*. New York: Oxford University Press.

Centeno, Miguel (2002). *Blood and Debt: War and the Nation-State in Latin America*. University Park, PA: Penn State University Press.

Chartock, Sarah (2013). "Corporatism with Adjectives? Conceptualizing Civil Society Incorporation and Indigenous Participation in Latin America," *Latin American Politics and Society*, 55(2): 52–76.

Chávez Gabriel (2009). *Autonomía: De la protesta a la propuesta*. Santa Cruz: La Hoguera.

Cheema, G. Shabbir, and Dennis Rondinelli (2007) (eds). *Decentralizing Governance: Emerging Concepts and Practices*. Washington: Brookings Institution Press.

Chumacero, Juan Pablo (2009). "Trece años de reforma agraria en Bolivia," in Juan Pablo Chumacero (ed.), *Informe 2009: Reconfigurando territorios*. La Paz: Fundación Tierra.

Coffe, Hilde (2008). "Social Democratic Parties as Buffers against the Extreme Right," *Contemporary Politics*, 14(2): 179–95.

Collier, David, and Ruth Collier (1991). *Shaping the Political Arena*. Princeton: Princeton University Press.

Conaghan, Catherine (1988). *Restructuring Domination: Industrialists and the State in Ecuador*. Pittsburgh: University of Pittsburgh Press.

Conaghan, Catherine (2006). *Fujimori's Peru: Deception in the Public Sphere*. Pittsburgh: University of Pittsburgh Press.

Conaghan, Catherine (2011). "Ecuador: Rafael Correa and the Citizen's Revolution," in Steven Levitsky and Kenneth Roberts (eds), *The Resurgence of the Latin American Left*. Baltimore: Johns Hopkins University Press.

Conaghan, Catherine (2015). "Surveil and Sanction: Rafael Correa's Regulatory Revolution," paper presented at the 2015 Congreso Latinoamericano y Caribeño de Ciencias Sociales, FLACSO.

Conaghan, Catherine, and James Malloy (1994). *Unsettling Statecraft: Democracy and Neoliberalism in the Central Andes*. Pittsburgh: University of Pittsburgh Press.

Conterno, Elena (2007). *La agenda a cuatro años de iniciado el proceso*. Lima: USAID.

Corrales, Javier (2003). "Market Reforms," in Jorge Dominguez and Michael Shifter (eds), *Constructing Democratic Governance in Latin America*. Baltimore: Johns Hopkins University Press.

Cotler, Julio (1978). *Clases, estado y nación en el Perú*. Lima: Instituto de Estudios Peruanos.

Crabtree, John (2014). "Funding Local Government: Use (and Abuse) of Peru's Canon System," *Bureau of Latin American Research*, 33(4): 452–67.

Cyr, Jennifer (2017). *The Fates of Parties: Institutional Crisis, Continuity, and Change*. New York: Cambridge University Press.

Dahl, Robert (1970). *After the Revolution: Authority in a Good Society*. New Haven: Yale University Press.

Dahl, Robert, and Charles Lindblom (1976). *Politics, Economics and Welfare*. Chicago: University of Chicago Press.

Dargent, Eduardo (2011). "Agents or Actors? Assessing the Autonomy of Economic Technocrats in Colombia and Peru," *Comparative Politics*, 43(3): 313–32.

Dargent, Eduardo (2013). "Estado, política y sociedad durante el boom de los commodities," *Argumentos*, 5(7): 1–11.

Dargent, Eduardo (2014). *Technocracy and Democracy in Latin America*. New York: Cambridge University Press.

Dargent, Eduardo, and Paula Muñoz (2016). "Patronage, Subnational Linkages, and Party-Building: The Cases of Colombia and Peru," in Steven Levitsky, James Loxton, and Brandon Van Dyck (eds), *Challenges of Party Building in Latin America*. New York: Cambridge University Press.

Davies, Jon (1988). "From Municipal Socialism to . . . Municipal Capitalism?," *Local Government Studies*, 14(2): 19–22.

Davis, Diane (2010). "Irregular Armed Forces, Shifting Patterns of Commitment, and Fragmented Sovereignty in the Developing World," *Theory and Society*, 39(3): 397–413.

Davis, Michael (2015). "Beijing's Broken Promises," *Journal of Democracy*, 26(2): 101–10.

de Echave, José (2012). "La minería Peruana y los escenarios de transición," in Alejandra Alayza and Eduardo Gudynas (eds), *Transiciones: Postextractivismo y alternativas al extractivismo en el Perú*. Lima: CEPES.

de Echave, José, and Alejandro Diez (2013). *Más allá de Conga*. Lima: RedGE.

de la Torre, Carlos (2015). *De Velasco a Correa: Populismos y elecciones en Ecuador, 1944–2013*. Quito: Universidad Andina Simón Bolívar.

de la Torre, Patricia (2004). *Stato Nostro: La cara oculta de la beneficencia en el Ecuador*. Quito: Abya-Yala.

Degregori, Carlos Iván (1996). *Las rondas campesinas y la derrota de Sendero Luminoso*. Lima: IEP.

del Río, Marco Antonio (2012). "La economía cruceña: 1810–2010," in Colección Investigacruz, *Santa Cruz y sus 200 años de independencia*. Santa Cruz: El País.

Delgado, Alina (2013). "Guayaquil City Profile," *Cities*, 31: 515–32.

Dickovick, Tyler (2011). *Decentralization and Recentralization in the Developing World*. University Park, PA: Penn State University Press.

Dickovick, Tyler, and Kent Eaton (2013). "Latin America's Resurgent Centre: National Government Strategies after Decentralisation," *Journal of Development Studies*, 49(11): 1453–66.

Doner, Richard, and Eric Hershberg (1999). "Flexible Production and Political Decentralization in the Developing World: Elective Affinities in the Pursuit of Competitiveness," *Studies in Comparative International Development*, 34(1): 45–82.

Dunkerley, James (2007). "Evo Morales, the 'Two Bolivias' and the Third Bolivian Revolution," *Journal of Latin American Studies*, 39: 133–66.

Durand, Francisco (2010). *La mano invisible en el Estado*. Lima: Fondo Editorial Pedagógico de San Marcos.

Durand, Francisco (2016). *Cuando el poder extractivo captura el estado: Lobbies, puertas giratorias y paquetazo ambiental en Perú*. Lima: Oxfam.

Eaton, Kent (2002). *Politicians and Economic Reform in New Democracies: Argentina and the Philippines in the 1990s*. University Park, PA: Penn State University Press.

Eaton, Kent (2004). *Politics beyond the Capital: The Design of Subnational Institutions in South America*. Stanford: Stanford University Press.

Eaton, Kent (2006). "Decentralization's Non-Democratic Roots: Authoritarianism and Subnational Reform in South America," *Latin American Politics and Society*, 48(1): 1–26.

Eaton, Kent (2007). "Backlash in Bolivia: Regional Autonomy as a Reaction against Indigenous Mobilization," *Politics and Society*, 35/1: 71–102.

Eaton, Kent (2010). "Subnational Economic Nationalism?: The Contradictory Effects of Decentralization in Peru," *Third World Quarterly*, 31(7): 1205–22.

Eaton, Kent (2012). "Decentralisation and Federalism," in Peter Kingstone and Deborah Yashar (eds), *The Routledge Handbook of Latin American Politics*. Abingdon: Routledge, 33–47.

Eaton, Kent (2013). "The Centralism of '21st Century Socialism': Recentralising Politics in Venezuela, Ecuador and Bolivia," *Journal of Latin American Studies*, 45 (3): 421–50.

Eaton, Kent, Kai Kaiser, and Paul Smoke (2010). *The Political Economy of Decentralization Reforms: Implications for Aid Effectiveness*. Washington: World Bank.

Erickson, Peter, and Kevin Tempest (2014). "Advancing Climate Ambition: How City-Scale Actions Can Contribute to Global Climate Goals," *Stockholm Environment Institute Working Paper*, 6: 3–23.

Evans, Peter (2002). *Livable Cities? The Politics of Urban Livelihood and Sustainability*. Berkeley and Los Angeles: University of California Press.

Fabricant, Nicole, and Nancy Postero (2013). "Contested Bodies, Contested States: Performance, Emotions, and New Forms of Regional Governance in Santa Cruz, Bolivia," *Journal of Latin American and Caribbean Anthropology*, 18(2): 187–211.

Faguet, Jean-Paul (2013). *Decentralization and Popular Democracy: Governance from below in Bolivia*. Ann Arbor: University of Michigan Press.

Fairfield, Tasha (2015a). *Private Wealth and Public Revenue in Latin America*. New York: Cambridge University Press.

Fairfield, Tasha (2015b). "Structural Power in Comparative Political Economy: Perspectives from Policy Formulation in Latin America," *Business and Politics*, 17(3): 411–41.

Falleti, Tulia (2010). *Decentralization and Subnational Politics in Latin America*. New York: Cambridge University Press.

Farthing, Linda, and Benjamin Kohl (2010). "Social Control: Bolivia's New Approach to Coca Reduction," *Latin American Perspectives*, 37(4): 197–213.

Fenwick, Tracy Beck (2016). *Avoiding Governors: Federalism, Democracy, and Poverty Alleviation in Brazil and Argentina*. Notre Dame: University of Notre Dame Press.

Ferreira, Reymi (2010). *Las logías en Santa Cruz*. 2nd edn. Santa Cruz: Unión.

Fiszbein, Ariel (1997). "The Emergence of Local Capacity: Lessons from Colombia," *World Development*, 25(7): 1029–43.

Fitzgerald, Valpy (2005). "The Conflict of Economic Doctrines in Latin America," in Valpy Fitzgerald and Rosemary Thorp (eds), *Economic Doctrines in Latin America: Origins, Embedding and Evolution*. New York: Palgrave.

Flores-Macias, Gustavo (2012). *After Neoliberalism?: The Left and Economic Reforms in Latin America*. New York: Oxford University Press.

Frank, Jonas (2004). *Decentralization in Ecuador: Actors, Institutions and Incentives*. Baden-Baden: Nomos.

Freidenberg, Flavia, and Manuel Alcantara (2001). *Los dueños del poder: Partidos políticos en Ecuador*. Quito: FLACSO.

Freidenberg, Flavia, and Julieta Suárez-Cao (2014). *Territorio y poder: Nuevos actores y competencia política en los sistemas de partidos multinivel en América Latina*. Salamanca: Ediciones Universidad de Salamanca.

Fukuyama, Francis (2004). *State Building: Governance and World Order in the 21st Century*. Ithaca, NY: Cornell University Press.

Gamarra, Eduardo (1997). "Hybrid Presidentialism and Democratization: The Case of Bolivia," in Scott Mainwaring and Mathew Shugart (eds), *Presidentialism and Democracy in Latin America*. New York: Cambridge University Press.

Gamboa, César, and Sébastien Snoeck (2012) (eds). *Análisis crítico de la consulta previa en el Perú*. Lima: Grupo de Trabajo sobre Pueblos Indígenas de la Coordinadora Nacional de Derechos Humanos.

Garay, Candelaria (2016). *Social Policy Expansion in Latin America*. New York: Cambridge University Press.

Geddes, Barbara (1996). *Politician's Dilemma: Building State Capacity in Latin America*. Berkeley and Los Angeles: University of California Press.

Geddes, Michael (2014). "Neoliberalism and Local Governance: Radical Developments in Latin America," *Urban Studies*, 51(15): 3147–63.

Geddes, Michael, and Helen Sullivan (2012). "Localities, Leadership and Neoliberalization: Conflicting Discourses, Competing Practices," *Critical Policy Studies*, 5(4): 391–413.

George, Stephen (2004). "Multi-Level Governance and the European Union," in Ian Bache and Matthew Flinders (eds), *Multi-Level Governance*. Oxford: Oxford University Press.

Gervasoni, Carlos (2010). "A Rentier Theory of Subnational Regimes," *World Politics*, 62(2): 302–40.

Ghezzi, Piero, and José Gallardo (2013). *Qué se puede hacer con el Perú?* Lima: Fondo Editorial.

Gibson, Edward (1996). *Class and Conservative Parties: Argentina in Comparative Perspective*. Baltimore: Johns Hopkins University Press.

Gibson, Edward (2012). *Boundary Control: Subnational Authoritarianism in National Democracies*. New York: Cambridge University Press.

Gil, Vladimir (2009). *Aterrizaje minero*. Lima: Instituto de Estudios Peruanos.

Gilbert de Babra, Marcia (2006). "Educación en Guayaquil: Políticas y estrategias," *Al Andar*, June, 1: 1–10.

Giraudy, Agustina (2015). *Democrats and Autocrats: Pathways of Subnational Undemocratic Regime Continuity within Democratic Countries*. Oxford: Oxford University Press.

Girolami, Monica (2006). "Gobernabilidad en Guayaquil: Las alianzas como alternativa para la gestión municipal," *Al Andar*, October, 2: 8–14.

Goldfrank, Benjamin (2011). *Deepening Local Democracy: Participation, Decentralization and the Left*. University Park, PA: Penn State University Press.

Goldfrank, Benjamin, and Andrew Schrank (2009). "Municipal Neoliberalism and Municipal Socialism: Urban Political Economy in Latin America," *International Journal of Urban and Regional Research*, 33(2): 443–62.

Gonzales de Olarte, Efraín (1982). *Economías regionales del Perú*. Lima: Instituto de Estudios Peruanos.

Gonzales de Olarte, Efraín (2000). *Neocentralismo y neoliberalismo en el Perú*. Lima: Instituto de Estudios Peruanos.

Gordon, David (2016). "The Politics of Accountability in Networked Urban Climate Governance," *Global Environmental Politics*, 16(2): 82–100.

Gorski, Philip (2003). *The Disciplinary Revolution: Calvinism and the Rise of the State in Early Modern Europe*. Chicago: University of Chicago Press.

Gourevitch, Peter (1986). *Politics in Hard Times: Comparative Responses to International Economic Crises*. Ithaca, NY: Cornell University Press.

Greenwood, Justin (2011). *Interest Representation in the European Union*. New York: Palgrave Macmillan.

Grindle, Merilee (2007). *Going Local: Decentralization, Democratization, and the Promise of Good Governance*. Princeton: Princeton University Press.

Grindle, Merilee, and Francisco Thoumi (1993). "Muddling toward Adjustment: The Political Economy of Economic Policy Change in Ecuador," in Robert Bates and Anne Krueger (eds), *Political and Economic Interactions in Economic Policy Reform*. Oxford: Blackwell.

Grompone, Romeo, and Martín Tanaka (2009) (eds). *Entre el crecimiento económico y la insatisfación social*. Lima: Instituto de Estudios Peruanos.

Grupo Propuesta Ciudadana (2011). *El programa minero de solidaridad con los pueblos y los fondos sociales: reporte de vigilancia*. Lima: Grupo Propuesta Ciudadana.

Guerrero, Rafael (1980). *Los oligarcas del cacao*. Quito: El Conejo.

Guerrero, Rafael (1994). *Regionalismo y democracia social en los origenes del CFP*. Quito: CAP.

Gunlicks, Arthur (2003). *The Länder and German Federalism*. Manchester: Manchester University Press.

Gustafson, Bret (2006). "Spectacles of Autonomy and Crisis," *Journal of Latin American Anthropology*, 11(2): 351–79.

Gustafsson, Maria-Therese (2016). "Private Conflict Regulation and the Influence of Peasant Communities over Natural Resources," *Latin American Research Review*, 51(2): 86–106.

Hacker, Jacob, and Paul Pierson (2002). "Business Power and Social Policy: Employers and the Formation of the American Welfare State," *Politics and Society*, 30(2): 277–325.

Haggard, Stephan (1990). *Pathways from the Periphery*. Ithaca, NY: Cornell University Press.

Haggard, Stephan, and Robert Kaufman (1995). *The Political Economy of Democratic Transitions*. Princeton: Princeton University Press.

Haggard, Stephan, and Matthew McCubbins (2001) (eds). *Presidents, Parliaments and Policy*. New York: Cambridge University Press.

Hagopian, Frances, and Scott Mainwaring (2005) (eds). *The Third Wave of Democratization in Latin America: Advances and Setbacks*. New York: Cambridge University Press.

Harbers, Imke (2015). "Taxation and the Unequal Reach of the State: Mapping State Capacity in Ecuador," *Governance*, 28(3): 373–91.

Harvey, David (2009). "Reshaping Economic Geography: The World Development Report 2009," *Development and Change*, 40: 1269–77.

Heller, Patrick (1999). *The Labor of Development: Workers in the Transformation of Capitalism in Kerala, India*. Ithaca, NY: Cornell University Press.

Heller, Patrick (2001). "Moving the State: The Politics of Democratic Decentralization in Kerala, South Africa, and Porto Alegre," *Politics & Society*, 29(1): 131–63.

Helmke, Gretchen, and Julio Rios-Figueroa (2014) (eds). *Courts in Latin America*. New York: Cambridge University Press.

Herbst, Jeffrey (2000). *States and Power in Africa: Comparative Lessons in Authority and Control*. Princeton: Princeton University Press.

Herrera, Veronica (forthcoming). *Water and Politics: Clientelism and Reform in Urban Mexico*. Ann Arbor: University of Michigan Press.

Hirschman, Albert (1970). *Exit, Voice and Loyalty*. Cambridge, MA: Harvard University Press.

Hirschman, Albert (1979). "The Turn to Authoritarianism in Latin America and the Search for its Economic Determinants," in David Collier (ed.), *The New Authoritarianism in Latin America*. Princeton: Princeton University Press.

Hooghe, Liesbet (1996). *Cohesion Policy and European Integration: Building Multi-Level Governance*. Oxford: Oxford University Press.

Hooghe, Liesbet, and Gary Marks (2001). *Multi-Level Governance and European Integration*. Lanham, MD, and Oxford: Rowman & Littlefield.

Hooghe, Liesbet, and Gary Marks (2010). "Types of Multi-Level Governance," in Henrik Enderlein, Sonja Walti, and Michael Zurn (eds), *Handbook on Multi-Level Governance*. London: Edward Elgar, 17–31.

Hooghe, Liesbet, and Gary Marks (2016). *Community, Scale and Regional Governance: A Postfunctionalist Theory of Governance, Volume II*. Oxford: Oxford University Press.

Huber, Evelyne (2002). "Conclusion: Actors, Institutions and Policies," in Evelyne Huber (ed.), *Capitalism: Lessons for Latin America*. University Park, PA: Penn State University Press.

Hurtado, Osvaldo (1977). *El poder político en el Ecuador*. Quito: Planeta.

Isaac, Thomas (2000). *Local Democracy and Development: People's Campaign for Decentralised Planning*. New Delhi: LeftWord Books.

Isch, Gustavo (2011). "Comunicación, esfera pública y democracia en el gobierno de la 'Revolución Ciudadana,'" MA thesis, FLACSO/Ecuador.

Iskenderian Aguilera, Emir (2010). "Un período defensivo para la burguesía cruceña: Ataques confirmados o atribuídos a la UJC," *Artículo Primero*, 19: 85–101.

Jaskoski, Maiah (2014). "Environmental Licensing and Conflict in Peru's Mining Sector: A Path-Dependent Analysis," *World Development*, 64: 873–83.

Jeffery, Charlie (2000). "Subnational Mobilization and European Integration: Does it Make Any Difference?," *Journal of Common Market Studies*, 38(1): 1–23.

Jeffery, Charlie, Nicole Pamphilis, Carolyn Rowe, and Ed Turner (2014). "Regional Policy Variation in Germany: The Diversity of Living Conditions in a 'Unitary Federal State,'" *Journal of European Public Policy*, 21(9): 1350–66.

Jessop, Robert (1997). "A Neo-Gramscian Approach to the Regulation of Urban Regimes," in Mickey Lauria (ed.), *Reconstructing Urban Regime Theory: Regulating Urban Politics in a Global Economy*. Thousand Oaks, CA: SAGE Publications.

Joiner, Emily (2007). *Murky Waters: A Critical and Purposeful Look at Water and Sanitation Services in Guayaquil, Ecuador*. Guayaquil: Observatorio de Servicios Públicos.

Jones, Barry, and Michael Keating (1995) (eds). *The European Union and the Regions*. Oxford: Oxford University Press.

Kahler, Miles (1990). "Orthodoxy and its Alternatives: Explaining Approaches to Stabilization and Adjustment," in Joan Nelson (ed.), *Economic Crisis and Policy Choice*. Princeton: Princeton University Press.

Kasza, Gregory (1981). "Regional Conflict in Ecuador: Quito and Guayaquil," *Inter-American Economic Affairs*, 35(2): 19–56.

Kaufman, Robert (1986). "Democratic and Authoritarian Responses to the Debt Issue: Argentina, Brazil, Mexico," in Miles Kahler (ed.), *The Politics of International Debt*. Ithaca, NY: Cornell University Press.

Kaufman, Robert, and Barbara Stallings (1989) (eds). *Debt and Democracy in Latin America*. Boulder, CO: Westview Press.

Kaup, Brent (2010). "A Neoliberal Nationalization? The Constraints on Natural Gas-Led Development in Bolivia," *Latin American Perspectives*, 37(3): 123–38.

Keating, Michael (1999). "Rethinking the Region: Culture, Institutions and Economic Development in Catalonia and Galicia," paper presented at the ECPR Workshop on Regionalism Revisited.

Kenney, George (2004). *Fujimori's Coup and the Breakdown of Democracy in Latin America*. Notre Dame: University of Notre Dame.

Kirshner, Joshua (2010). "Migrants' Voices: Negotiating Autonomy in Santa Cruz," *Latin American Perspectives*, 37(4): 108–24.

Klein, Herbert (2003). *A Concise History of Bolivia*. New York: Cambridge University Press.

Kohli, Atul (2004). *State-Directed Development: Political Power and Industrialization in the Global Periphery*. New York: Cambridge University Press.

Kurtz, Marcus (2004). "The Dilemmas of Democracy in the Open Economy: Lessons from Latin America," *World Politics*, 56: 262–302.

Kurtz, Marcus (2013). *Latin American State Building in Comparative Perspective*. New York: Cambridge University Press.

Laserna, Roberto (2004). *La democracia en el Ch'enko*. La Paz: Fundación Milenio.

Leopold, Ellen, and David McDonald (2012). "Municipal Socialism Then and Now: Some Lessons for the Global South," *Third World Quarterly*, 33(10): 1837–53.

Levitsky, Steven, James Loxton, and Brandon Van Dyck (2016) (eds). *Challenges of Party-Building in Latin America*. New York: Cambridge University Press.

Levitsky, Steven, and Kenneth Roberts (2011) (eds). *The Resurgence of the Latin American Left*. Baltimore: Johns Hopkins University Press.

Levitsky, Steven, and Mauricio Zavaleta (2016). "Why No Party Building in Peru?," in Steven Levitsky, James Loxton, and Brendan Van Dyck (eds), *Challenges of Party Building in Latin America*. New York: Cambridge University Press.

Lindblom, Charles (1977). *Politics and Markets*. New York: Basic Books.

Linz, Juan, and Alfred Stepan (1996). *Problems of Democratic Transition and Consolidation*. Baltimore: Johns Hopkins University Press.

Logan, John, and Harvey Molotch (1987). *Urban Fortunes: The Political Economy of Place*. Berkeley and Los Angeles: University of California Press.

Loveman, Mara (2005). "The Modern State and the Primitive Accumulation of Symbolic Power," *American Journal of Sociology*, 110(6): 1651–83.

Lucero, José Antonio (2008). *Struggles of Voice: The Politics of Indigenous Representation in the Andes*. Pittsburgh: University of Pittsburgh Press.

Luedtke, Adam (2005). "A Europe of the Regions: Rhetoric or Reality?," *International Studies Review*, 7(1): 101–3.

McClintock, Cynthia (1981). *Peasant Cooperatives and Political Change in Peru*. Princeton: Princeton University Press.

McMann, Kelly (2006). *Economic Autonomy and Democracy: Hybrid Regimes in Russia and Kyrgyzstan*. New York: Cambridge University Press.

McNulty, Stephanie (2011). *Voice and Vote: Decentralization and Participation in Post-Fujimori Peru*. Stanford: Stanford University Press.

Madrid, Raúl (2012). *The Rise of Ethnic Politics in Latin America*. New York: Cambridge University Press.

Mahon, Rianne, and Laura Macdonald (2010). "Anti-Poverty Politics in Toronto and Mexico City," *Geoforum*, 41: 209–17.

Maiguashca, Juan (1994) (ed.). *Historia y región en el Ecuador: 1830–1972*. Quito: FLACSO.

Mainwaring, Scott, and Timothy Scully (1995) (eds). *Building Democratic Institutions: Party Systems in Latin America*. Stanford: Stanford University Press.

Malloy, James (1970). *Bolivia: The Uncompleted Revolution*. Pittsburgh: University of Pittsburgh Press.

Mann, Michael (1986). *The Sources of Social Power: A History of Power from the Beginning to AD 1760*. Cambridge: Cambridge University Press.

Mansilla, H.C.F. (2007). *Problemas de la autonomía en el Oriente Boliviano*. Santa Cruz: El País.

Mansuri, Ghazala, and Vijayendra Rao (2013). *Localizing Development: Does Participation Work?* Washington: World Bank.

Marca, Juan Pablo (2012). *Septiembre 2008 en el proceso autonómico cruceño*. Santa Cruz: Editorial Universidad Autónoma Gabriel René Moreno.

Martínez, Gabriel (2006). "The Political Economy of the Ecuadorian Financial Crisis," *Cambridge Journal of Economics*, 30(4): 567–85.

Mauceri, Philip (1995). "State Reform, Coalitions, and the Neoliberal *Autogolpe* in Peru," *Latin American Research Review*, 30(1): 7–37.

May, Peter, and Ashley Jochim (2013). "Policy Regime Perspectives: Policies, Politics, and Governing," *Policy Studies Journal*, 41(3): 426–52.

Mayorga, Fernando (2007). *Encrucijadas: Ensayos sobre democracia y reforma estatal en Bolivia*. La Paz: Editorial Gente Común.

Mayorga, René Antonio Mayorga (2005). "Bolivia's Democracy at the Crossroads," in Frances Hagopian and Scott Mainwaring (eds), *The Third Wave of Democratization in Latin America*. New York: Cambridge University Press.

Meléndez, Carlos (2009). "Movilización sin movimientos: El caso de los conflictos entre comunidades y la empresa minera Yanacocha en Cajamarca," in Romeo Grompone and Martin Tanaka (eds), *Entre el crecimiento económico y la insatisfacción social*. Lima: Instituto de Estudios Peruanos.

Meyer, Enrique (2009). *Ugly Stories of the Peruvian Agrarian Reform*. Durham:, NC: Duke University Press.

Molina, Carlos Hugo (2013). *La base ideológica del desarrollo cruceño*. Santa Cruz: El País.

Monge, Carlos (2012). "Las políticas del Presidente Ollanta Humala en relación con la minería y los hidrocarburos," *Cuadernos Descentralistas*, 29: 63–77.

Montero, Alfred (2002). *Shifting States in Global Markets: Subnational Industrial Policy in Contemporary Brazil and Spain*. University Park, PA: Penn State University Press.

Montinola, Gabriela, Yingyi Qian, and Barry Weingast (1995). "Federalism, Chinese Style: The Political Basis for Economic Success," *World Politics*, 48(1): 50–81.

Montúfar, César (2013). "Rafael Correa and his Plebiscitary Citizen's Revolution," in Carlos de la Torre and Cynthia Arnson (eds), *Latin American Populism in the Twenty-First Century*. Baltimore: Johns Hopkins University Press.

Moravcsik, Andrew (1998). *The Choice for Europe: Social Purpose and State Power from Rome to Maastricht*. Ithaca, NY: Cornell University Press.

Muñoz, Francisco (1999). "Introducción," in Francisco Muñoz (ed.), *Descentralización*. Quito: Tramasocial Editorial.

Muñoz, Paula, and Andrea García (2011). "Balance de las elecciones regionales 2010," in María Ana García and Omar Coronel (eds), *El nuevo poder en las regiones*. Lima: Pontificia Universidad Católica del Perú, 8–17.

Murillo, M. Victoria (2003). *Labor Unions, Partisan Coalitions, and Market Reforms in Latin America*. New York: Cambridge University Press.

Murphy, Alexander (1996). "The Sovereign State System as Political–Territorial Ideal: Historical and Contemporary Considerations," in Thomas Biersteker and Cynthia Weber (eds), *State Sovereignty as Social Construct*. New York: Cambridge University Press, 81–112.

Niedzwiecki, Sara (2016). "Social Policies, Attribution of Responsibility, and Political Alignments: A Subnational Analysis of Argentina and Brazil," *Comparative Political Studies*, 49(4): 457–98.

Niedzwiecki, Sara (forthcoming). *Multilevel Social Policies and Politics in Latin America.*

Noboa, Ricardo (2004). *El país del no.* Guayaquil: Edino.

North, Liisa (2004). "State Building, State Dismantling, and Financial Crises in Ecuador," in Jo-Marie Burt and Philip Mauceri (eds), *Politics in the Andes: Identity, Conflict, Reform.* Pittsburgh: University of Pittsburgh Press.

O'Donnell, Guillermo (1973). *Modernization and Bureaucratic Authoritarianism.* Berkeley and Los Angeles: Institute of International Studies.

O'Donnell, Guillermo (1993). "On the State, Democratization and Some Conceptual Problems," *World Development*, 21/(8): 1355–70.

O'Donnell, Guillermo (1994). "Delegative Democracy," *Journal of Democracy*, 51: 55–69.

Oates, Wallace (1972). *Fiscal Federalism.* New York: Harcourt Brace Jovanovich.

Oficina Nacional de Diálogo y Sostenibilidad (2013). "Mesas de Diálogo, Mesas de Desarrollo, y Conflictos Sociales en el Perú," *Willaqniki*, 5: 7–16.

Oi, Jean (1999). *Rural China Takes Off: The Institutional Foundations of Economic Reform.* Berkeley and Los Angeles: University of California Press.

Orijuela, José Carlos (2014). "Converging Divergence: The Diffusion of the Green State in Latin America," *Studies in Comparative International Development*, 49: 242–65.

Oxhorn, Philip, and Graciela Ducatenzeiler (1998) (eds). *What Kind of Democracy? What Kind of Market? Latin America in the Age of Neoliberalism.* University Park, PA: Penn State University Press.

Oxhorn, Philip, Joseph Tulchin, and Andrew Selee (2004) (eds). *Decentralization, Democratic Governance and Civil Society in Comparative Perspective.* Baltimore: Johns Hopkins University Press.

Pachano, Simón (2007). *La trama de Penelope: Procesos políticos e instituciones en el Ecuador.* Quito: FLACSO.

Pallares, Amalia (2003). "Entre Singapur y Tahuantinsuyo: estado, región y la nación imaginada," *Revista Ecuatoriana de Historia*, 19: 223–36.

Panfichi, Aldo (2011). "Contentious Representation and its Impact in Contemporary Peru," in John Crabtree (ed.), *Fractured Politics: Peruvian Democracy Past and Present.* London: University of London Press.

Parayil, Govindan (2000) (ed.). *The Kerala Model.* London: ZED.

Paredes, Maritza (2008). "El caso de Tambogrande," in Martin Scurrah (ed.), *Defendiendo Derechos y Promoviendo Cambios.* Lima: Instituto de Estudios Peruanos, 269–300.

Parnell, Susan, and Jennifer Robinson (2012). "(Re)Theorizing Cities from the Global South: Looking beyond Neoliberalism," *Urban Geography*, 33(4): 593–617.

Pasotti, Eleonora (2010). *Political Branding in Cities: The Decline of Machine Politics in Bogota, Naples and Chicago.* New York: Cambridge University Press.

Paul, Darel (2002). "Re-Scaling IPE: Subnational States and the Regulation of the Global Political Economy," *Review of International Political Economy*, 9(3).

Pedraza, Gustavo (2011). "Nuevo poder, cambio y resistencia: Santa Cruz en la década de la confrontación," in Gustavo Pedraza (ed.), *Repensar Santa Cruz.* Santa Cruz: Fundación Boliviana para la Democracia Multipartidaria.

Peña, Claudia (2011). *Vos confias?: Capital social, identidad y desarrollo en Santa Cruz.* La Paz: Friedrich Ebert Stiftung.

Peña, Paula (2003). *La permanente construcción de lo cruceño.* La Paz: Fundación PIEB.

Petras, James, and Henry Veltmeyer (2009). *What's Left in Latin America?: Regime Change in New Times*. Farnham: Ashgate Publishing.

Piattoni, Simona, and Justus Schönlau (2015). *Shaping EU Policy from Below: EU Democracy and the Committee of the Regions*. London: Edward Elgar.

Pineo, Ronn (1994). "Guayaquil y su región en el segundo boom cacaotero," in Juan Maiguasha (ed.), *Historia y región en el Ecuador: 1830–1972*. Quito: FLACSO, 251–94.

Pinto, Gustavo (2009). "Estado, estructura y poder en Santa Cruz," in Paula Peña (ed.), *Estados de la investigación: Santa Cruz*, i. La Paz: Fundación PIEB.

Piore, Michael, and Charles Sabel (1986). *The Second Industrial Divide: Possibilities for Prosperity*. New York: Basic Books.

Plata, Wilfred (2008). "Discurso autonomista de las elites de Santa Cruz," in Ximena Soruco (ed.), *Los barones del oriente*. Santa Cruz: Fundación Tierra, 101–71.

Ponce, Aldo, and Cynthia McClintock (2014). "The Explosive Combination of Inefficient Local Bureaucracies and Mining Production: Evidence from Localized Societal Protests in Peru," *Latin American Politics and Society*, 56/3: 118–40.

Portes, Alejandro, and Bryan Roberts (2005). "The Free-Market City: Latin American Urbanization in the Years of the Neoliberal Experiment," *Studies in Comparative International Development*, 40(1): 43–82.

Post, Alison (2014). *Foreign and Domestic Investment in Argentina: The Politics of Privatized Infrastructure*. New York: Cambridge University Press.

Postero, Nancy (2006). *Now We Are Citizens: Indigenous Politics in Postmulticultural Bolivia*. Stanford: Stanford University Press.

Postero, Nancy (2010). "Morales's MAS Government: Building Indigenous Popular Hegemony in Bolivia," *Latin American Perspectives*, 37(3): 18–34.

Prado, Fernando (2007) (ed.). *Poder y elites en Santa Cruz*. Santa Cruz: El País.

Pribble, Jennifer (2015). "The Politics of Building Municipal Institutional Effectiveness in Chile," *Latin American Politics and Society*, 57(3): 100–21.

Pribble, Jennifer, and Evelyne Huber (2011). "Social Policy and Redistribution under Left Governments in Chile and Uruguay," in Steven Levitsky and Kenneth Roberts (eds), *The Resurgence of the Latin American Left*. Baltimore: Johns Hopkins University Press.

Przeworski, Adam (1991). *Democracy and the Market: Political and Economic Reforms in Eastern Europe and Latin America*. New York: Cambridge University Press.

Przeworski, Adam, and Michael Wallerstein (1988). "Structural Dependence of the State on Capital," *American Political Science Review*, 82(1): 11–29.

Qian, Yingyi, and Joseph Stiglitz (1996). "Institutional Innovations and the Role of Local Government in Transition Economies: The Case of Guangdong Province of China," in John McMillan and Barry Naughton (eds), *Reforming Asian Socialism: The Growth of Market Institutions*. Ann Arbor: University of Michigan Press.

Quilley, Stephen (2000). "Manchester First: From Municipal Socialism to the Entrepreneurial City," *International Journal of Urban and Regional Research*, 24(3): 601–15.

Quinones, Patricia (2013). "Concesiones, participación y conflicto en Puno: El caso del proyecto minero Santa Ana," in Javier Torres (ed.), *Los limites de la expansión minera en el Perú*. Lima: Asociación SER.

Quintero, Rafael, and Erika Silva (1991). "Región y representación política en el Ecuador contemporáneo," in Rafael Quintero (ed.), *La cuestión regional y el poder*. Quito: Corporación Editora Nacional.

Rada, Alfredo (2004). "Octubre y la Tierra," *Artículo Primero*, 8/16: 149–60.

Ramírez Gallegos, Franklin (2012). "Perspectivas del proceso de democratización en Ecuador: cambio político e inclusión social (2005–2010)," in Anja Dargatz and Moria Zuazo (eds), *Democracias en transformación: Qué hay de nuevo en los Estados andinos?* La Paz: Friedrich Ebert Stiftung.

Remy, María Isabel (2013). "Descentralización y gestión territorial en el Perú," in Bruno Revesz (ed.), *Miradas Cruzadas: Políticas Públicas y Desarrollo Regional en el Perú*. Lima: Instituto de Estudios Peruanos.

República del Perú (2013). *Evaluación del Proceso de descentralización a 10 años de su inicio*. Lima: Comisión de Descentralización, Congreso de la República.

Revesz, Bruno (2009). "Tambogrande: de la defensa del agro a la defensa del derecho a decidir," in Jose de Echave (ed.), *Minería y conflicto social*. Lima: Instituto de Estudios Peruanos.

Revesz, Bruno, and Alejandro Diáz (2006). "El triángulo sin cúpula," in Eduardo Toche (ed.), *Peru hoy: Nuevos rostros en la escena nacional*. Lima: DESCO.

Riker, William (1964). *Federalism: Origin, Operation, Significance*. Boston: Little, Brown, and Company.

Roberts, Brian (2015). *Managing Systems of Secondary Cities*. Washington: Inter-American Development Bank.

Roberts, Kenneth (1996). "Economic Crisis and the Demise of the Legal Left in Peru," *Comparative Politics*, 29(1): 69–92.

Roberts, Kenneth (2015). *Changing Course in Latin America: Party Systems in the Neoliberal Era*. New York: Cambridge University Press.

Roca, José Luis (1980). *Fisonomía del regionalismo boliviano*. La Paz: Editorial Los Amigos del Libro.

Roca, José Luis (2001). *Economía y sociedad en el oriente boliviano*. Santa Cruz: COTAS.

Rodden, Jonathan (2004). "Comparative Federalism and Decentralization: On Meaning and Measurement," *Comparative Politics*, 36: 481–500.

Rodríguez, Esther, and Pascha Bueno Hansen (forthcoming). *De la Gran Transformación a la Gran Traición: Ollanta Humala's State Policy*.

Rodríguez, Linda Alexander (1985). *The Search for Public Policy: Regional Politics and Government Finances in Ecuador, 1830–1940*. Berkeley and Los Angeles: University of California Press.

Rodrik, Dani (2010). "Who Needs the Nation State?," *Economic Geography*, 89(1): 1–19.

Sabel, Charles, and Jonathan Zeitlin (2012). "Experimentalist Governance," in David Levi-Faur (ed.), *The Oxford Handbook of Governance*. New York: Oxford University Press.

Salmond, Alex (2014). "A Partnership of Equals," *New Statesman*, February 2, 143(5199): 22–5.

Sanborn, Cynthia, and Luis Dammert (2013). *Extracción de recursos naturales, desarrollo económico e inclusión social: Perú*. Lima: Centro de Investigación de la Universidad del Pacífico.

Sandoval, Dunia (2003). *Santa Cruz: Economía y poder (1952–1993)*. La Paz: PIEB.

Santillana, Miguel (2013). "Bambi Boys en Acción," *Correo*, March 15.

Sassen, Saskia (1998). *Globalization and its Discontents*. New York: New Press.

Savitch, Hank, and Paul Kantor (2004). *Cities in the International Market Place*. Princeton: Princeton University Press.

Saylor, Ryan (2014). *State Building in Boom Times: Commodities and Coalitions in Latin America and Africa*. Oxford: Oxford University Press.

Schamis, Hector (1999). "Distributional Coalitions and the Politics of Economic Reform in Latin America," *World Politics*, 51(2): 236–68.

Schuldt, Jurgen (2012). "El necesario cambio de rumbo," *Cuadernos Descentralistas*, 29: 21–30.

Scott, Allen (1998). *Regions and the World Economy: The Coming Shape of Global Production, Competition, and Political Order*. Oxford: Oxford University Press.

Scurrah, Martin (2008). "Incidencia política y conflicto: Algunos temas comunes a los casos extractivos," in Martin Scurrah (ed.), *Defendiendo derechos y promoviendo cambios*. Lima: Instituto de Estudios Peruanos.

Seawright, Jason (2012). *Party-System Collapse: The Roots of Crisis in Peru and Venezuela*. Stanford: Stanford University Press.

Seifert Bonifaz, Manuel (2014). *Colapso de los partidos nacionales y auge de los partidos regionales*. Lima: Pontificia Universidad Católica del Perú.

Sharma, Ruchir (2013). "The Rise of the Rest of India," *Foreign Affairs*, 92(5): 75–85.

Sheahan, John (2002). "Alternative Models of Capitalism in Latin America," in Evelyne Huber (ed.), *Models of Capitalism: Lessons for Latin America*. University Park, PA: Penn State University Press.

Silva, Karen (2013). "Comunicación y política: Los medios y la construcción del capital política de los líderes del Partido Social Cristiano en Guayaquil," MA thesis, FLACSO/ Ecuador.

Silva, Verónica (2016). "Constructing a State in the Face of Regional Power: The Case of Guayaquil," *Latin American Perspectives*, 43(1): 93–108.

Simmons, Erica (2016). *Meaningful Resistance: Market Reforms and the Roots of Social Protest in Latin America*. New York: Cambridge University Press.

Simon, Yehude (2011). *Mi visión de Perú: más allá de las ideologías*. Lima: Biblioteca Nacional de Perú.

Singh, Prerna (2011). "We-ness and Welfare: A Longitudinal Analysis of Social Development in Kerala, India," *World Development*, 39(2).

Singh, Prerna (2015). *Collective Identity and the Common Good: Subnationalism and Social Development in India*. New York: Cambridge University Press.

Sinha, Aseema (2003). "Rethinking the Developmental State Model: Divided Leviathan and Subnational Comparisons in India," *Comparative Politics*, 35(4): 459–76.

Sinha, Aseema (2004). "Ideas, Interests and Institutions in Policy Change: A Comparison of West Bengal and Gujarat," in Rob Jenkins (ed.), *Comparing Politics across India's States: Case Studies of Democracy in Practice*. New York: Oxford University Press.

Skocpol, Theda (1979). *States and Social Revolutions*. New York: Cambridge University Press.

Smith, William, Carlos Acuña, and Eduardo Gamarra (1994). *Democracy, Markets, and Structural Reform in Latin America*. Miami: North–South Center Press.

Smoke, Paul, Eduardo Gomez, and George Peterson (2007) (eds). *Decentralization in Asia and Latin America: Towards a Comparative Interdisciplinary Perspective*. Cheltenham: Edward Elgar.

Snyder, Richard (2001). "Scaling Down: The Subnational Comparative Method," *Studies in Comparative International Development*, 36(1): 93–110.

Snyder, Richard (2006). *Politics after Neoliberalism: Reregulation in Mexico*. New York: Cambridge University Press.

Soifer, Hillel (2015). *State Building in Latin America*. New York: Cambridge University Press.

Soifer, Hillel (2016). "Regionalism, Ethnic Diversity, and Variation in Public Good Provision by National States," *Comparative Political Studies*, 49/10: 1341–71.

Soifer, Hillel, and Matthias vom Hau (2008). "Unpacking the Strength of the State: The Utility of State Infrastructural Power," *Studies in Comparative International Development*, 43: 219–30.

Soruco, Ximena (2008). "De la goma a la soya: El proyecto histórico de la élite cruceña," in Ximena Soruco (ed.), *Los barones del oriente*. Santa Cruz: Fundación Tierra.

Spektorowski, Alberto (2003). "Ethnoregionalism: The Intellectual New Right and the Lega Nord," *Global Review of Ethnopolitics*, 2(3–4): 55–70.

Spitzer, Steven, and Andrew T. Scull (2001). "Privatization and Capitalist Development: The Case of the Private Police," *Social Problems*, 25(1): 18–29.

Stepan, Alfred (1978). *The State and Society: Peru in Comparative Perspective*. Princeton: Princeton University Press.

Stone, Clarence (1989). *Regime Politics: Governing Atlanta*. Lawrence, KS: University Press of Kansas.

Swyngedouw, Erik (2004). *Social Power and the Urbanization of Water*. Oxford: Oxford University Press.

Tanaka, Martin (2002). *La dinámica de los actores regionales y el proceso de descentralización: Es despertar del letargo?* Lima: Instituto de Estudios Peruanos.

Tanaka, Martin (2005). *Democracia sin partidos: Los problemas de representación y las propuestas de reforma política*. Lima: Instituto de Estudios Peruanos.

Tanaka, Martín (2006). "From Crisis to Collapse of the Party Systems and Dilemmas of Democratic Representation," in Scott Mainwaring, Ana María Bejarano, and Eduardo Pizarro (eds), *The Crisis of Democratic Representation in the Andes*. Stanford: Stanford University Press.

Tendler, Judith (1968). *Electric Power in Brazil: Entrepreneurship in the Public Sector*. Cambridge. MA: Harvard University Press.

Tendler, Judith (1998). *Good Government in the Tropics*. Baltimore: Johns Hopkins University Press.

Thelen, Kathleen (2003). "How Institutions Evolve: Insights from Comparative–Historical Analysis," in James Mahoney and Dietrich Reuschemeyer (eds), *Comparative Historical Analysis in the Social Sciences*. New York: Cambridge University Press.

Thorp, Rosembary, and Geoffrey Bertram (1978). *Peru 1890–1977: Growth and Policy in an Open Economy*. London: Macmillan.

Thun, Eric (2004). "'Keeping up with the Jones': Decentralization, Policy Imitation, and Industrial Development in China," *World Development*, 32(8): 1289–308.

Tockman, Jason, and John Cameron (2014). "Indigenous Autonomy and the Contradictions of Plurinationalism in Bolivia," *Latin American Politics and Society*, 46(3): 46–69.

Trebat, Thomas (1983). *Brazil's State-Owned Enterprises: A Case Study of the State as Entrepreneur*. Cambridge: Cambridge University Press.

Ungar, Mark (2007–8). "The Privatization of Citizen Security in Latin America: From Elite Guards to Neighborhood Vigilantes," *Social Justice*, 34(3–4): 20–37.

United Nations (2014). *World Urbanization Prospects: The 2014 Revision*. New York: United Nations, Department of Economic and Social Affairs.

United Nations (2015). *World Population Prospects: The 2015 Revision*. New York: United Nations, Department of Economic and Social Affairs.

Urenda, Juan Carlos (2003). *Autonomías departamentales*. Santa Cruz: El País.

Urenda, Juan Carlos (2005). *Separando la paja del trigo: Bases para construir las autonomías departamentales*. Santa Cruz: El País.

Urenda, Juan Carlos (2009). *El sueño imperturbable: El proceso autonómico boliviano*. Santa Cruz: El País.

Valdivia, Gabriela (2010). "Agrarian Capitalism and Struggles over Hegemony in the Bolivian Lowlands," *Latin American Perspectives*, 37(4): 67–87.

Valverde, Carlos (2012). *Maten a Rozsa! El rompecabezas de una conspiración*. Santa Cruz: El País.

Van Cott, Donna (2008). *Radical Democracy in the Andes: Ethnic Parties and the Quality of Democracy in Latin America*. New York: Cambridge University Press.

Verdesoto, Luis (2001). *Descentralizar: Grados de autonomía para enriquecer a la democracia*. Quito: Abya-Yala.

Vergara, Alberto (2011). "United by Discord, Divided by Consensus: National and Subnational Articulation in Bolivia and Peru," *Journal of Politics in Latin America*, 3(3): 65–93.

Vergara, Alberto (2015). *La danza hostil: Poderes subnacionales y estado central en Bolivia y Peru (1952–2012)*. Lima: Instituto de Estudios Peruanos.

Vergara, Alberto, and Daniel Encinas (2016). "Continuity by Surprise: Explaining Institutional Stability in Contemporary Peru," *Latin American Research Review*, 51/1): 159–80.

Vogel, David (1987). "Political Science and the Study of Corporate Power: A Dissent from the New Conventional Wisdom," *British Journal of Political Science*, 17(4): 385–408.

Wade, Robert (1996). "Globalization and its Limits: Reports of the Death of the National Economy Are Greatly Exaggerated," in Suzanne Berger and Ronald Dore (eds), *National Diversity and Global Capitalism*. Ithaca, NY: Cornell University Press, 60–88.

Waldmann, Adrián (2008). *El hábitus camba*. Santa Cruz: El País.

Wampler, Brian (2007). *Participatory Budgeting in Brazil: Contestation, Cooperation, Accountability*. University Park, PA: Penn State University Press.

Waterbury, John (1993). *Exposed to Innumerable Delusions: Public Enterprise and State Power in Egypt, India, Mexico, and Turkey*. New York: Cambridge University Press.

Webber, Jeffery (2011). *From Rebellion to Reform in Bolivia: Class Struggle, Indigenous Liberation, and the Politics of Evo Morales*. London: Haymarket Books.

Weingast, Barry (2014). "Second Generation Fiscal Federalism: Political Aspects of Decentralization and Economic Development," *World Development*, 53: 14–25.

Weisbrot, Mark, Jake Johnston, and Stephan Lefebvre (2013). *Ecuador's New Deal: Reforming and Regulating the Financial Sector*. Washington: Center for Economic and Policy Research.

Whitehead, Laurence (1972). *National Power and Local Power: The Case of Santa Cruz de la Sierra, Bolivia*. Cambridge: Cambridge University Press.

Wibbels, Erik (2005). *Federalism and the Market: Intergovernmental Conflict and Economic Reform in the Developing World*. New York: Cambridge University Press.

Willis, Eliza, Christopher Garman, and Stephan Haggard (1999). "Decentralization in Latin America," *Latin American Research Review*, 34(1): 7–56.

Wilson, Carter (2000). "Policy Regimes and Policy Change," *Journal of Public Policy*, 20(3): 247–74.

Wolff, Jonas (2016). "Business Power and the Politics of Post-Neoliberalism: Relations between Governments and Economic Elites in Bolivia and Ecuador," *Latin American Politics and Society*, 58(2): 124–47.

Wong, Daniel (2005). *Regeneración urbana: Marca de Guayaquil*. Guayaquil: Poligráfica.

World Bank (2009). *Reshaping Economic Geography: World Development Report 2009*. Washington: World Bank.

World Bank (2011). *The Changing Wealth of Nations: Measuring Sustainable Development in the New Millennium*. Washington: World Bank.

Yang, Dali (1997). *Beyond Beijing: Liberalization and the Regions in China*. London: Routledge.

Yashar, Deborah (2005). *Contesting Citizenship in Latin America*. New York: Cambridge University Press.

Zas Friz, Jonny (2004). *La insistencia de la voluntad: El actual proceso peruano de descentralización política y sus antecedentes inmediatos (1980–2004)*. Lima: Defensoría del Pueblo.

Zegada, María Teresa (2010). "El rol de la oposición política en Bolivia," in Luís García and Fernando García (eds), *Mutaciones del campo político en Bolivia*. La Paz: UNDP.

Ziblatt, Daniel (2006). *Structuring the State: The Formation of Italy and Germany and the Puzzle of Federalism*. Princeton: Princeton University Press.

Ziblatt, Daniel (2008). "Why Some Cities Provide More Public Goods than Others: A Subnational Comparison of the Provision of Public Goods in German Cities in 1912," *Studies in Comparative International Development*, 43: 273–89.

Zuazo Moira, Jean-Paul Faguet, and Gustavo Bonifaz (2012) (eds). *Descentralización y democratización en Bolivia*. La Paz: Friedrich Ebert Stiftung.

Index

The manufacturer's authorised representative in the EU for product safety is Oxford University Press España S.A. of el Parque Empresarial San Fernando de Henares, Avenida de Castilla, 2 – 28830 Madrid (www.oup.es/en or product.safety@oup.com). OUP España S.A. also acts as importer into Spain of products made by the manufacturer.

www.ingramcontent.com/pod-product-compliance
Lightning Source LLC
LaVergne TN
LVHW011800200926
848484LV00003B/746
* 9 7 8 0 1 9 8 8 0 0 5 7 6 *